ViKiNG SAGAS

Erik the Red, Grettir the Strong, and Kormac the Skald

Louis Moe.

Red and Black Publishers, St Petersburg, FL

Erik the Red's Saga translated 1880 by Rev John Sephton
The Saga of Grettir the Strong translated 1914 by G.H Hight
The Life and Death of Kormac the Skald translated 1901 by W.G.Collingwood

Library of Congress Cataloging-in-Publication Data

Viking sagas : Erik the Red, Grettir the Strong, and Kormac the Skald /
[translators, John Sephton, G.H. Hight, W.G. Collingwood]
       p. cm.
"Erik the Red's Saga translated 1880 by Rev John Sephton ; The Saga
of Grettir the Strong translated 1914 by G.H Hight ; The Life and Death
of Kormac the Skald translated 1901 by W.G.Collingwood."
  ISBN 978-1-934941-09-6
1. Eiríkr Rauði Þorvaldsson, fl. 985--Criticism and
interpretation. 2. Grettir Ásmundarson, 996-1031--Criticism and interpretation.
3. Kormákr Ögmundarson, ca. 935-970--Criticism and interpretation. 4. Sagas—
Translations into English. I. Sephton, John, b. 1835
translator. II. Hight, George Ainslie, b. 1851, translator. III. Collingwood,
W. G. (William Gershom), 1854-1932 translator.
  PT7269.A25V55 2008
  869'.6308--dc22

                                                    2008008821

Red and Black Publishers, PO Box 7542, St Petersburg, Florida, 33734

Contact us at: info@RedandBlackPublishers.com

        Printed and manufactured in the United States of America

Contents

Erik the Red's Saga

laf, who was called Olaf the White, was styled a warrior king. He was the son of King Ingjald, the son of Helgi, the son of Olaf, the son of Gudred, the son of Halfdan Whiteleg, king of the Uplands (in Norway). He led a harrying expedition of sea-rovers into the west, and conquered Dublin, in Ireland, and Dublinshire, over which he made himself king. He married Aud the Deep-minded, daughter of Ketil Flatnose, son of Bjorn the Ungartered, a noble man from Norway. Their son was named Thorstein the Red. Olaf fell in battle in Ireland, and then Aud and Thorstein went into the Sudreyjar (the Hebrides). There Thorstein married Thorid, daughter of Eyvind the Easterling, sister of Helgi the Lean; and they had many children. Thorstein became a warrior king, and formed an alliance with Earl Sigurd the Great, son of Eystein the Rattler. They conquered Caithness, Sutherland, Ross, and Moray, and more than half Scotland. Over these Thorstein was king until the Scots plotted against him, and he fell there in battle. Aud was in Caithness when she heard of Thorstein's death. Then she caused a merchant-ship to be secretly built in the wood, and when she was ready, directed her course out into the Orkneys. There she gave in marriage Thorstein the Red's daughter, Gro, who became mother of Grelad, whom

Earl Thorfinn, the Skullcleaver, married. Afterwards Aud set out to seek Iceland, having twenty free men in her ship. Aud came to Iceland, and passed the first winter in Bjarnarhofn (Bjornshaven) with her brother Bjorn. Afterwards she occupied all the Dale country between the Dogurdara (day-meal river) and the Skraumuhlaupsa (river of the giantess's leap), and dwelt at Hvamm. She had prayer meetings at Krossholar (Crosshills), where she caused crosses to be erected, for she was baptised and deeply devoted to the faith. There came with her to Iceland many men worthy of honour, who had been taken captive in sea-roving expeditions to the west, and who were called bondmen. One of these was named Vifil; he was a man of high family, and had been taken captive beyond the western main, and was also called a bondman before Aud set him free. And when Aud granted dwellings to her ship's company, Vifil asked why she gave no abode to him like unto the others. Aud replied, "That it was of no moment to him, for," she said, "he would be esteemed in whatever place he was, as one worthy of honour." She gave him Vifilsdalr (Vifilsdale), and he dwelt there and married. His sons were Thorbjorn and Thorgeir, promising men, and they grew up in their father's house.

There was a man named Thorvald, the son of Asvald, the son of Ulf, the son of Yxna-Thoris. His son was named Erik. Father and son removed from Jadar (in Norway) to Iceland, because of manslaughters, and occupied land in Hornstrandir, and dwelt at Drangar. There Thorvald died, and Erik then married Thjodhild, daughter of Jorund, the son of Atli, and of Thorbjorg the Ship-breasted, whom afterwards Thorbjorn, of the Haukadalr (Hawkdale) family, married; he it was who dwelt at Eriksstadr after Erik removed from the north. It is near Vatzhorn. Then did Erik's thralls cause a landslip on the estate of Valthjof, at Valthjofsstadr. Eyjolf the Foul, his kinsman, slew the thralls beside Skeidsbrekkur (slopes of the race-course), above Vatzhorn. In return Erik slew Eyjolf the Foul; he slew also Hrafn the Dueller, at Leikskalar (playbooths). Gerstein, and Odd of Jorfi, kinsman of Eyjolf, were found willing to follow up his death by a legal prosecution; and then was Erik banished from Haukadalr. He occupied then Brokey and Eyxney, and dwelt at Tradir, in Sudrey, the first winter. At this time did he lend to Thorgest pillars for seat-stocks, Afterwards Erik removed into Eyxney, and dwelt at Eriksstadr. He then claimed his pillars, and got them not. Then went Erik and fetched the pillars from Breidabolstadr, and Thorgest went after him. They fought at a short distance from the hay-yard at Drangar, and there fell two sons of Thorgest, and some other men. After that they both kept a large body of men together. Styr gave assistance to Erik, as also did Eyjolf, of Sviney, Thorbjorn Vifilsson, and the sons of Thorbrand, of Alptafjordr (Swanfirth). But the sons of Thord Gellir, as also Thorgeir, of Hitardalr (Hotdale), Aslak, of Langadalr (Longdale), and Illugi, his son, gave assistance to Thorgest. Erik and his people were outlawed at Thorsnes Thing. He prepared a ship in Eriksvagr (creek), and Eyjolf concealed him in Dimunarvagr while Thorgest and his people sought him among the islands. Erik said to his people that he purposed to seek for the land which Gunnbjorn, the son of Ulf the Crow, saw when he was driven westwards over the ocean, and discovered Gunnbjarnarsker (Gunnbjorn's rock or skerry). He promised that he would return to visit his friends if he found the land. Thorbjorn, and Eyjolf, and Styr accompanied Erik beyond the islands. They separated in the most friendly manner, Erik saying that he would be of the like assistance to them, if he should be able so to be, and they should happen to need him. Then he sailed oceanwards under Snoefellsjokull (snow mountain glacier), and arrived at the glacier called Blaserkr (Blue-shirt); thence he journeyed south to see if there were any inhabitants of the country. He passed the first winter at Eriksey, near the middle, of the Vestribygd (western settlement). The following spring he proceeded to Eriksfjordr, and fixed his abode there. During the summer he proceeded into the unpeopled districts in the west, and was there a long time, giving names to the places far and wide. The second winter he passed in Eriksholmar (isles), off Hvarfsgnupr (peak of disappearance, Cape Farewell); and the third summer he went altogether northwards, to Snoefell and into Hrafnsfjordr (Ravensfirth); considering then that he had come to the head of Eriksfjordr, he turned back, and passed the third winter in Eriksey, before the mouth of Eriksfjordr. Now, afterwards, during the summer, he proceeded to Iceland, and came to Breidafjordr (Broadfirth). This winter he was with Ingolf, at Holmlatr (Island-litter). During the spring, Thorgest and he fought, and Erik met with defeat. After that they were reconciled. In the summer Erik went to live in the land which he had discovered, and which he called Greenland, "Because," said he, "men will desire much the more to go there if the land has a good name."

Thorgeir Vifilsson married, and took to wife Arnora, daughter of Einar, from Laugarbrekka (the slope of the hot spring), the son of Sigmund, the eon of Ketil-Thistil, who had occupied Thistilsfjordr. The second daughter of Einar was named Hallveig. Thorbjorn Vifilsson took her to wife, and received with her the land of Laugarbrekka, at Hellisvollr (the cave-hill). To that spot Thorbjorn removed his abode, and became great and worshipful. He was the temple-priest, and had a magnificent estate. Thorbjorn's daughter was Gudrid, the fairest of women, and of peerless nobility in all her conduct. There was a man named Orm, who dwelt at Arnarstapi (eagle-rock), and he had a wife who was named Halldis. He was a well-to-do franklin, a great friend of Thorbjorn, and Gudrid lived at his house as his foster-child for a long time. There was a man named Thorgeir, who dwelt at Thorgeirsfjall (fell). He was mighty rich in cattle, and had been made a freedman. He had a son, whose name was Einar, a handsome man, well mannered, and a great dandy. Einar, at this time, was a travelling merchant, sailing from land to land with great success; and he always passed his winter either in Iceland or in Norway. Now after this, I have to tell how that one autumn, when Einar was in Iceland, he proceeded with his wares along Snoefellsnes, with the object of selling; he came to Arnarstapi; Orm invited him to stay there, and Einar accepted his invitation, because there was friendship between him and Orm's people, and his wares were earned into a certain outhouse. There he unpacked his merchandise, showed it to Orm and the housemen, and bade Orm take therefrom such things as he would. Orm accepted the offer, and pronounced Einar to be a goodly gallant traveller, and a great favourite of fortune. When now they were busy with the wares, a woman passed before the door of the outhouse; and Einar inquired of Orm who that fair woman might be, passing before the door. "I have not seen her here before," said he. "That is Gudrid, my foster-child," said Orm, "daughter of Thorbjorn the franklin, from Laugarbrekka." "She must be a good match," said Einar; "surely she has not been without suitors who have made proposals for her, has she?" Orm answered, "Proposals have certainly been made, friend, but this treasure is not to be had for the picking up; it is found that she will be particular in her choice, as well as also her father." "Well, in spite of that," quoth Einar, "she is the woman whom I have it in my mind to propose for, and I wish that in this suit of mine you approach her father on my part, and apply yourself to plead diligently for me, for which I shall pay you in return a perfect friendship. The franklin, Thorbjorn, may reflect that our families would be suitably joined in the bonds of affinity; for he is a man in a position of great honour, and owns a fine abode, but his personal property, I am told, is greatly on the decrease; neither I nor my father lack lands or personal property; and if this alliance should be brought about, the greatest assistance would accrue to Thorbjorn." Then answered Orm, "Of a surety I consider myself to be thy friend, and yet am I not willing to bring forward this suit, for Thorbjorn is of a proud mind, and withal a very ambitious man." Einar replied that he desired no other thing than that his offer of marriage should be made known. Orm then consented to undertake his suit, and Einar journeyed south again until he came home. A while after, Thorbjorn had a harvest-feast, as he was bound to have because of his great rank. There were present Orm, from Arnarstapi, and many other friends of Thorbjorn. Orm entered into conversation with Thorbjorn, and told him how that Einar had lately been to see him from Thorgeirsfjall, and was become a promising man.

He now began the wooing on behalf of Einar, and said that an alliance between the families would be very suitable on account of certain interests. "There may arise to thee, franklin," he said, "great assistance in thy means from this alliance." But Thorbjorn answered, "I did not expect the like proposal from thee, that I should give my daughter in marriage to the son of a thrall. And so thou perceivest that my substance is decreasing; well, then, my daughter shall not go home with thee, since thou considerest her worthy of so poor a match." Then went Orm home again, and each of the other guests to his own household, and Gudrid remained with her father, and stayed at home that winter.

Now, in the spring, Thorbjorn made a feast to his friends, and a goodly banquet was prepared. There came many guests, and the banquet was of the best. Now, at the banquet, Thorbjorn called for a hearing, and thus spake: "Here have I dwelt a long time. I have experienced the goodwill of men and their affection towards me, and I consider that our dealings with one another have been mutually agreeable. But now do my money matters begin to bring me uneasiness, although to this time my condition has not been reckoned contemptible. I wish, therefore, to break up my household before I lose my honour; to remove from the country before I disgrace my family. So now I purpose to look after the promises of Erik the Red, my friend, which he made when we separated at Breidafjordr. I purpose to depart for Greenland in the summer, if events proceed as I could wish." These tidings about this design appeared to the guests to be important, for Thorbjorn had long been beloved by his friends. They felt that he would only have made so public a declaration that it might be held of no avail to attempt to dissuade him from his purpose. Thorbjorn distributed gifts among the guests, and then the feast was brought to an end, and they departed to their own homesteads. Thorbjorn sold his lands, and bought a ship which had been laid up on shore at the mouth of the Hraunhofn (harbour of the lava field). Thirty men ventured on the expedition with him. There was Orm, from Arnarstapi, and his wife, and those friends of Thorbjorn who did not wish to be separated from him. Then they launched the ship, and set sail with a favourable wind. But when they came out into the open sea the favourable wind ceased, and they experienced great gales, and made but an ill-sped voyage throughout the summer. In addition to that trouble, there came fever upon the expedition, and Orm died, and Halldis, his wife, and half the company. Then the sea waxed rougher, and they endured much toil and misery in many ways, and only reached Herjolfsnes, in Greenland, at the very beginning of winter. There dwelt at Herjolfsnes the man who was called Thorkell. He was a useful man and most worthy franklin. He received Thorbjorn and all his ship's company for the winter, assisting them in right noble fashion. This pleased Thorbjorn well and his companions in the voyage.

At that time there was a great dearth in Greenland; those who had been out on fishing expeditions had caught little, and some had not returned. There was in the settlement the woman whose name was Thorbjorg. She was a prophetess (spae-queen), and was called Litilvolva (little sybil). She had had nine sisters, and they were all spae-queens, and she was the only one now living. It was a custom of Thorbjorg, in the winter time, to make a circuit, and people invited her to their houses, especially those who had any curiosity about the season, or desired to know their fate; and inasmuch as Thorkell was chief franklin thereabouts, he considered that it concerned him to know when the scarcity which overhung the settlement should cease. He invited, therefore, the spae-queen to his house, and prepared for her a hearty welcome, as was the custom whereever a reception was accorded a woman of this kind. A high seat was prepared for her, and a cushion laid thereon in which were poultry-feathers. Now, when she came in the evening, accompanied by the man who had been sent to meet her, she was dressed in such wise that she had a blue mantle over her, with strings for the neck, and it was inlaid with gems quite down to the skirt. On her neck she had glass beads. On her head she had a black hood of lambskin, lined with ermine. A staff she had in her hand, with a knob thereon; it was ornamented with brass, and inlaid with gems round about the knob. Around her she wore a girdle of soft hair, and therein was a large skin-bag, in which she kept the talismans needful to her in her wisdom. She wore hairy calf-skin shoes on her feet, with long and strong-looking thongs to them, and great knobs of latten at the ends. On her hands she had gloves of ermine-skin, and they were white and hairy within. Now, when she entered, all men thought it their bounden duty to offer her becoming greetings, and these she received according as the men were agreeable to her. The franklin Thorkell took the wise-woman by the hand, and led her to the seat prepared for her. He requested her to cast her eyes over his herd, his household, and his homestead. She remained silent altogether. During the evening the tables were set; and now I must tell you what food was made ready for the spae-queen. There was prepared for her porridge of kid's milk, and hearts of all kinds of living creatures there found were cooked for her. She had a brazen spoon, and a knife with a handle of walrus-tusk, which was mounted with two rings of brass, and the point of it was broken off. When the tables were removed, the franklin Thorkell advanced to Thorbjorg and asked her how she liked his homestead, or the appearance of the men; or how soon she would ascertain that which he had asked, and which the men desired to know. She replied that she would not give answer before the morning, after she had slept there for the night. And when the (next) day was far spent, the preparations were made for her which she required for the exercise of her enchantments. She begged them to bring to her those women who were acquainted with the lore needed for the exercise of the enchantments, and which is known by the name of Weird-songs, but no such women came forward. Then was search made throughout the homestead if any woman were so learned. Then answered Gudrid, "I am not skilled in deep learning, nor am I a wise-woman, although Halldis, my foster-mother, taught me, in Iceland, the lore which she called Weird-songs." "Then art thou wise in good season," answered Thorbjorg; but Gudrid replied, "That lore and the ceremony are of such a kind, that I purpose to be of no assistance therein, because I am a Christian woman." Then answered Thorbjorg, "Thou mightest perchance afford thy help to the men in this company, and yet be none the worse woman than thou wast before; but to Thorkell give I charge to provide here the things that are needful." Thorkell thereupon urged Gudrid to consent, and she yielded to his wishes. The women formed a ring round about, and Thorbjorg ascended the scaffold and the seat prepared for her enchantments. Then sang Gudrid the weird-song in so beautiful and excellent a manner, that to no one there did it seem that he had ever before heard the song in voice so beautiful as now. The spae-queen thanked her for the song. "Many spirits," said she, "have been present under its charm, and were pleased to listen to the song, who before would turn away from us, and grant us no such homage. And now are many things clear to me which before were hidden both from me and others. And I am able this to say, that the dearth will last no longer — the season improving as spring advances. The epidemic of fever which has long oppressed us will disappear quicker than we could have hoped. And thee, Gudrid, will I recompense straightway, for that aid of thine which has stood us in good stead; because thy destiny is now clear to me, and foreseen. Thou shalt make a match here in Greenland, a most honourable one, though it will not be a long-lived one for thee, because thy way lies out to Iceland; and there, shall arise from thee a line of descendants both numerous and goodly, and over the branches of thy family shall shine a bright ray. And so fare thee now well and happily, my daughter." Afterwards the men went to the wise-woman, and each enquired after what he was most curious to know. She was also liberal of her replies, and what she said proved true. After this came one from another homestead after her, and she then went there. Thorbjorn was invited, because he did not wish to remain at home while such heathen worship was performing. The weather soon improved when once spring began, as Thorbjorg had said, Thorbjorn made ready his ship, and went on until he came to Brattahlid (the steep slope). Erik received him with the utmost cordiality, saying he had done well to come there. Thorbjorn and his family were with him during the winter. And in the following spring Erik gave to Thorbjorn land at Stokknes, and handsome farm buildings were there built for him, and he dwelt there afterwards.

rik had a wife who was named Thjodhild, and two sons; the one was named Thorstein, and the other Leif. These sons of Erik were both promising men. Thorstein was then at home with his father; and there was at that time no man in Greenland who was thought so highly of as he. Leif had sailed to Norway, and was there with King Olaf Tryggvason. Now, when Leif sailed from Greenland during the summer, he and his men were driven out of their course to the Sudreyjar. They were slow in getting a favourable wind from this place, and they stayed there a long time during the summer, reaching Norway about harvest-tide. He joined the body-guard of King Olaf Tryggvason, and the king formed an excellent opinion of him, and it appeared to him that Leif was a well-bred man. Once upon a time the king entered into conversation with Leif, and asked him, "Dost thou purpose sailing to Greenland in summer?" Leif answered, "I should wish so to do, if it is your will." The king replied, "I think it may well be so; thou shalt go my errand, and preach Christianity in Greenland." Leif said that he was willing to undertake it, but that, for himself, he considered that message a difficult one to proclaim in Greenland. But the king said that he knew no man who was better fitted for the work than he. "And thou shalt carry," said he, "good luck with thee in it." "That can only be," said Leif, "if I carry yours with me." Leif set sail as soon as he was ready. He was tossed about a long time out at sea, and lighted upon lands of which before he had no expectation. There were fields of wild wheat, and the vine-tree in full growth. There were also the trees which were called maples; and they gathered of all this certain tokens; some trunks so large that they were used in house-building. Leif came upon men who had been shipwrecked, and took them home with him, and gave them sustenance during the winter. Thus did he show his great munificence and his graciousness when he brought Christianity to the land, and saved the shipwrecked crew. He was called Leif the Lucky. Leif reached land in Eriksfjordr, and proceeded home to Brattahlid. The people received him gladly. He soon after preached Christianity and catholic truth throughout the land, making known to the people the message of King Olaf Tryggvason; and declaring how many renowned deeds and what great glory accompanied this faith. Erik took coldly to the proposal to forsake his religion, but his wife, Thjodhild, promptly yielded, and caused a church to be built not very near the houses. The building was called Thjodhild's Church; in that spot she offered her prayers, and so did those men who received Christ, and they were many. After she accepted the faith, Thjodhild would have no intercourse with Erik, and this was a great trial to his temper.

After this there was much talk about making ready to go to the land which Leif had discovered. Thorstein, Erik's son, was chief mover in this, a worthy man, wise and much liked. Erik was also asked to go, and they believed that his luck and foresight would be of the highest use. He was for a long time against it, but did not say nay, when his friends exhorted him to go. They made ready the ship which Thorbjorn had brought there, and there were twenty men who undertook to start in her. They had little property, but chiefly weapons and food. On the morning when Erik left home he took a little box, which had in it gold and silver; he hid the money, and then went forth on his journey. He had proceeded, however, but a little way, when he fell from his horse, and broke his ribs and injured his shoulder, and cried out, "Aiai!" At this accident he sent word to his wife that she should take away the money that he had hidden, declaring his misfortune to be a penalty paid on account of having hid the money. Afterwards they sailed away out of Eriksfjordr with gladness, as their plan seemed to promise success. They were driven about for a long time on the open sea, and came not into the track which they desired. They came in sight of Iceland, and also met with birds from the coast of Ireland. Then was their ship tossed to and fro on the sea. They returned about harvest-tide, worn out by toil and much exhausted, and reached Eriksfjordr at the beginning of winter. Then spake Erik, "You were in better spirits in the summer, when you went forth out of the firth, than you are in now, and yet for all that there is much to be thankful for." Thorstein replied, "It is a chieftain's duty now to look after some arrangement for these men who are without shelter, and to find them food." Erik answered, "That is an ever-true saying, 'You know not until you have got your answer.' I will now take thy counsel about this." All those who had no other abodes were to go with the father and the son. Then came they to land, and went forth home.

Now, after this, I have to tell you how Thorstein, Erik's son, began wooing Gudrid, Thorbjorn's daughter. To his proposals a favourable answer was given, both by the maid herself, and also by her father. The marriage was also arranged, so that Thorstein went to take possession of his bride, and the bridal feast was held at Brattahlid in the autumn. The banquet went off well, and was numerously attended. Thorstein owned a homestead in the Vestribygd on the estate known as Lysufjordr (shining firth). The man who was called Thorstein owned the other half of the homestead. His wife was called Sigrid. Thorstein went, during the autumn, to Lysufjordr, to his namesake, both he and Gudrid. Their reception was a welcome one. They were there during the winter. When little of the winter was past, the event happened there that fever broke out on their estate. The overseer of the work was named Garth. He was an unpopular man. He took the fever first and died. Afterwards, and with but little intermission, one took the fever after another and died. Then Thorstein, Erik's son, fell ill, and also Sigrid, the wife of his namesake Thorstein. And one evening Sigrid left the house, and rested awhile opposite the outer door; and Gudrid accompanied her; and they looked back towards the outer door, and Sigrid screamed out aloud. Gudrid said, "We have come forth unwarily, and thou canst in no wise withstand the cold; let us even go home as quickly as possible." "It is not safe as matters are," answered Sigrid. "There is all that crowd of dead people before the door; Thorstein, thy husband, also, and myself, I recognise among them, and it is a grief thus to behold." And when this passed away, she said, "Let us now go, Gudrid; I see the crowd no longer." Thorstein, Erik's son, had also disappeared from her sight; he had seemed to have a whip in his hand, and to wish to smite the ghostly troop. Afterwards they went in, and before morning came she was dead, and a coffin was prepared for the body. Now, the same day, the men purposed to go out fishing, and Thorstein led them to the landing places, and in the early morning he went to see what they had caught. Then Thorstein, Erik's son, sent word to his namesake to come to him, saying that matters at home were hardly quiet; that the housewife was endeavouring to rise to her feet and to get under the clothes beside him. And when he was come in she had risen upon the edge of the bed. Then took he her by the hands and laid a pole-axe upon her breast. Thorstein, Erik's son, died near nightfall. Thorstein, the franklin, begged Gudrid to lie down and sleep, saying that he would watch over the body during the night. So she did, and when a little of the night was past, Thorstein, Erik's son, sat up and spake, saying he wished Gudrid to be called to him, and that he wished to speak with her. "God wills," he said, "that this hour be given to me for my own, and the further completion of my plan." Thorstein, the franklin, went to find Gudrid, and waked her; begged her to cross herself, and to ask God for help, and told her what Thorstein, Erik's son, had spoken with him; "and he wishes," said he, "to meet with thee. Thou art obliged to consider what plan thou wilt adopt, because I can in this issue advise thee in nowise." She answered, "It may be that this, this wonderful thing, has regard to certain matters, which are afterwards to be had in memory; and I hope that God's keeping will test upon me, and I will, with God's grace, undertake the risk and go to him, and know what he will say, for I shall not be able to escape if harm must happen to me. I am far from wishing that he should go elsewhere; I suspect, moreover, that the matter will be a pressing one." Then went Gudrid and saw Thorstein. He appeared to her as if shedding tears. He spake in her ear, in a low voice, certain words which she alone might know; but this he said so that all heard, "That those men would be blessed who held the true faith, and that all salvation and mercy accompanied it; and that many, nevertheless, held it lightly." "It is," said he, "no good custom which has prevailed here in Greenland since Christianity came, to bury men in unconsecrated ground with few religious rites over them. I wish for myself, and for those other men who have died, to be taken to the church; but for Garth, I wish him to be burned on a funeral pile as soon as may be, for he is the cause of all those ghosts which have been among us this winter." He spake to Gudrid also about her own state, saying that her destiny would be a great one, and begged her to beware of marrying Greenland men. He begged her also to pay over their property to the Church and some to the poor; and then he sank down for the second time. It had been a custom in Greenland, after Christianity was brought there, to bury men in unconsecrated ground on the farms where they died. An upright stake was placed over a body, and when the priests came afterwards to the place, then was the stake pulled out, consecrated water poured therein, and a funeral service held, though it might be long after the burial. The bodies were removed to the church in Eriksfjordr, and funeral services held by the priests. After that died Thorbjorn. The whole property then went to Gudrid. Erik received her into his household, and looked well after her stores.

There was a man named Thorfinn Karlsefni, son of Thord Horsehead, who dwelt in the north (of Iceland), at Reynines in Skagafjordr, as it is now called. Karlsefni was a man of good family, and very rich. His mother's name was Thorun. He engaged in trading journeys, and seemed a goodly, bold, and gallant traveller. One summer Karlsefni prepared his ship, intending to go to Greenland. Snorri, Thorbrand's son, from Alptafjordr, resolved to travel with him, and there were thirty men in the company. There was a man named Bjarni, Grimolf's son, a man of Breidafjordr (Broadfirth); another called Thorhall, son of Gamli, a man from the east of Iceland. They prepared their ship the very same summer as Karlsefni, with intent also to go to Greenland. They had in the ship forty men. The two ships launched out into the open sea as soon as they were ready. It is not recorded how long a voyage they had. But, after this, I have to tell you that both these ships came to Eriksfjordr about autumn. Erik rode down to the ships with other men of the land, and a market-fair was promptly instituted. The captains invited Gudrid to take such of the merchandise as she wished, and Erik displayed on his part much magnificence in return, inasmuch as he invited both these ships' companies home with him to pass the winter in Brattahlid. The merchants accepted the invitation, and went home with Erik. Afterwards their merchandise was removed to Brattahlid, where a good and large outhouse was not lacking in which to store the goods. The merchants were well pleased to stay with Erik during the winter. When now Yule was drawing nigh, Erik began to look more gloomy than he was wont to be. Presently Karlsefni entered into conversation with him, and said, "Art thou in trouble, Erik? It appears to me that thou art somewhat more taciturn than thou hast been; still thou helpest us with much liberality, and we are bound to reward thee according as we have means thereto. Say now what causes thy cheerlessness." Erik answered, "You receive hospitality well, and like worthy men. Now, I have no mind that our intercourse together should be expensive to you; but so it is, that it will seem to me an ill thing if it is heard that you never spent a worse Yule than this, just now beginning, when Erik the Red entertained you at Brattahlid, in Greenland." Karlsefni answered, "It must not come to such a pass; we have in our ships malt, meal, and corn, and you have right and title to take therefrom whatever you wish, and to make your entertainment such as consorts with your munificence." And Erik accepted the offer. Then was preparation made for the Yule-feast, and so magnificent was it that the men thought they had scarcely ever seen so grand a feast. And after Yule, Karlsefni broached to Erik the subject of a marriage with Gudrid, which he thought might be under Erik's control, and the woman appeared to him to be both beautiful and of excellent understanding. Erik answered and said, that for his part he would willingly undertake his suit, and said, moreover, that she was worthy of a good match. It is also likely, he thought, that she will be following out her destiny, should she be given to him; and, moreover, the report which comes to me of him is good. The proposals were now laid before her, and she allowed the marriage with her to be arranged which Erik wished to promote. However, I will not now speak at length how this marriage took place; the Yule festival was prolonged and made into a marriage-feast. Great joy was there in Brattahlid during the winter. Much playing at backgammon and telling of stories went on, and many things were done that ministered to the comfort of the household.

During this time much talk took place in Brattahlid about making ready to go to Vinland the Good, and it was asserted that they would there find good choice lands. The discourse came to such conclusion that Karlsefni and Snorri prepared their ship, with the intention of seeking Vinland during the summer. Bjarni and Thorhall ventured on the same expedition, with their ship and the retinue which had accompanied them. There was a man named Thorvard; he married Freydis, natural daughter of Erik the Red; he set out with them likewise, as also Thorvald, a son of Erik. There was a man named Thorvald; he was a son-in-law of Erik the Red. Thorhall was called the Sportsman; he had for a long time been Erik's companion in hunting and fishing expeditions during the summers, and many things had been committed to his keeping. Thorhall was a big man, dark, and of gaunt appearance; rather advanced in years, overbearing in temper, of melancholy mood, silent at all times, underhand in his dealings, and withal given to abuse, and always inclined towards the worst. He had kept himself aloof from the true faith when it came to Greenland. He was but little encompassed with the love of friends, but yet Erik had long held conversation with him. He went in the ship with Thorvald and his man, because he was widely acquainted with the unpeopled districts. They had the ship which Thorbjorn had brought to Greenland, and they ventured on the expedition with Karlsefni and the others; and most of them in this ship were Greenlanders. There were one hundred and sixty men in their ships. They sailed away from land; then to the Vestribygd and to Bjarneyjar (the Bear Islands). Thence they sailed away from Bjarneyjar with northerly winds. They were out at sea two half-days. Then they came to land, and rowed along it in boats, and explored it, and found there flat stones, many and so great that two men might well lie on them stretched on their backs with heel to heel. Polar-foxes were there in abundance. This land they gave name to, and called it Helluland (stone-land). Then they sailed with northerly winds two half-days, and there was then land before them, and on it a great forest and many wild beasts. An island lay in the south-east off the land, and they found bears thereon, and called the island Bjarney (Bear Island); but the mainland, where the forest was, they called Markland (forest-land). Then, when two half-days were passed, they saw land, and sailed under it. There was a cape to which they came. They cruised along the land, leaving it on the starboard side. There was a harbourless coast-land, and long sandy strands. They went to the land in boats, and found the keel of a ship, and called the place Kjalar-nes (Keelness). They gave also name to the strands, calling them Furdustrandir (wonder-shore), because it was tedious to sail by them. Then the coast became indented with creeks, and they directed their ships along the creeks. Now, before this, when Leif was with King Olaf Tryggvason, and the king had requested him to preach Christianity in Greenland, he gave him two Scotch people, the man called Haki, and the woman called Hækja. The king requested Leif to have recourse to these people if ever he should want fleetness, because they were swifter than wild beasts. Erik and Leif had got these people to go with Karlsefni. Now, when they had sailed by Furdustrandir, they put the Scotch people on land, and requested them to run into the southern regions, seek for choice land, and come back after three half-days were passed. They were dressed in such wise that they had on the garment which they called *biafal*. It was made with a hood at the top, open at the sides, without sleeves, and was fastened between the legs. A button and a loop held it together there; and elsewhere they were without clothing. Then did they cast anchors from the ships, and lay there to wait for them. And when three days were expired the Scotch people leapt down from the land, and one of them had in his hand a bunch of grapes, and the other an ear of wild wheat.

They said to Karlsefni that they considered they had found good and choice land. Then they received them into their ship, and proceeded on their journey to where the shore was cut into by a firth. They directed the ships within the firth. There was an island lying out in front of the firth, and there were great currents around the island, which they called Straums-ey (Stream-island). There were so many birds on it that scarcely was it possible to put one's feet down for the eggs. They continued their course up the firth, which they called Straumsfjordr, and carried their cargo ashore from the ships, and there they prepared to stay. They had with them cattle of all kinds, and for themselves they sought out the produce of the land thereabout. There were mountains, and the place was fair to look upon. They gave no heed to anything except to explore the land, and they found large pastures. They remained there during the winter, which happened to be a hard one, with no work doing; and they were badly off for food, and the fishing failed. Then they went out to the island, hoping that something might be got there from fishing or from what was drifted ashore. In that spot there was little, however, to be got for food, but their cattle found good sustenance. After that they called upon God, praying that He would send them some little store of meat, but their prayer was not so soon granted as they were eager that it should be. Thorhall disappeared from sight, and they went to seek him, and sought for three half-days continuously. On the fourth half-day Karlsefni and Bjarni found him on the peak of a crag. He lay with his face to the sky, with both eyes and mouth and nostrils wide open, clawing and pinching himself, and reciting something. They asked why he had come there. He replied that it was of no importance; begged them not to wonder thereat; as for himself, he had lived so long, they needed not to take any account of him. They begged him to go home with them, and he did so. A little while after a whale was driven ashore, and the men crowded round it, and cut it up, and still they knew not what kind of whale it was. Even Karlsefni recognised it not, though he had great knowledge of whales. It was cooked by the cook-boys, and they ate thereof; though bad effects came upon all from it afterwards. Then began Thorhall, and said, "Has it not been that the Redbeard has proved a better friend than your Christ? this was my gift for the poetry which I composed about Thor, my patron; seldom has he failed me." Now, when the men knew that, none of them would eat of it, and they threw it down from the rocks, and turned with their supplications to God's mercy. Then was granted to them opportunity of fishing, and after that there was no lack of food that spring. They went back again from the island, within Straumsfjordr, and obtained food from both sides; from hunting on the mainland, and from gathering eggs and from fishing on the side of the sea.

When summer was at hand they discussed about their journey, and made an arrangement. Thorhall the Sportsman wished to proceed northwards along Furdustrandir, and off Kjalarnes, and so seek Vinland; but Karlsefni desired to proceed southwards along the land and away from the east, because the land appeared to him the better the further south he went, and he thought it also more advisable to explore in both directions. Then did Thorhall make ready for his journey out by the islands, and there volunteered for the expedition with him not more than nine men; but with Karlsefni there went the remainder of the company. And one day, when Thorhall was carrying water to his ship, he drank, and recited this verse:

"The clashers of weapons did say when I came here that I should have the best of drink (though it becomes me not to complain before the common people). Eager God of the war-helmet! I am made to raise the bucket; wine has not moistened my beard, rather do I kneel at the fountain."

Afterwards they put to sea, and Karlsefni accompanied them by the island. Before they hoisted sail Thorhall recited a verse:

"Go we back where our countrymen are. Let us make the skilled hawk of the sand-heaven explore the broad ship-courses; while the dauntless rousers of the sword-storm, who praise the land, and cook whale, dwell on Furdustrandir."

Then they left, and sailed northwards along Furdustrandir and Kjalarnes, and attempted there to sail against a wind from the west. A gale came upon them, however, and drove them onwards against Ireland, and there were they severely treated, enthralled, and beaten. Then Thorhall lost his life.

Karlsefni proceeded southwards along the land, with Snorri and Bjarni and the rest of the company. They journeyed a long while, and until they arrived at a river, which came down from the land and fell into a lake, and so on to the sea. There were large islands off the mouth of the river, and they could not come into the river except at high flood-tide. Karlsefni and his people sailed to the mouth of the river, and called the land Hop. There they found fields of wild wheat wherever there were low grounds; and the vine in all places were there was rough rising ground. Every rivulet there was full of fish. They made holes where the land and water joined and where the tide went highest; and when it ebbed they found halibut in the holes. There was great plenty of wild animals of every form in the wood. They were there half a month, amusing themselves, and not becoming aware of anything. Their cattle they had with them. And early one morning, as they looked around, they beheld nine canoes made of hides, and snout-like staves were being brandished from the boats, and they made a noise like flails, and twisted round in the direction of the sun's motion. Then Karlsefni said, "What will this betoken?" Snorri answered him, "It may be that it is a token of peace; let us take a white shield and go to meet them." And so they did. Then did they in the canoes row forwards, and showed surprise at them, and came to land. They were short men, ill-looking, with their hair in disorderly fashion on their heads; they were large-eyed, and had broad cheeks. And they stayed there awhile in astonishment. Afterwards they rowed away to the south, off the headland.

They had built their settlements up above the lake. And some of the dwellings were well within the land, but some were near the lake. Now they remained there that winter. They had no snow whatever, and all their cattle went out to graze without keepers. Now when spring began, they beheld one morning early, that a fleet of hide-canoes was rowing from the south off the headland; so many were they as if the sea were strewn with pieces of charcoal, and there was also the brandishing of staves as before from each boat. Then they held shields up, and a market was formed between them; and this people in their purchases preferred red cloth; in exchange they had furs to give, and skins quite grey. They wished also to buy swords and lances, but Karlsefni and Snorri forbad it. They offered for the cloth dark hides, and took in exchange a span long of cloth, and bound it round their heads; and so matters went on for a while. But when the stock of cloth began to grow small, then they split it asunder, so that it was not more than a finger's breadth. The Skroelingar (Esquimaux) gave for it still quite as much, or more than before.

Now it came to pass that a bull, which belonged to Karlsefni's people, rushed out of the wood and bellowed loudly at the same time. The Skroelingar, frightened thereat, rushed away to their canoes, and rowed south along the coast. There was then nothing seen of them for three weeks together. When that time was gone by, there was seen approaching from the south a great crowd of Skroelingar boats, coming down upon them like a stream, the staves this time being all brandished in the direction opposite to the sun's motion, and the Skroelingar were all howling loudly. Then took they and bare red shields to meet them. They encountered one another and fought, and there was a great shower of missiles. The Skroelingar had also war-slings, or catapults. Then Karlsefni and Snorri see that the Skroelingar are bringing up poles, with a very large ball attached to each, to be compared in size to a sheep's stomach, dark in colour; and these flew over Karlsefni's company towards the land, and when they came down they struck the ground with a hideous noise. This produced great terror in Karlsefni and his company, so that their only impulse was to retreat up the country along the river, because it seemed as if crowds of Skroelingar were driving at them from all sides. And they stopped not until they came to certain crags. There they offered them stern resistance. Freydis came out and saw how they were retreating. She called out, "Why run you away from such worthless creatures, stout men that ye are, when, as seems to me likely, you might slaughter them like so many cattle? Let me but have a weapon, I think I could fight better than any of you." They gave no heed to what she said. Freydis endeavoured to accompany them, still she soon lagged behind, because she was not well; she went after them into the wood, and the Skroelingar directed their pursuit after her. She came upon a dead man; Thorbrand, Snorri's son, with a flat stone fixed in his head; his sword lay beside him, so she took it up and prepared to defend herself therewith. Then came the Skroelingar upon her. She let down her sark and struck her breast with the naked sword. At this they were frightened, rushed off to their boats, and fled away. Karlsefni and the rest came up to her and praised her zeal. Two of Karlsefni's men fell, and four of the Skroelingar, notwithstanding they had overpowered them by superior numbers. After that, they proceeded to their booths, and began to reflect about the crowd of men which attacked them upon the land; it appeared to them now that the one troop will have been that which came in the boats, and the other troop will have been a delusion of sight. The Skroelingar also found a dead man, and his axe lay beside him. One of them struck a stone with it, and broke the axe. It seemed to them good for nothing, as it did not withstand the stone, and they threw it down.

Karlsefni and his company were now of opinion that though the land might be choice and good, there would be always war and terror overhanging them, from those who dwelt there before them. They made ready, therefore, to move away, with intent to go to their own land. They sailed forth northwards, and found five Skroelingar in jackets of skin, sleeping near the sea, and they had with them a chest, and in it was marrow of animals mixed with blood; and they considered that these must have been outlawed. They slew them. Afterwards they came to a headland and a multitude of wild animals; and this headland appeared as if it might be a cake of cow-dung, because the animals passed the winter there. Now they came to Straumsfjordr, where also they had abundance of all kinds. It is said by some that Bjarni and Freydis remained there, and a hundred men with them, and went not further away. But Karlsefni and Snorri journeyed southwards, and forty men with them, and after staying no longer than scarcely two months at Hop, had come back the same summer. Karlsefni set out with a single ship to seek Thorhall, but the rest of the company remained behind. He and his people went northwards off Kjalarnes, and were then borne onwards towards the west, and the land lay on their larboard-side, and was nothing but wilderness. And when they had proceeded for a long time, there was a river which came down from the land, flowing from the east towards the west. They directed their course within the river's mouth, and lay opposite the southern bank.

ne morning Karlsefni's people beheld as it were a glittering speak above the open space in front of them, and they shouted at it. It stirred itself, and it was a being of the race of men that have only one foot, and he came down quickly to where they lay. Thorvald, son of Erik the Red, sat at the tiller, and the One-footer shot him with an arrow in the lower abdomen. He drew out the arrow. Then said Thorvald, "Good land have we reached, and fat is it about the paunch."Then the One-footer leapt away again northwards. They chased after him, and saw him occasionally, but it seemed as if he would escape them. He disappeared at a certain creek. Then they turned back, and one man spake this ditty:

"Our men chased (all true it is) a One-footer down to the shore; but the wonderful man strove hard in the race.... Hearken, Karlsefni."

Then they journeyed away back again northwards, and saw, as they thought, the land of the One-footers. They wished, however, no longer to risk their company. They conjectured the mountains to be all one range; those, that is, which were at Hop, and those which they now discovered; almost answering to one another; and it was the same distance to them on both sides from Straumsfjordr. They journeyed back, and were in Straumsfjordr the third winter. Then fell the men greatly into backsliding. They who were wifeless pressed their claims at the hands of those who were married. Snorri, Karlsefni's son, was born the first autumn, and he was three winters old when they began their journey home. Now, when they sailed from Vinland, they had a southern wind, and reached Markland, and found five Skroelingar; one was a bearded man, two were women, two children. Karlsefni's people caught the children, but the others escaped and sunk down into the earth. And they took the children with them, and taught them their speech, and they were baptized. The children called their mother Voetilldi, and their father Uvoegi. They said that kings ruled over the land of the Skroelingar, one of whom was called Avalldamon, and the other Valldidida. They said also that there were no houses, and the people lived in caves or holes. They said, moreover, that there was a land on the other side over against their land, and the people there were dressed in white garments, uttered loud cries, bare long poles, and wore fringes. This was supposed to be Hvitramannaland (whiteman's land). Then came they to Greenland, and remained with Erik the Red during the winter.

Bjarni, Grimolf's son, and his men were carried into the Irish Ocean, and came into a part where the sea was infested by ship-worms. They did not find it out before the ship was eaten through under them; then they debated what plan they should follow. They had a ship's boat which was smeared with tar made of seal-fat. It is said that the ship-worm will not bore into the wood which has been smeared with the seal-tar. The counsel and advice of most of the men was to ship into the boat as many men as it would hold. Now, when that was tried, the boat held not more than half the men. Then Bjarni advised that it should be decided by the casting of lots, and not by the rank of the men, which of them should go into the boat; and inasmuch as every man there wished to go into the boat, though it could not hold all of them; therefore, they accepted the plan to cast lots who should leave the ship for the boat. And the lot so fell that Bjarni, and nearly half the men with him, were chosen for the boat. So then those left the ship and went into the boat who had been chosen by lot so to do. And when the men were come into the boat, a young man, an Icelander, who had been a fellow-traveller of Bjarni, said, "Dost thou intend, Bjarni, to separate thyself here from me." "It must needs be so now," Bjarni answered. He replied, "Because, in such case, thou didst not so promise me when I set out from Iceland with thee from the homestead of my father." Bjarni answered, "I do not, however, see here any other plan; but what plan dost thou suggest?" He replied, "I propose this plan, that we two make a change in our places, and thou come here and I will go there." Bjarni answered, "So shall it be; and this I see, that thou labourest willingly for life, and that it seems to thee a grievous thing to face death." Then they changed places. The man went into the boat, and Bjarni back into the ship; and it is said that Bjarni perished there in the Worm-sea, and they who were with him in the ship; but the boat and those who were in it went on their journey until they reached land, and told this story afterwards.

The next summer Karlsefni set out for Iceland, and Snorri with him, and went home to his house in Reynines. His mother considered that he had made a shabby match, and she was not at home the first winter. But when she found that Gudrid was a lady without peer, she went home, and their intercourse was happy. The daughter of Snorri, Karlsefni's son, was Hallfrid, mother of Bishop Thorlak, the son of Runolf. Hallfrid and Runolf had a son, whose name was Thorbjorn; his daughter was Thorun, mother of Bishop Bjarn. Thorgeir was the name of a son of Snorri, Karlsefni's son; he was father of Yngvild, the mother of the first Bishop Brand. And here ends this story.

The Saga of Grettir the Strong

Chapter I
The Family and Early Wars of Onund the Son of Ofeig

There was a man named Onund, the son of Ofeig Clumsyfoot, who was the son of Ivar Horsetail. Onund was the brother of Gudbjorg, the mother of Gudbrand Knob, the father of Asta, the mother of King Olaf the Saint. His mother came from the Upplands, while his father's relations were mostly in Rogaland and Hordland. He was a great viking and used to harry away in the West over the sea. He was accompanied on these expeditions by one Balki, the son of Blaeing from Sotanes, and by Orm the Wealthy. Another comrade of theirs was named Hallvard. They had five ships, all well equipped. They plundered the Hebrides, reaching the Barra Isles, where there ruled a king named Kjarval, who also had five ships. These they attacked; there was a fierce battle between them, in which Onund's men fought with the utmost bravery. After many had fallen on both sides, the battle ended with the king taking to flight with a single ship; the rest were captured by Onund's force, along with much booty. They stayed there for the winter, and spent the succeeding three summers harrying the coasts of Ireland and Scotland, after which they returned to Norway.

Chapter II
The Battle Of Hafrsfjord

At that time Norway was very disturbed. Harald Shockhead, the son of Halfdan the Black, till then king of the Upplands, was aiming at the supreme kingship. He went into the North and fought many battles there, in which he was always victorious. Then he marched harrying through the territories to the South, bringing them into subjection wherever he came. On reaching Hordland he was opposed by a motley multitude led by Kjotvi the Wealthy, Thorir Long-chin, and Soti and King Sulki from South Rogaland. Geirmund Swarthyskin was then away in the West, beyond the sea, so he was not present at the battle, although Hordland belonged to his dominion.

Onund and his party had arrived that autumn from the western seas, and when Thorir and Kjotvi heard of their landing they sent envoys to ask for their aid, promising to treat them with honour.

They were very anxious for an opportunity of distinguishing themselves, so they joined Thorir's forces, and declared that they would be in the thickest part of the battle. They met King Harald in a fjord in Rogaland called Hafrsfjord. The forces on each side were very large, and the battle was one of the greatest ever fought in Norway. There are many accounts of it, for one always hears much about those people of whom the saga is told. Troops had come in from all the country around and from other countries as well, besides a multitude of vikings. Onund brought his ship alongside of that of Thorir Long-chin in the very middle of the battle. King Harald made for Thorir's ship, knowing him to be a terrible berserk, and very brave. The fighting was desperate on either side. Then the king ordered his berserks, the men called Wolfskins, forward. No iron could hurt them, and when they charged nothing could withstand them. Thorir defended himself bravely and fell on his ship fighting valiantly. The whole ship from stem to stern was cleared and her fastenings were cut, so that she fell out of the line of battle. Then they attacked Onund's ship, in the forepart of which he was standing and fighting manfully. The king's men said: "He bears himself well in the forecastle. Let us give him something to remind him of having been in the battle." Onund was stepping out with one foot on to the bulwark, and as he was striking they made a thrust at him with a spear; in parrying it he bent backwards, and at that moment a man on the forecastle of the king's ship struck him and took off his leg below the knee, disabling him at a blow. With him fell the greater number of his men. They carried him to a ship belonging to a man named Thrand, a son of Bjorn and brother of Eyvind the Easterner. He was fighting against King Harald, and his ship was lying on the other side of Onund's. Then there was a general flight. Thrand and the rest of the vikings escaped any way they could, and sailed away westwards. They took with them Onund and Balki and Hallvard Sugandi. Onund recovered and went about for the rest of his life with a wooden leg, wherefore he was called Onund Treefoot as long as he lived.

Chapter III
Meeting Of Defeated Chiefs In The West And Marriage Of Onund

There were then in the western parts many distinguished men who had fled from their homes in Norway before King Harald, for he declared all who fought against him outlaws, and seized their property. As soon as Onund had recovered from his wound, Thrand went with his party to Geirmund Swarthyskin, who was the most eminent of the vikings in the West. They asked him whether he was not going to try and regain his kingdom in Hordland, and offered to join him, hoping by this means to do something for their own properties, for Onund was very wealthy and his kindred very powerful. Geirmund answered that Harald had such a force that there was little hope of gaining any honour by fighting when the whole country had joined against him and been beaten. He had no mind, he said, to become the king's thrall, and to beg for that which he had once possessed in his own right. Seeing that he was no longer in the vigour of his youth he preferred to find some other occupation. So Onund and his party returned to the Southern Islands, where they met many of their friends.

There was a man named Ofeig, nicknamed Grettir. He was the son of Einar, the son of Olvir the Babyman. He was a brother of Oleif the Broad, the father of Thormod Shaft. Another son of Olvir was named Steinolf, the father of Una, whom Thorbjorn the Salmon-man married. A third son of Olvir was Steinmod, who was the father of Konal, the father of Alfdis of the

Barra Isles. Konal's son was named Steimnod; he was the father of Halldora, whom Eilif, the son of Ketil the One-handed, married.

Ofeig Grettir married Asny, the daughter of Vestar, the son of Haeing. His sons were Asmund the Beardless and Asbjorn, and his daughters were named Aldis, Aesa, and Asvor. Ofeig had fled from the wrath of King Harald into the West over the sea, along with his kinsman Thormod Shaft and all their families. They ravaged far and wide in the western seas. Thrand and Onund Treefoot were going West to Ireland to join Thrand's brother, Eyvind the Easterner, who had command of the Irish defences. Eyvind's mother was named Hlif; she was the daughter of Hrolf, the son of Ingjald, the son of King Frodi, while Thrand's mother was Helga, the daughter of Ondott Crow. The father of Eyvind and Thrand was Bjorn, the son of Hrolf of Ar. He had had to leave Gautland because he had burnt in his house Sigfast the father-in-law of King Solvi. Then he went to Norway and spent the winter with Grim the Hersir, a son of Kolbjorn the Sneak, who wanted to murder him for his money. Thence Bjorn went to Ondott Crow, who lived in Hvinisfjord in Agdir. There he was well received, stayed the winter, and went campaigning with Ondott in the summer until his wife Hlif died. Eventually Ondott gave Bjorn his daughter Helga, and Bjorn then no longer went out to fight. Eyvind had taken over his father's ships and become a great chief in the western parts. He married Rafarta, the daughter of the Irish king Kjarval. Their sons were Helgi the Lean and Snaebjorn.

When Thrand and Onund came to the Southern Islands they found there Ofeig Grettir and Thormod Shaft, with whom they became very friendly, for each thought the others had risen from the dead, their last meeting having been in Norway when the war was at its worst. Onund was very silent, and Thrand, when he noticed it, asked what was on his mind. Onund answered with a verse:

> "No joy is mine since in battle I fought.
> Many the sorrows that o'er me lower.
> Men hold me for nought; this thought is the worst
> of all that oppresses my sorrowing heart."

Thrand said: "Why, you still seem as full of vigour as ever you were. You may yet settle down and marry. You shall have my good word and my interest if you will only tell me whom you fancy."

Onund said he behaved nobly; but said there had once been a time when his chances of making a profitable marriage had been better.

Thrand said: "Ofeig has a daughter named Aesa; we might mention it if you like."

Onund said he would like it, and soon afterwards Ofeig was approached on the subject. He received the proposal favourably, saying he knew the man to be of good lineage and to have some wealth in movable property, though his lands were not worth much. "But," he said, "I do not think he is very wise. Why, my daughter is quite a child."

Thrand said that Onund was more vigorous than many a man whose legs were sounder.

So with the aid of Thrand the terms were settled. Ofeig was to give his daughter a portion in cash, for neither would reckon anything for his lands in Norway. Soon afterwards Thrand was betrothed to the daughter of Thormod Shaft. Both the maids were to remain plighted for three years.

Then they went on fighting expeditions in the summer, remaining in the Barra Isles during the winter.

Chapter IV
Fight With Vikings Vigbjod And Vestmar

There were two Vikings from the Southern Isles, named Vigbjod and Vestmar; they were abroad both summer and winter. They had eight ships, and harried mostly round the coast of Ireland, where they did many an evil deed until Eyvind undertook the defence of the coast, when they retired to the Hebrides to harry there, and right in to the Scotch firths. Thrand and Onund went out against them and learned that they had sailed to an island called Bot. Onund and Thrand followed them thither with five ships, and when the vikings sighted them and saw how many there were, they thought their own force was sufficient, so they took to their arms and advanced to the attack. Onund ordered his ships to take up a position between two rocks where there was a deep but narrow channel, open to attack from one side only, and by not more than five ships at once. Onund was a very wily man. He sent his five ships forward into the channel so that, as there was plenty of sea room behind them, they could easily retire by merely backing their oars. One ship he brought under an island lying on their beam, and carried a great stone to a place on the front of the rock where it could not be seen from the enemy's ships. The Vikings came boldly on, thinking they had caught them in a trap. Vigbjod asked who they were that he had hemmed in. Thrand answered that he was a brother of Eyvind the Easterner, and the man with him was his comrade, Onund Treefoot. The Vikings laughed and said:

"Trolls take the rascal Treefoot
and lay him even with the ground.
Never yet did I see men go to battle
who could not carry themselves."

Onund said that could not be known until it was tried. Then the ships came together. There was a great battle in which both sides fought bravely. When the battle was thick Onund ordered his ships to back their oars. The vikings seeing it thought they were taking to flight, and pushed on with all their might, coming under the rock just at the moment when the party which had been dispatched for that purpose arrived. They launched upon the vikings stones so huge that nothing could hold against them. A number of the vikings were killed, and others were so injured that they could fight no more. Then the vikings tried to escape, but could not, as their ships were in the narrowest part of the channel and were impeded both by the current and by the enemy's ships. Onund's men vigorously attacked the wing commanded by Vigbjod while Thrand engaged Vestmar, but effected little. When the men on Vigbjod's ship had been somewhat reduced, Onund's men, he himself with them, prepared to board her. On seeing that, Vigbjod spurred on his men resolutely. He turned against Onund, most of whose men gave way. Onund was a man of immense strength and he bade his followers observe how it fared with them. They shoved a log under the stump of his leg, so that he stood pretty firm. The viking dashed forward, reached Onund and hewed at him with his sword, which cut right through his shield and into the log beneath his leg, where it remained fixed. As Vigbjod bent down to pull his sword clear again, Onund dealt him a blow on his shoulder, severing his arm and disabling him. When Vestmar saw his comrade fall, he sprang on to the outermost ship and escaped along with all who could get on to her. Then they examined the dead. Vigbjod had already expired. Onund went up to him and said:

"Bloody thy wounds. Didst thou see me flee?
'One-leg' no hurt received from thee.
Braver are many in word than in deed.
Thou, slave, didst fail when it came to the trial."

They took a large quantity of booty and returned to the Barra Isles in the autumn.

Chapter V
Visit Of Onund And Thrand To Eyvind In Ireland

The following summer they made ready for a voyage to the West, to Ireland. At the same time Balki and Hallvard sailed westwards, to Iceland, where they had heard that good land was available for occupation. Balki took up some land at Hrutafjord, and had his abode in two places called Balkastad. Hallvard occupied Sugandafjord and Skalavik as far as Stigi, where he lived.

Thrand and Onund went to visit Eyvind the Easterner, who welcomed joyfully his brother Thrand; but when he heard that Onund had also come, he became very angry and wanted to fight him. Thrand asked him not to do so, and said it would ill become him to quarrel with men from Norway, especially with such as had given no offence. Eyvind said that he had given offence before, when he made war on Kjarval the king, and that he should now pay for it. The brothers had much to say to each other about the matter, till at last Thrand said that he and Onund should share their fortune together. Then Eyvind allowed himself to be appeased. They stayed there a long time in the summer and went with Eyvind on his expeditions. Eyvind found Onund to be a man of the greatest valour. In the autumn they went to the Hebrides, and Eyvind made over to Thrand all his share in their father Bjorn's patrimony in the event of Bjorn dying before Thrand. They stayed in the Hebrides until they married and some years after.

Chapter VI
Death Of Bjorn; Disputes Over His Property In Norway

The next thing that happened was the death of Thrand's father Bjorn. When the news of it reached Grim the Hersir he proceeded against Ondott Crow and claimed Bjorn's estate. Ondott held Thrand to be the rightful heir of his father, but Grim contended that Thrand was away in the

West. Bjorn, he said, came from Gautland, and the succession to the estate of all foreigners passed to the king. Ondott said that he would hold the property on behalf of Thrand, who was his daughter's son. Grim then departed, having effected nothing by his claim.

Thrand, when he heard of his father's death, prepared to leave the Hebrides, and Onund Treefoot decided to go with him. Ofeig Grettir and Thormod Shaft went to Iceland with all their belongings, landing at Eyrar in the South. They spent the first winter with Thorbjorn the Salmon-man, and then occupied Gnupverjahrepp. Ofeig took the outer part lying between the rivers Thvera and Kalfa, and lived at Ofeigsstad near Steinsholt, while Thormod took the eastern part, living at Skaptaholt. Thormod's daughters were named Thorvor and Thorve; the former afterwards became the mother of Thorodd the Godi at Hjalli, Thorve of Thorstein the Godi the father of Bjarni the Wise.

We now return to Thrand and Onund, who sailed back from the West to Norway. A strong wind blew in their favour, so that they arrived at the house of Ondott Crow before any one knew of their journey. He welcomed Thrand and told him of the claim which Grim the Hersir had raised for Bjorn's estate.

"To my thinking, kinsman," he said, "it is better that the property should go to you than to the king's thralls. It is a fortunate thing for you that no one knows of your having come here, for I expect that Grim will make an attack upon one or the other of us if he can. I should prefer if you would take over your property and stay in other countries."

Thrand said that he would do so. He took over the property and prepared to leave Norway. Before leaving he asked Onund Treefoot whether he would not come to Iceland. Onund said he wanted first to visit some of his relations and friends in the South.

"Then," said Thrand, "we must part. I should be glad if you would give my kinsmen your support, for our enemies will certainly try to take revenge upon them when I am gone. I am going to Iceland, and I want you to come there too."

Onund said he would come, and they parted with great friendship. Thrand went to Iceland, where he met with a welcome from Ofeig and Thormod Shaft. He took up his dwelling at Thrandarholt to the west of Thjorsa.

Chapter VII
Murder Of Ondott Crow, And The Vengeance Therefor

Onund went to Rogaland in the South and visited many of his relations and friends. He lived there in concealment with a man named Kolbeinn. He there learned that King Harald had taken all his property and given it into the charge of a man named Harekr, one of his officials. Onund went by night to Harekr's house and caught him at home; he was led to execution. Then Onund took possession of all the loose property which he found and burnt the building.

That autumn Grim the Hersir murdered Ondott Crow because he had not succeeded in getting the property for the king. Ondott's wife Signy carried off all their loose property that same night to a ship and escaped with her sons Asmund and Asgrim to her father Sighvat. A little later she sent her sons to Hedin, her foster-father in Soknadal, where they remained for a time and then wanted to return to their mother. They left at last, and at Yule-tide came to Ingjald the Trusty at Hvin. His wife Gyda persuaded him to take them in, and they spent the winter there.

In the spring Onund came to northern Agdir, having learned of the murder of Ondott. He met Signy and asked her what assistance they would have of him. She said they were most anxious to punish Grim for the death of Ondott. So the sons were sent for, and when they met Onund Treefoot they all joined together and had Grim's doings closely watched.

In the summer there was a beer-brewing at Grim's for a jarl named Audun, whom he had invited. When Onund and the sons of Ondott heard of it, they appeared at his house unexpectedly and set fire to it. Grim the Hersir and about thirty men were burnt in the house. They captured a quantity of valuables. Then Onund went into the forest, while the two brothers took the boat of their foster-father Ingjald, rowed away and lay in hiding a little way off. Soon jarl Audun appeared, on his way to the feast, as had been arranged, but on arriving he missed his host. So he collected his men around him and stayed there a few nights, quite unaware of Onund and his companions. He slept in a loft with two other men. Onund knew everything that was going on in the house and sent for the two brothers to come to him. On their arrival he asked them whether they preferred to keep watch on the house or to attack the jarl. They chose to attack. They then battered the entrance of the loft with beams until the door gave way. Asmund seized the two men who were with the jarl and threw them to the ground with such violence that they were well-nigh killed.

Asgrim rushed at the jarl and demanded of him weregild for his father, for he had been in league with Grim and took part in the attack when Ondott was murdered. The jarl said he had no money about him and asked for time. Asgrim then placed the point of his spear against his breast and ordered him to pay up on the spot. Then the jarl took a necklace from his neck and gave it to him with three gold rings and a velvet mantle. Asgrim took the things and bestowed a name upon the jarl. He called him Audun Nannygoat.

When the farmers and people about heard of the disturbances they all came out to help the jarl. Onund had a large force with him, and there was a great battle in which many a good farmer and many a follower of the jarl were slain. The brothers returned to Onund and reported what had occurred with the jarl. Onund said it was a pity they had not killed him. It would, he said, have been something to make up for the losses which he had suffered from King Harald. They said the disgrace was far worse for the jarl as it was, and they went off to Surnadal to Erik Beery, a Landman there, who took them all in for the winter. At Yule-tide they had a great drinking bout with a man named Hallsteinn, nicknamed Stallion. Erik opened the feast and entertained them generously. Then it was Hallsteinn's turn, and they began to quarrel. Hallsteinn struck Erik with a deer's horn, for which Erik got no revenge, but had to go home with it, to the great annoyance of Ondott's sons. A little later Asgrim went to Hallsteinn's house and gave him a severe wound. All the people who were present started up and attacked Asgrim. He defended himself vigorously and escaped in the dark, leaving them under the belief that they had killed him. Onund and Asmund, on hearing that Asgrim had been killed, were at a loss what they could do in the matter. Erik's advice was that they should betake themselves to Iceland, for it would never do for them to remain in the land where the king could get at them. This they determined to do. Each of them had his own ship and they made ready for the voyage to Iceland. Hallsteinn was laid low with his wound and died before Onund sailed with his party. Kolbeinn, the man who was mentioned before, went in the ship with Onund.

Chapter VIII
Onund And Asmund Sail To Iceland

nund and Asmund set sail directly when they were ready and their ships kept together. Onund said:

"Hallvard and I were aforetime deemed
worthy in storm of swords to bear us.
With one foot now I step on the ship
towards Iceland. The poet's day is o'er."

They had a rough passage with cross winds, mostly from the south, so that they drifted away to the north. They made Iceland right in the North, at Langanes, where they regained their reckonings. The ships were near enough to each other for them to speak together. Asmund said they had better make for Eyjafjord, and this was agreed to. They kept under the land and heavy weather set in from the south-east. Just as Onund was tacking, the yard was carried away; they lowered the sail and were driven out to sea. Asmund got under the lee of Hrisey, where he waited until a fair wind set in which took him up to Eyjafjord. Helgi the Lean gave him the whole of Kraeklingahlid, and he lived at South-Glera. A few years later his brother Asgrim came to Iceland and took up his residence at North-Glera. His son was Ellidagrim the father of Asgrim.

Chapter IX
Onund Settles In Kaldbak

nund Treefoot was driven away from the shore for several days, after which the wind shifted and blew towards the land. Then they made land again, which those of them who had been there before recognised as the western coast of the Skagi peninsula. They sailed in to Strandafloi, almost to Sudrstrandir. There came rowing towards them a ten-oared boat with six men on board, who hailed the sea-going ship and asked who was their captain. Onund told them his name and asked whence they came. They said they were the men of Thorvald from Drangar. Then Onund asked whether all the land round that coast was occupied; they answered there was very little left at Sudrstrandir and none at all in the North. So Onund asked his men whether they would seek some land further to the West or take that of which they had just been told. They said they would first explore a little further. They sailed in along the coast of the bay and anchored off a creek near Arnes, where they put off in a boat to the shore.

Here dwelt a wealthy man named Erik Snare, who had taken the land between Ingolfsfjord and Ofaera in Veidileysa. On hearing that Onund had arrived in those parts, he offered to let him have such portion as he needed from his own lands, adding that there was little land which had not already been taken up. Onund said he would first like to see what there was.

Then they went further into the bay past some fjords and came to Ofaera, where Erik said: "Here is what there is to see. From here down to the lands of Bjorn is unoccupied." A high range of mountains, on which snow had fallen, rose from beside the river. Onund looked at the mountains and spoke a verse:

"My lands and my might have drifted away
as drifts the ship on the ocean.
My friends and my home I have left behind me,
and bartered my acres for Kaldbak."

"Many a man," answered Erik, "has lost so much in Norway that it may not be mended. I expect too that nearly all the lands in the main districts have been taken, so that I will not urge you to leave these parts and seek elsewhere. I will keep to my word and let you have whatever lands of my own you may require."

Onund said he would take advantage of his offer, and in the end he took some of the Ofaera land and the three creeks Byrgisvik, Kolbeinsvik, and Kaldbaksvik as far as Kaldbak's Cliff. Afterwards Erik gave him Veidileysa with Reykjarfjord and the outer part of Reykjanes on that side. Nothing was settled about the drift which came to the coast, because there was so much of it that every one could have what he wanted. Onund made his home in Kaldbak and had a large household. His property increased and he had another house in Reykjarfjord. Kolbeinn lived in Kolbeinsvik and for some years Onund lived quietly at home.

Chapter X
Ofeig Grettir Is Killed. Visit Of Onund To Aud The Deep-Minded

Onund was a man of such valour that few, even of those whose limbs were sound, could measure themselves against him. His name, too, was renowned throughout the whole country on account of his ancestry. It happened that a dispute arose between Ofeig Grettir and one Thorbjorn called Jarlakappi, which ended in Ofeig being killed by Thorbjorn in Grettisgeil near Haell. The feud was taken up by Ofeig's sons who assembled a large force of men. Onund Treefoot was sent for, and in the spring he rode South to Hvamm, where he stayed with Aud the Deep-Minded. He had been with her over the sea in the West, and she received him with welcome. Her grandson, Olaf Feilan, was then grown up, and Aud was very infirm. She consulted Onund concerning her kinsman Olaf, for whom she wished to ask in marriage Alfdis of the Barra Isles, the cousin of Onund's wife Aesa. Onund thought it a very suitable match, and Olaf rode with him to the South. Then Onund met friends and kinsmen, who made him their guest. The matter of the dispute was talked over between them, and finally laid before the Kjalarnes Thing, for the All-Thing had not yet been established. Eventually it was settled by arbitration and heavy weregilds were imposed for the murder. Thorbjorn Jarlakappi was exiled. His son was Solmund, the father of Svidukari. These kinsmen were long abroad after that. Thrand invited Onund and Olaf with his party to stay with him, as did Thormod Shaft. The matter of Olaf's marriage was then pressed, and an agreement easily arrived at, for Aud's rank and influence were well known to them. The settlement was arranged and Onund's party rode home again. Aud thanked him for his aid in behalf of Olaf, who married Alfdis of the Barra Isles that autumn. Then Aud the Deep-Minded died, as is told in the Laxdaela Saga.

Chapter XI
Death Of Onund. Disputes Between The Sons Of Onund And Of Erik

nund and Aesa had two sons; the elder was named Thorgeir, the younger Ofeig Grettir. Soon afterwards Aesa died and Onund married a second wife, Thordis Thorgrim's daughter of Gnup in Midfjord, a kinsman of Skeggi of Midfjord. By her Onund had a son named Thorgrim, who grew up quickly to manhood, tall and strong, wise and a good manager. Onund continued to live at Kaldbak until his old age. He died a natural death and lies in Treefoot's howe. He was the boldest and most active one-legged man that ever came to Iceland.

Among Onund's sons Thorgrim was the foremost, although the others were older. When he was twenty-five years old his hair was grey, whence they nick-named him Greyhead. His mother Thordis married again, taking as her second husband Audun Skokull. They had a son named Asgeir of Asgeirsa. Thorgrim Greyhead and his brothers had a large property, which they managed together without dividing it up.

Erik lived, as was mentioned, at Arnes. He had married Alof, the daughter of Ingolf of Ingolfsfjord, by whom he had a son named Flosi, a very promising young man with many friends.

There came to that part of Iceland three brothers, named Ingolf, Ofeig, and Eyvind, and took the three fjords which are called by their names, where they lived. Eyvind had a son named Olaf. He at first lived at Eyvindsfjord, but went later to Drangar. He was a most capable man.

So long as their fathers were living no disputes arose among these men; but when Erik was dead it occurred to Flosi that those of Kaldbak had no legal title to the lands which Erik had given to Onund. Out of this serious dissensions arose between them. Thorgrim and his brothers continued in possession of the lands as before, but they would not join in games together.

Thorgeir, the eldest brother, was managing the farm at Reykjarfjord, and often rowed out fishing, as the fjords were full of fish. The men of Vik now laid their plans. Flosi had a man in Arnes named Thorfinn, and sent him to fetch Thorgeir's head. This man hid himself in the boatshed. One morning when Thorgeir was preparing to row out with two other men, one of whom was named Brand, Thorgeir was walking ahead with a leather skin on his back containing some drink. It was very dark, and as he passed the boat-house Thorfinn sprang out upon him and dealt him a blow with an axe between his shoulders. The axe went into something and made a squeaking noise. Thorfinn let go his axe, feeling quite sure that no bandages would be needed, and being very anxious to escape as fast as he could. He ran North, and reaching Arnes before the day had quite broken, said that he had killed Thorgeir and that Flosi must protect him. The only thing to be done was to offer some compensation in money. "That," he said, "will be the best thing for us after such a terrible piece of work."

Flosi said he must first learn more about it, and that he thought Thorfinn seemed very frightened after his doughty deed.

We must now tell what had happened to Thorgeir. He turned round when he was struck, but the blow had gone into the leather bottle, and he was unhurt. They could make no search for the man because it was dark, so they rowed on down the fjord to Kaldbak, where they told what had happened. People made great game of the affair and called him Thorgeir Bottleback, a name which stuck to him ever after. A verse was made:

"In days gone by men bathed their blades
in the streaming gore of a foeman's wound.
But now a wretch of all honour bereft
reddens his dastard axe in whey."

Chapter XII
Battle At Rifsker

At that time there came over Iceland a famine the like of which
had never been seen before. Nearly all the fisheries failed, and also the drift
wood. So it continued for many years.

One autumn some traders in a sea-going ship, who had been driven out
of their course, were wrecked at Vik. Flosi took in four or five of them with
their captain, named Steinn. They all found shelter in the neighbourhood of
Vik and tried to rig up a ship out of the wreckage, but were not very
successful. The ship was too narrow in the bow and stern and too broad
amidships. In the spring a northerly gale set in which lasted nearly a week,
after which men began to look for drift.

There was a man living in Reykjanes named Thorsteinn. He found a
whale stranded on the south side of the promontory at the place now called
Rifsker. It was a large rorqual, and he at once sent word by a messenger to
Flosi in Vik and to the nearest farms.

At Gjogr lived a man named Einar, a tenant of the Kaldbak men whom
they employed to look after the drift on that side of the fjord. He got to
know of the whale having been stranded and at once rowed across the fjord
in his boat to Byrgisvik, whence he sent a messenger to Kaldbak. When
Thorgrim and his brother heard the news they got ready to go with all speed
to the spot. There were twelve of them in a ten-oared boat, and six others,
with Ivar and Leif, sons of Kolbeinn. All the farmers who could get away
went to the whale.

In the meantime Flosi had sent word to his kinsmen in the North at
Ingolfsfjord and Ofeigsfjord and to Olaf the son of Eyvind who lived at
Drangar. The first to arrive were Flosi and the men of Vik, who at once
began to cut up the whale, carrying on shore the flesh as it was cut. At first
there were about twenty men, but more came thronging in. Then there came
the men of Kaldbak with four ships. Thorgrim laid claim to the whale and
forbade the men of Vik to cut, distribute, or carry away any portion of it.

Flosi called upon him to show proof that Erik had in express words given over the drift to Onund; if not, he said he would prevent them by force. Thorgrim saw that he was outnumbered and would not venture on fighting. Then there came a ship across the fjords, the men rowing with all their might. They came up; it was Svan of Hol from Bjarnarfjord with his men, and he at once told Thorgrim not to let himself be robbed. The two men had been great friends, and Svan offered Thorgrim his aid, which the brothers accepted, and they attacked valiantly. Thorgeir Bottleback was the first to get on to the whale where Flosi's men were. Thorfinn, who was spoken of before, was cutting it up, standing near the head on the place where he had been carving. "Here I bring you your axe," said Thorgeir. Then he struck at Thorfinn's neck and cut off his head. Flosi was up on the beach and saw it. He urged on his men to give it them back. They fought for a long time and the Kaldbak people were getting the best of it. Most of them had no weapons but the axes with which they were cutting up the whale and short knives. The men of Vik were driven from the whale on to the sandbanks. The men from the East, however, were armed and able to deal wounds. Their captain Steinn cut off the leg of Kolbeinn's son Ivar, and Ivar's brother Leif beat one of Steinn's men to death with a rib of the whale. Then they fought with anything they could get, and men were slain on both sides. At last Olaf came up with a number of ships from Drangar and joined Flosi; the men of Kaldbak were then overpowered by numbers. They had already loaded their ships, and Svan told them to get on board. They therefore retired towards the ships, the men of Vik after them. Svan on reaching the sea struck at Steinn their captain, wounding him badly, and then sprang into his own ship. Thorgrim gave Flosi a severe wound and escaped. Olaf wounded Ofeig Grettir fatally, but Thorgeir carried him off and sprang on to his ship with him. The Kaldbak men rowed into the fjord and the two parties separated.

The following verse was composed on these doings:

"Hard were the blows which were dealt at Rifsker;
no weapons they had but steaks of the whale.
They belaboured each other with rotten blubber.
Unseemly methinks is such warfare for men."

After this they made peace, and the dispute was laid before the All-Thing. On the side of the Kaldbak men were Thorodd the Godi, Skeggi of Midfjord, and many others from the South. Flosi was exiled, along with several others who had been with him. He was put to great expense, for he insisted upon paying all the fines himself. Thorgrim and his brothers were unable to show that they had paid any money either for the land or for the drift which Flosi claimed. The Lawman was Thorkell Mani, and the question was referred to him. He declared that by law something must have been paid, though not necessarily the full value.

"There was a case in point," he said, "between my grandfather Ingolf and a woman named Steinvor the Old. He gave her the whole of Rosmhvalanes and she gave him a dirty cloak for it; the transfer was afterwards held to be valid. That was a much more important affair than this. My advice is that the land be divided in equal portions between the two; and henceforward it shall be legally established that all drift shall be the property of the owner of the land upon which it has been stranded."

This was agreed to. Thorgrim and his brothers were to give up Reykjarfjord with all on that side, and were to keep Kamb. For Ofeig a large sum of money was paid, and Thorfinn was assessed at nothing at all; Thorgeir received compensation for the attack made upon his life, and all the parties were reconciled. Flosi went to Norway with Steinn the captain and sold his lands in Vik to Geirmund Hvikatimbr, who lived there thenceforward.

The ship which Steinn's sailors had built was rather a tub. She was called Trekyllir—Tree-sack. Flosi went on his journey in her, but was driven back to Oxarfjord; out of this arose the saga of Bodmod the Champion and Grimolf.

Chapter XIII
Thorgrim Settles At Bjarg And Marries. His Son Asmund Visits Norway And Marries Twice

After these events Thorgrim and his brothers divided up the property between them. Thorgrim took the movable property and Thorgeir the lands. Then Thorgrim went inland to Midfjord and bought some land at Bjarg with the aid of Skeggi. He married Thordis, the daughter of Asmund from Asmund's peak who had land in Thingeyrasveit. They had a son named Asmund, a great man and strong, also wise, and notable for his abundance of hair, which turned grey very early. He was called Longhair.

Thorgrim occupied himself with the management of his estate and kept all the men of his household hard at work. Asmund did not want to work, so that he and his father got on rather badly together. This continued until Asmund was grown up, when he asked his father to give him the means to go abroad. Thorgrim said he should have little enough, but he gave him some ready cash. So Asmund went away and soon increased his capital. He sailed to diverse lands, became a great trader and very wealthy. He was popular and enjoyed good credit, and had many friends among the leading men of Norway.

One autumn Asmund was in the East on a visit to a certain magnate named Thorsteinn. His family came from the Upplands, and he had a sister named Rannveig who had excellent prospects. Asmund asked this girl in marriage and obtained her through the interest of her brother Thorsteinn; he settled there for a time and was highly thought of. He and Rannveig had a son named Thorsteinn, who became a handsome man, strong, and with a powerful voice. He was very tall and rather sluggish in his movements, wherefore he was nicknamed Dromund. When young Thorsteinn was half grown up his mother fell ill and died, and Asmund cared no more for Norway. Thorsteinn was taken over by his mother's relations along with his property, while Asmund went on voyages and became famous.

Asmund came in his ship to Hunavain, where Thorkell Krafla was chief of the Vatnsdalers. On hearing of Asmund's arrival Thorkell went to the ship and invited him to stay, and Asmund went to visit him in Marsstadir in Vatnsdal where he lived. Thorkell was a son of Thorgrim, the Godi of Karnsa, and a man of great experience. This was soon after the arrival of Bishop Fridrek and Thorvald the son of Kodran, who were living at Laekjamot when these events happened, preaching Christianity for the first time in the North of the island. Thorkell and many of his men received the prima signatio. Many things might be told of the dealings between the bishop's men and the Northerners, which, however, do not belong to this saga.

There was a girl named Asdis who was being brought up in Thorkell's house. She was a daughter of Bard the son of Jokull, the son of Ingimund the Old, the son of Thorsteinn, the son of Ketil Raum. Her mother's name was Aldis, whom we have already heard of as the daughter of Ofeig Grettir. Asdis was not betrothed as yet, and was a most desirable match, both on account of her connections and her wealth. Asmund now became sick of travelling about and wanted to settle down in Iceland. So he spoke up and asked for Asdis as his wife. Thorkell knew all about him and knew that he was a man of wealth, able to manage his affairs, so the marriage was arranged. Asmund married Asdis, and became a close friend of Thorkell. He was a great man of affairs, learned in the law and very strenuous. Soon afterwards Thorgrim Greyhead died at Bjarg; Asmund succeeded to his property and took up his residence at Bjarg.

Chapter XIV
Asmund's Children. Grettir's Childhood

Asmund Longhair now set up a large and sumptuous household in Bjarg, where he maintained a numerous retinue and became very popular. His children were as follows: The eldest was Atli, an able and accomplished man, tactful and easy to deal with; he was much liked by all. His second son was called Grettir. He was very hard to manage in his bringing up. He spoke little and was rough in his manners and quarrelsome, both in words and deeds. He got little affection from his father Asmund, but his mother loved him dearly. Grettir was a handsome man in appearance, with a face rather broad and short, red-haired and somewhat freckled; not very precocious in his youth. There was a daughter named Thordis, who afterwards married Glum the son of Ospak, Kjallak's son from Skridinsenni. Another daughter was named Rannveig; she married Gamli the son of Thorhall of Vineland, and they dwelt at Melar in Hrutafjord and had a son named Grim. Glum and Thordis had a son named Ospak who fell into a dispute with Odd the son of Ofeig, which is told of in the "Saga of the Banded Men."

Grettir grew up at Bjarg until he was ten years old, when he began to develop a little. Asmund told him that he must do some work. Grettir said that would not suit him very well, but asked what he was to do.

"You must mind the geese," said Asmund.

"That is wretched work, only fit for an idiot," Grettir answered.

"You do that properly," his father said, "and we shall get on better together."

So Grettir went to mind the geese. There were fifty of them, and a number of goslings. Before long he began to find them troublesome, and the goslings would not come on quickly enough. This put him out, for he could never control his temper. Soon afterwards some wanderers found the goslings lying outside dead, and the geese with their wings broken. This was in the autumn. Asmund was very much annoyed and asked Grettir whether he had killed the birds. Grettir grinned and answered:

> "Always when winter is coming on
> I like to wring the goslings' necks.
> If among them there are geese
> I treat the creatures all alike."

"You shan't twist any more of their necks," said Asmund.

"The friend aye warns his friend of ill," answered Grettir.

"I will give you other work to do."

"He knoweth most who most hath tried. But what am I to do now?" Grettir asked.

"You shall rub my back when I am sitting by the fire, as I am in the habit of having it done."

"Warm work for the hands." he answered. "It is only fit for an idiot."

This for a time was Grettir's occupation. As the autumn advanced Asmund wanted more warmth, and was constantly telling Grettir to rub his back hard. It was the custom in those days for people to have large rooms with long fires in them in their houses, where men sat by the fire in the evenings on benches, sleeping afterwards at the side away from the fires. By day the women carded their wool there.

One evening when Grettir had to scratch Asmund's back his father said to him: "Now you will have to put aside your laziness, you good-for-nothing you."

Grettir answered: "'Tis ill to rouse a hasty temper."

"You are fit for nothing at all," said Asmund.

Grettir saw some wood-combs lying on one of the benches; he took up one of them and drew it along Asmund's back. Asmund sprang up and was going to thrash him with his stick, but he escaped. His mother came up and asked what they were fighting about. Grettir answered in a verse:

> "Oh lady, the giver of treasure, I see,
> has dire intent to burn my hands.
> With nails uncut I was stroking his back.
> Clearly I see the bird of wounds."

His mother was much vexed with Grettir for what he had done and said he would not grow up very prudent. The affair did not improve the relations between Asmund and his son.

Soon after this Asmund spoke to Grettir and told him to look after his horses. Grettir said that would be better than back-fire-warming.

"You are to do what I tell you," said Asmund. "I have a dun mare with a dark stripe down her back whom I call Keingala. She is very knowing about the weather and about rain coming. When she refuses to graze it never fails that a storm will follow. You are then to keep the horses under shelter in the stables, and when cold weather sets in keep them to the north of the ridge. I hope you will perform this duty better than the two which I gave you before."

Grettir said: "That is cold work, and fit for a man to do; but it seems to me rash to trust to the mare, when to my knowledge no one has done so before."

So Grettir took to minding the horses, and went on until Yule-tide was past, when very cold weather set in, with snow, so that grazing was difficult. He was very badly provided with clothes and little hardened to the weather. He began to feel it very cold, and Keingala always chose the windiest places whatever the weather was. She never came to the meadow early enough to get home before nightfall. Grettir then thought he would play a trick upon Keingala to pay her out for her wanderings. One morning early he came to the stables, opened the door and found Keingala standing in front of the manger. She had taken the whole of the fodder which had been given to all the horses for herself. Grettir jumped upon her back, with a sharp knife in his hand which he drew across her shoulder and along her back on both sides. The horse was fat and fresh; she shied back very frightened and kicked out till her hoofs rattled against the walls. Grettir fell off, but picked himself up and tried to mount her again. There was a sharp struggle, which ended in his shaving all the skin on her back down to her flank. Then he drove the horses out to the meadow. Keingala would not take a bite except off her back, and soon after noon she bolted off to the stables. Grettir locked the door and went home. Asmund asked him where the horses were; he said he had looked after them as usual. Asmund said there must be a storm close at hand if the horses would not stay out in such weather as there was then.

Grettir said: "Many seem wise who are lacking in wit."

The night passed and there was no storm. Grettir drove out the horses, but Keingala could not endure the pasture. Asmund thought it very strange that no change came in the weather. On the third morning he went himself to the horses and on seeing Keingala he said: "Ill indeed have the horses fared in this beautiful weather! Thy back will not deceive me, my Bleikala."

"The likely may happen—also the unlikely," said Grettir.

Asmund stroked the back of the horse and all her coat came off on his hand. He could not understand how she had got into that state and thought Grettir must have done it. Grettir grinned and said nothing. Asmund went home and became very abusive. He heard his wife say: "My son's watching of the horses must have prospered well."

Then he spoke a verse:

> "He has cheated me sorely, and Keingala shorn.
> 'Tis the pride of a woman that urges her tongue.
> Artful he holds my commands in derision.
> Consider my verses, oh wife of my heart."

"I do not know," she said, "which seems to me the more perverse, for you to make him work, or for him always to get out of it in the same way."

"Now there shall be an end to it," said Asmund. "He must have something worse than merely making good the damage."

"Let neither speak of it to the other," said Grettir, and so it remained.

Asmund had Keingala killed. Many more childish pranks did Grettir play which are not told in the saga. He now began to grow very big, but men did not clearly know what strength he had because he had never been tried in wrestling. He kept making verses and ditties which were always a little ironical. He did not sleep in the common room and was generally very silent.

Chapter XV
Games At Midfjordvatn

There were then a good many youths growing up in Midfjord. A certain Skaldtorfa, whose home was in Torfustadir, had a son named Bersi, an accomplished young man and a clever poet. Two brothers named Kormak and Thorgils lived at Mel and had with them a youth named Odd, who was dependent upon them, and was nicknamed Odd the Needy-Skald. Another was named Audun; he grew up in Audunarstad in Vididal, a pleasant good-natured youth and the strongest of his age in the North. Kalf the son of Asgeir and his brother Thorvald lived at Asgeirsa. Grettir's brother Atli was then growing to a man; he was most gracious in manners and universally liked.

These youths used to play at ball together at Midfjord Water. Those from Midfjord and from Vididal used to meet there, and there came many from Vestrhop and Vatnsnes with some from Hrutafjord. Those who came from afar used to lodge there. Those who were about equal in the ball-game were matched together, and generally they had much fun in the autumn. Grettir went to the sports when he was fourteen years old at the request of his brother Atli. The parties were made up. Grettir was matched against Audun, the youth already mentioned, who was a few years the elder. Audun struck the ball over Grettir's head so that he could not reach it, and it bounded far away over the ice. Grettir lost his temper, thinking he had done it out of mischief, but he fetched the ball, brought it back and going up to Audun drove it straight into his forehead, so that the skin was broken.

Audun then struck at Grettir with the bat that he was holding, but Grettir ducked and the blow missed him. Then they seized each other with their arms and wrestled. It was evident to the people around that Grettir was stronger than they had supposed, for Audun was very strong indeed of body. They struggled long together until at last Grettir was thrown. Audun then set his knees on his stomach and dealt unmercifully with him. Atli and Bersi and a number of the others ran up and separated them. Grettir said they need not hold him like a mad dog, and added: "The thrall alone takes instant vengeance, the coward never."

The rest had no mind to let the affair create discord among them, and the brothers Kalf and Thorvald tried to reconcile them. Audun and Grettir were distantly related to each other. The games went on and there was no further disturbance.

Chapter XVI
Grettir Kills Skeggi And Is Outlawed For Three Years

Thorkell Krafla now began to grow very old. He was a great chieftain and held the Vatnsdal Godord. He was a close friend of Asmund Longhair, as befitted the near relations in which they stood to each other. He had, therefore, been in the habit of riding every year in the spring to Bjarg to visit his kinsmen there, and he did so in the spring which followed the events just related. Asmund and Asdis received him with both hands. He stayed there three nights and many a matter did the kinsmen discuss together. Thorkell asked Asmund what his heart told him about his sons, and what professions they were likely to follow. Asmund said that Atli would probably be a great landowner, very careful and wealthy.

"A useful man, like yourself," said Thorkell. "But what can you tell me of Grettir?"

"I can only say," he replied, "that he will be a strong man; but headstrong and quarrelsome. A heavy trial has he been to me."

"That does not look very promising, kinsman!" said Thorkell. "But how are we to arrange our journey to the Thing in the summer?"

"I am getting difficult to move," he said. "I would rather stay at home."

"Would you like Atli to go for you?"

"I don't think I can spare him," Asmund said, "because of the work and the provisioning. Grettir will not do anything. But he has quite wit enough to carry out the duties at the Thing on my behalf under your guidance."

"It shall be as you please," said Thorkell.

Then Thorkell made himself ready and rode home; Asmund dismissed him with presents.

A little later Thorkell journeyed to the Thing with sixty men. All the men of his godord went with him. They passed through Bjarg, where Grettir joined them. They rode South through the heath called Tvidaegra. There was very little grazing to be had in the hills, so they rode quickly past them into the cultivated land. When they reached Fljotstunga they thought it was time to sleep, so they took the bits from their horses and turned them loose with their saddles. They lay there well on into the day, and when they woke began to look for their horses. Every horse had gone off in a different direction and some had been rolling. Grettir could not find his horse at all. The custom was at that time that men should find their own provisions at the Thing, and most of them carried their sacks over their saddles. When Grettir found his horse its saddle was under its belly, and the sack of provisions gone. He searched about but could not find it. Then he saw a man running very fast and asked him who he was. He said his name was Skeggi and that he was a man from Ass in Vatnsdal in the North.

"I am travelling with Thorkell," he said. "I have been careless and lost my provision-bag."

"Alone in misfortune is worst. I also have lost my stock of provisions; so we can look for them together."

Skeggi was well pleased with this proposal, and so they went about seeking for a time. Suddenly, when Grettir least expected it, Skeggi started running with all his might along the moor and picked up the sack. Grettir saw him bend and asked what it was that he had picked up.

"My sack," he said.

"Who says so besides yourself?" Grettir asked. "Let me see it! Many a thing is like another."

Skeggi said no one should take from him what was his own. Grettir seized hold of the sack and they both pulled at it for a time, each trying to get his own way.

"You Midfjord men have strange notions," said Skeggi, "if you think that because a man is not so wealthy as you are, he is not to dare to hold to his own before you."

Grettir said it had nothing to do with a man's degree, and that each should have that which was his own.

Skeggi replied: "Audun is now too far away to strangle you as he did at the ball-play."

"That is well," said Grettir; "but however that may have been you shall not strangle me."

Skeggi then seized his axe and struck at Grettir, who on seeing it seized the handle of the axe with his left hand and pulled it forward with such force that Skeggi at once let go. The next moment it stood in his brain and he fell dead to the earth. Grettir took the sack, threw it across his saddle and rode back to his companions.

Thorkell rode on, knowing nothing of what had happened. Soon Skeggi was missed in the company, and when Grettir came up they asked him what news he had of Skeggi. He answered in a verse:

"Hammer-troll ogress has done him to death.
Thirsting for blood the war-fiend came.
With hard-edged blade she gaped, o'er his head,
nor spared she his teeth. I saw it myself."

Then Thorkell's men sprang up and said it was impossible that a troll should have taken the man in full daylight. Thorkell was silent for a moment. Then he said: "There must be something more in it. Grettir must have killed him. What was it that really happened, Grettir?"

Grettir then told him all about their fight. Thorkell said: "It is a most unfortunate occurrence, because Skeggi was entrusted to my service, and was a man of good family. I will take the matter upon myself and pay whatever compensation is adjudged. But a question of banishment does not lie with me. Now, Grettir, there are two things for you to choose between. Either you can go on to the Thing with us and take the chance of what may happen there, or you can turn back and go home."

Grettir decided to go on to the Thing, and to the Thing he went. The matter was taken up by the heirs of the man slain. Thorkell gave his hand to pay the compensation and Grettir was to be banished for three years.

On their way back from the Thing all the chiefs halted at Sledaass before they parted company. It was then that Grettir lifted a stone lying in the grass, which is still known as Grettishaf. Many went afterwards to see this stone and were astounded that so young a man should have lifted such a mountain.

Grettir rode home to Bjarg and told his father about his adventures. Asmund was much put out and said he would be a trouble to everybody.

Chapter XVII
Grettir Sails For Norway And Is Wrecked On Haramarsey

There dwelt at Reydarfell on the banks of the Hvita a man named Haflidi, a mariner, owning a ship of his own which was lying in dock in the Hvita river. He had as his mate a man named Bard who had a young and pretty wife. Asmund sent a man to Haflidi asking him to take Grettir and look after him. Haflidi answered that he had heard that Grettir was very difficult to get on with, but out of friendship for Asmund he took him. Grettir, therefore, prepared to go to sea. His father would not give him any outfit for his voyage beyond his bare provisions and a little wadmal. Grettir asked him to give him some sort of weapon. Asmund answered: "You have never been obedient to me. Nor do I know what you would do with a weapon that would be of any profit. I shall not give you any."

Grettir said: "Work not done needs no reward."

Father and son parted with little love between them. Many wished him a good voyage, but few a safe return. His mother went with him along the road. Before they parted she said: "You have not been sent off in the way that I should have wished, my son, or in a way befitting your birth. The most cruel thing of all, I think, is that you have not a weapon which you can use. My heart tells me that you will want one."

Then she took from under her mantle a sword all ready for use, a valuable possession. She said: "This was the sword of Jokull, my father's father and of the ancient Vatnsdal men, in whose hands it was blessed with victory. I give it to you; use it well."

Grettir thanked her warmly and said it would be more precious to him than any other possession though of greater value. Then he went on his way and Asdis wished him all possible happiness. He rode South over the heath and did not stop till he reached his ship. Haflidi received him well and asked him about his outfit for the voyage. Grettir spoke a verse:

> "Oh trimmer of sails I my father is wealthy,
> but poorly enough he sent me from home.
> My mother it was who gave me this sword.
> True is the saying: The mother is best."

Haflidi said it was evident that she had most thought for him.

Directly they were ready and had a wind they got under way. When they were out of shallow water they hoisted their sail. Grettir made himself a corner under the ship's boat, whence he refused to stir either to bale or to trim the sails or to do any work in the ship, as it was his duty to do equally with the other men; nor would he buy himself off. They sailed to the South, rounded Reykjanes and left the land behind them, when they met with stormy weather. The ship was rather leaky and became very uneasy in the gale; the crew were very much exhausted. Grettir only let fly satirical verses at them, which angered them sorely.

One day when it was very stormy and very cold the men called out to Grettir to get up and work; they said their claws were quite frozen. He answered:

"Twere well if every finger were froze
on the hands of such a lubberly crew."

They got no work out of him and liked him even worse than before, and
said they would pay him out on his person for his squibs and his mutinous
behaviour.

"You like better," they said, "to pat the belly of Bard the mate's wife
than to bear a hand in the ship. But we don't mean to stand it."

The weather grew steadily worse; they had to bale night and day, and
they threatened Grettir. Haflidi when he heard them went up to Grettir and
said: "I don't think your relations with the crew are very good. You are
mutinous and make lampoons about them, and they threaten to pitch you
overboard. This is most improper."

"Why cannot they mind their own business?" Grettir rejoined. "But I
should like one or two to remain behind with me before I go overboard."

"That is impossible," said Haflidi. "We shall never get on upon those
terms. But I will make you a proposal about it."

"What is that?"

"The thing which annoys them is that you make lampoons about them.
Now I suggest that you make a lampoon about me. Then, perhaps, they will
become better disposed towards you."

"About you I will never utter anything but good," said he. "I am not
going to compare you with the sailors."

"But you might compose a verse which should at first appear foul, but
on closer view prove to be fair."

"That," he answered, "I am quite equal to."

Haflidi then went to the sailors and said: "You have much toil; and it
seems that you don't get on with Grettir."

"His lampoons," they answered, "annoy us more than anything else."

Then Haflidi, speaking loud, said: "It will be the worse for him some
day."

Grettir, when he heard himself being denounced, spoke a verse:

"Other the words that Haflidi spake
when he dined on curds at Reydarfell.
But now two meals a day he takes
in the steed of the bays mid foreland shores."

The sailors were very angry and said he should not lampoon Haflidi for
nothing. Haflidi said: "Grettir certainly deserves that you should take him
down a little, but I am not going to risk my good name because of his ill-
temper and caprice. This is not the time to pay him out, when we are all in
such danger. When you get on shore you can remember it if you like."

"Shall we not endure what you can endure?" they said. "Why should a lampoon hurt us more than it does you?"

Haflidi said so it should be, and after that they cared less about Grettir's lampoons.

The voyage was long and fatiguing. The ship sprung a leak, and the men began to be worn out. The mate's young wife was in the habit of stitching Grettir's sleeves for him, and the men used to banter him about it. Haflidi went up to Grettir where he was lying and said:

> "Arise from thy den! deep furrows we plough!
> Remember the word thou didst speak to the fair.
> Thy garment she sewed; but now she commands
> that thou join in the toil while the land is afar."

Grettir got up at once and said:

> "I will rise, though the ship be heavily rolling.
> The woman is vexed that I sleep in my den.
> She will surely be wrath if here I abide
> while others are toiling at work that is mine."

Then he hurried aft where they were baling and asked what they wanted him to do. They said he would do little good. He replied: "A man's help is something." Haflidi told them not to refuse his help. "Maybe," he said, "he is thinking of loosening his hands if he offers his services."

In those days in sea-going ships there were no scuppers for baling; they only had what is called bucket or pot-baling, a very troublesome and fatiguing process. There were two buckets, one of which went down while the other came up. The men told Grettir to take the buckets down, and said they would try what he could do. He said the less tried the better, and went below and filled his bucket. There were two men above to empty the buckets as he handed them. Before long they both gave in from fatigue. Then four others took their places, but the same thing happened. Some say that before they were done eight men were engaged in emptying the buckets for him. At last the ship was baled dry. After this, the seamen altered their behaviour towards Grettir, for they realised the strength which was in him. From that time on he was ever the forwardest to help wherever he was required.

They now held an easterly course out to sea. It was very dark. One night when they least expected it, they struck a rock and the lower part of the ship began to fill. The boats were got out and the women put into them with all the loose property. There was an island a little way off, whither they carried as much of their property as they could get off in the night. When the day broke, they began to ask where they were. Some of them who had been about the country before recognised the coast of Sunnmore in Norway. There was an island lying a little off the mainland called Haramarsey, with a large settlement and a farm belonging to the Landman on it.

Chapter XVIII
Adventure In The Howe Of Kar The Old

The name of the Landman who lived in the island was Thorfinn. He was a son of Kar the Old, who had lived there for a long time. Thorfinn was a man of great influence.

When the day broke, the people on the island saw that there were some sailors there in distress and reported it to Thorfinn, who at once set about to launch his large sixteen-oared boat. He put out as quickly as possible with some thirty men to save the cargo of the trader, which then sank and was lost, along with much property. Thorfinn brought all the men off her to his house, where they stayed for a week drying their goods. Then they went away to the South, and are heard of no more in this story.

Grettir stayed behind with Thorfinn, keeping very quiet and speaking little. Thorfinn gave him his board, but took little notice of him. Grettir held rather aloof, and did not accompany him when he went abroad every day. This annoyed Thorfinn, but he did not like to refuse Grettir his hospitality; he was a man who kept open house, enjoyed life and liked to see other men happy. Grettir liked going about and visiting the people in the other farms on the island. There was a man named Audun, who dwelt at Vindheim. Grettir went to see him daily and became very intimate with him, sitting there all day long.

One evening very late when Grettir was preparing to return home, he saw a great fire shoot up on the headland below Audun's place, and asked what new thing that might be. Audun said there was no pressing need for him to know.

"If they saw such a thing in our country," said Grettir, "they would say the fire came from some treasure."

"He who rules that fire," answered the man, "is one whom it will be better not to inquire about."

"But I want to know," Grettir said.

"On that headland," said Audun, "there is a howe, wherein lies Kar the Old, the father of Thorfinn. Once upon a time father and son had a farm-property on the island; but ever since Kar died his ghost has been walking and has scared away all the other farmers, so that now the whole island belongs to Thorfinn, and no man who is under Thorfinn's protection suffers any injury."

"You have done right to tell me," said Grettir. "Expect me here to-morrow morning, and have tools ready for digging."

"I won't allow you to have anything to do with it," said Audun, "because I know that it will bring Thorfinn's wrath down upon you."

Grettir said he would risk that.

The night passed; Grettir appeared early the next morning, and the bondi, who had got all the tools for digging ready, went with Grettir to the howe. Grettir broke open the grave, and worked with all his might, never stopping until he came to wood, by which time the day was already spent. He tore away the woodwork; Audun implored him not to go down, but Grettir bade him attend to the rope, saying that he meant to find out what it was that dwelt there. Then he descended into the howe. It was very dark and the odour was not pleasant. He began to explore how it was arranged, and found the bones of a horse. Then he knocked against a sort of throne in which he was aware of a man seated. There was much treasure of gold and silver collected together, and a casket under his feet, full of silver. Grettir took all the treasure and went back towards the rope, but on his way he felt himself seized by a strong hand. He left the treasure to close with his aggressor and the two engaged in a merciless struggle. Everything about them was smashed. The howedweller made a ferocious onslaught. Grettir for some time gave way, but found that no holding back was possible. They did not spare each other. Soon they came to the place where the horse's bones were lying, and here they struggled for long, each in turn being brought to his knees. At last it ended in the howedweller falling backwards with a horrible crash, whereupon Audun above bolted from the rope, thinking that Grettir was killed. Grettir then drew his sword Jokulsnaut, cut off the head of the howedweller and laid it between his thighs. Then he went with the treasure to the rope, but finding Audun gone he had to swarm up the rope with his hands. First he tied the treasure to the lower end of the rope, so that he could haul it up after him. He was very stiff from his struggle with Kar, but he turned his steps towards Thorfinn's house, carrying the treasure along with him. He found them all at supper. Thorfinn cast a severe glance at him and asked what he had found so pressing to do that he could not keep proper hours like other men.

"Many a trifle happens at eve," he replied.

Then he brought out all the treasure which he had taken from the howe and laid it on the table. One thing there was upon which more than anything else Grettir cast his eyes, a short sword, which he declared to be finer than any weapon which he had ever seen. It was the last thing that he showed. Thorfinn opened his eyes when he saw the sword, for it was an heirloom of his family and had never been out of it.

"Whence came this treasure?" he asked.

Grettir then spake a verse:

> "Scatterer of gold! 'twas the lust of wealth
> that urged my hand to ravish the grave.
> This know; but none hereafter, I ween,
> will be fain to ransack Fafnir's lair."

Thorfinn said: "You don't seem to take it very seriously; no one ever before had any wish to break open the howe. But since I know that all treasure which is hidden in the earth or buried in a howe is in a wrong place I hold you guilty of no misdeed, especially since you have brought it to me."

Grettir answered:

> "The monster is slain!
> in the dismal tomb I have captured a sword,
>   dire wounder of men.
> Would it were mine I a treasure so rare
> I never would suffer my hand to resign."

"You have spoken well," Thorfinn answered. "But before I can give you the sword you must display your prowess in some way. I never got it from my father whilst he lived."

Grettir said: "No one knows to whom the greatest profit will fall ere all is done."

Thorfinn took the treasure and kept the sword in his own custody near his bed. The winter came on bringing Yule-tide, and nothing more happened that need be told of.

Chapter XIX
Berserks At Haramarsey

The following summer jarl Erik the son of Hakon was preparing to leave his country and sail to the West to join his brother-in-law King Knut the Great in England, leaving the government of Norway in the hands of Hakon his son, who, being an infant, was placed under the government and regency of Erik's brother, jarl Sveinn.

Before leaving Erik summoned all his Landmen and the larger bondis to meet him. Erik the jarl was an able ruler, and they had much discussion regarding the laws and their administration. It was considered a scandal in the land that pirates and berserks should be able to come into the country and challenge respectable people to the holmgang for their money or their women, no weregild being paid whichever fell. Many had lost their money and been put to shame in this way; some indeed had lost their lives. For this reason jarl Erik abolished all holmgang in Norway and declared all robbers and berserks who disturbed the peace outlaws. Thorfinn the son of Kar of Haramarsey, being a man of wise counsel and a close friend of the jarl, was present at the meeting.

The worst of these ruffians were two brothers named Thorir Paunch and Ogmund the Bad. They came from Halogaland and were bigger and stronger than other men. When angry they used to fall into the berserk's fury, and nothing escaped that was before them. They used to carry off men's wives, keep them for a week or two and then send them back. Wherever they came they committed robberies and other acts of violence. Jarl Erik had declared them outlaws throughout Norway. The man who had been most active in getting them outlawed was Thorfinn, and they were determined to pay him out in full for his hostility.

The jarl's expedition is told of in his saga, and the government of Norway was left in the hands of jarl Sveinn, with the regency.

Thorfinn returned home and remained there until about Yule-tide, as has already been told. Towards Yule-tide he made ready to go on a journey to his farm called Slysfjord on the mainland, whither he had invited a number of his friends. He could not take his wife with him, because their grown-up daughter was lying sick, so they both had to stay at home. Grettir and eight of the serving men remained with them. Thorfinn went with thirty freemen to the Yule festival, at which there was much gladness and merriment.

Yule-eve set in with bright and clear weather. Grettir, who was generally abroad in the daytime, was watching the vessels which came along the coast, some from the North, some from the South, meeting at the places agreed upon for their drinking-bouts. The bondi's daughter was then better and could go out with her mother. So the day passed. At last Grettir noticed a ship rowing up to the island, not large, covered with shields amidships and painted above the water-line. They were rowing briskly and making for Thorfinn's boat-houses. They ran the boat on to the beach and all sprang ashore. Grettir counted the men; there were twelve in all, and their aspect did not look peaceful.

After hauling up their boat out of the water they all made for the boat-house where Thorfinn's great boat, mentioned already, was stowed. She always required thirty men to put her to sea, but the twelve shoved her along the beach at once. Then they brought their own boat into the boat-house. It was very evident to Grettir that they did not mean to wait for an invitation, so he went up to them, and greeting them in a friendly way asked who they were and who was their captain. The man whom he addressed answered him at once, saying his name was Thorir, called Paunch; the others were his brother Ogmund with their companions. "I think," he added, "that your master Thorfinn has heard our names mentioned. But is he at home?"

"You must be men who have luck," said Grettir, "you have come most opportunely, if you are the people I take you for. The bondi has gone from home with all his freedmen and will not be back until after Yule. The goodwife is at home with her daughter, and if I had any grudge to repay, I would come just as you do, for there is everything here which you want, ale to drink and other delights."

Thorir was silent while Grettir went on talking. Then he turned to Ogmund and said: "Has anything not happened as I said it would? I should not be sorry to punish Thorfinn for having got us outlawed. This man seems ready to tell us everything; we don't have to drag the words out of his mouth."

"Every one is master of his own words," said Grettir. "If you will come home with me I will give you what entertainment I can."

They thanked him and said they would accept his invitation. When they reached the house Grettir took Thorir by the hand and led him into the hall. He was very talkative. The mistress was in the hall decorating it and putting all in order. On hearing what Grettir said, she came to the door and asked who it was that Grettir was welcoming so warmly.

Grettir answered: "It will be advisable, mistress, to be civil to these men who have come. They are the bondi Thorir Paunch and his followers, and have come, all twelve of them, to spend Yule-tide here. It is fortunate for us, for we have had little company till now."

She said: "I don't call them bondis, nor are they decent men, but arrant robbers and malefactors. I would gladly pay a large portion of my property for them not to have come just at this time. It is an ill return that you make to Thorfinn for having saved you from shipwreck and kept you this winter like a free man, destitute as you were."

"You would do better," said Grettir, "if you first took off the wet clothes from your guests instead of casting reproaches upon me. You will have plenty of time for that."

Then Thorir said: "Don't be angry, mistress! You shall lose nothing by your husband being away, for you shall have a man in his place and so shall your daughter and all the other women."

"That is spoken like a man," said Grettir. "The women shall be quite contented with what they get."

Then all the women fled and began to weep, being overcome by terror. Grettir said to the berserks: "Give me all the things which you want to lay aside, your weapons and your wet clothes, for the men will not obey us while they are frightened."

Thorir said he cared little for the women's whining. "But," he said, "we mean to treat you in a different way from the other men of the house. It seems to me that we may make a comrade of you."

"See to that yourselves," said Grettir. "But I do not look upon all men alike."

Then they laid aside most of their weapons. Grettir said: "I think now you had better sit down at the table and have some drink. You must be thirsty after your rowing."

They said they were quite ready for a drink, but did not know where the cellar was. Grettir asked whether they would let him arrange for their entertainment, which they willingly agreed to. So Grettir went and fetched some ale which he gave them to drink. They were very tired and drank enormously. He kept them well plied with the strongest ale there was, and they sat there for a long time whilst he told them funny stories. There was a tremendous din amongst them all, and the servants had no wish to approach them. Thorir said: "I never yet met with a stranger who treated me like this man. What reward shall we give you for all that you have done, Grettir?"

Grettir replied: "I don't expect any reward for my services at present. But if when you depart we are still as good friends as we seem to be now, I should very much like to join your company, and though I may not be able to do as much work as any of you, I will not be a hindrance in any doughty undertaking."

They were delighted, and wanted to swear fellowship with him at once. Grettir said that could not be, "for," he added, "there is truth in the saying that Ale is another man, and such a thing should not be done hastily, so let it remain at what I said; we are both little in the habit of restraining ourselves."

They declared that they did not mean to go back. The night was now coming on and it was getting very dark. Grettir noticed that they were rather fuddled, and asked whether they did not think it was time to go to bed. Thorir said: "So it is; but I have to fulfil my promise to the mistress." Grettir then went out and called out loud: "Go to bed, women! Such is the will of Thorir the bondi."

The women execrated him and could be heard howling like wolves. The berserks then left the room. Grettir said: "Let us go outside; I will show you the room in which Thorfinn keeps his clothes."

They were agreeable and all went out to an enormous outhouse, which was very strongly built, and had a strong lock on the outer door. Adjoining it was a large and well-built privy, with only a wooden partition between it and the room of the outhouse, which was raised above the ground and had to be reached by steps. The berserks then began skylarking and pushing

Grettir about. He fell down the in steps, as if in sport, and in a moment was out of the house, had pulled the bolt, slammed the door to, and locked it. Thorir and his mates thought at first that the door had swung to of itself, and paid little attention; they had a light with them by which Grettir had been showing them all Thorfinn's treasures, and they continued looking at them for some time.

Grettir went off to the homestead, and on reaching the door cried out very loud, asking where the mistress was. She was silent, being afraid to answer. He said: "Here is rather good sport to be had. Are there any arms which are good for anything?"

"There are arms," she said; "but I don't know for what purpose you want them."

"We will talk about that afterwards; but now let each do what he can; it is the last chance."

"Now indeed were God in the dwelling," she said, "if anything should happen to save us. Over Thorfinn's bed there hangs the great halberd which belonged to Kar the Old; there, too, is a helmet and a corselet and a good short sword. The weapons will not fail if your heart holds firm."

Grettir took the helmet and spear, girt the sword about him and went quickly out. The mistress called to her men and bade them follow their brave champion. Four of them rushed to their arms, but the other four durst not go near them.

Meantime the berserks thought that Grettir was a long time away and began to suspect some treachery. They rushed to the door and found it locked. They strained at the woodwork till every timber groaned. At last they tore down the wooden partition and so gained the passage where the privy was, and thence the steps. Then the berserks' fury fell upon them and they howled like dogs.

At that moment Grettir returned, and taking his halberd in both hands he thrust it right through Thorir's body just as he was about to descend the steps. The blade was very long and broad. Ogmund the Bad was just behind pushing him on, so that the spear passed right up to the hook, came out at his back between the shoulderblades and entered the breast of Ogmund. They both fell dead, pierced by the spear. Then all the others dashed down as they reached the steps. Grettir tackled them each in turn, now thrusting with the spear, now hewing with the sword, while they defended themselves with logs lying on the ground or with anything else which they could get. It was a terrible trial of a man's prowess to deal with men of their strength, even unarmed.

Grettir slew two of the Halogaland men there in the enclosure. Four of the serving-men then came up. They had not been able to agree upon which arms each should take, but they came out to the attack directly the berserks were running away; when these turned against them they fell back on the house. Six of the ruffians fell, all slain by Grettir's own hand; the other six then fled towards the landing place and took refuge in the boat-house, where they defended themselves with oars. Grettir received a severe blow from one of them and narrowly escaped a serious hurt.

The serving-men all went home and told great stories of their own exploits. The lady wanted to know what had become of Grettir, but they could not tell her. Grettir slew two men in the boat-house, but the other four got away, two in one direction, two in another. He pursued those who were nearest to him. The night was very dark. They ran to Vindheim, the place spoken of before, and took refuge in a barn, where they fought for a long time until at last Grettir killed them. By this time he was terribly stiff and exhausted. The night was far spent; it was very cold and there were driving snow-storms. He felt little inclination to go after the two who yet remained, so he went back home. The goodwife kindled a light and put it in a window in the loft at the top of the house, where it served him as a guide, and he was able to find his way home by the light. When he came to the door the mistress came to meet him and bade him welcome.

"You have earned great glory," she said, "and have saved me and my household from a disgrace never to be redeemed if you had not delivered us."

"I think I am much the same person as I was last evening when you spoke so roughly to me," said Grettir.

"We knew not then the might that was in you," she said, "as we know it now. Everything in the house shall be yours, so far as it is fitting for me to bestow and right for you to receive. I doubt not that Thorfinn will reward you in a better way when he comes home."

"There is little that I want as a reward at present," said Grettir. "But I accept your offer until your husband returns. I think now that you will be able to sleep in peace undisturbed by the berserks."

Grettir drank little before he retired and lay all night in his armour. In the morning, directly the day broke, all the men of the island were called together to go forth and search for the two berserks who had escaped. They were found at the end of the day lying under a rock, both dead from cold and from their wounds; they were carried away and buried in a place on the shore beneath the tide, with some loose stones over them, after which the islanders returned home, feeling that they could live in peace. When Grettir came back to the house and met the mistress he spoke a verse:

"Near the surging sea the twelve lie buried.
I stayed not my hand but slew them alone.
Great lady! what deed that is wrought by a man
shall be sung of as worthy if this be deemed small."

She answered: "Certainly you are very unlike any other man now living." She set him in the high seat and gave him the best of everything. So it remained until Thorfinn returned.

Chapter XX
Thorfinn's Return. Grettir Visits The North

When Yule-tide was past, Thorfinn made ready for his homeward journey and dismissed his many guests with gifts. He sailed with all his men and landed near the place where the boat-houses were.

They saw a ship lying on the sand which they at once recognized as his great boat. Thorfinn had heard nothing of the vikings and told his men to put him on shore, "for I suspect," he said, "that they are not friends who have been at work here."

Thorfinn was the first to land, and went straight to the boat-house, where he saw a craft which he knew at once to be that of the berserks. He said to his men: "I suspect that things have taken place here such that I would give the whole island and everything that is in it for them not to have happened."

They asked how that was.

"Vikings have been here, men whom I know as the worst in all Norway, namely Thorir Paunch and Ogmund the Bad. They will not have dealt gently with us. I mistrust that Icelander."

Then he spoke many things to his men. Grettir was at home and detained the men from going down to the shore. He said he did not care if the bondi got a little fright from what he saw. The goodwife asked his leave to go down, and he said she was mistress of her own ways, but that he was not going. So she hurried away to greet Thorfinn and embraced him joyfully. He was rejoiced to see her and said: "God be praised that I see you well and my daughter too. But what has happened to you since I left?"

"It has ended well," she said. "But we were nigh to suffering a disgrace which could never have been wiped out, had not your winter-guest aided us."

Thorfinn said: "Let us sit down and you shall tell me everything."

Then she told him fully all that had happened, praising highly Grettir's courage and resourcefulness. Thorfinn was silent while she was speaking, and when she had finished he said: "True indeed is the word, 'Long shall a man be tried'. But where is Grettir?"

"He is at home in the hall," she answered.

Then they went up to the house. Thorfinn went to Grettir and turned towards him and thanked him with the fairest words for his courageous conduct.

"I will say a word to you," he said, "which few would say to their friend. I would it might happen that you should need the help of a man, for you to know whether I count for anything or not; I cannot repay what you have done for me as long as you are not in straits. You shall have in my house whatever you desire, and shall be in the highest honour in my household."

Grettir thanked him and said he would have accepted his offer even if he had made it earlier.

Grettir stayed there the rest of the winter in high favour with Thorfinn. The fame of his deed spread through all Norway, especially in those parts where the berserks had ravaged most mercilessly. In the spring Thorfinn asked him what he would like to do. He said he would go North to Vagar while the fair was on there. Thorfinn said that any money which he required should be at his service; Grettir said he did not want more just then than enough to pay for his living. Thorfinn said that was his due, and brought him to a ship, where he gave him the excellent shortsword. Grettir kept it as long as he lived; it was a most precious possession. Thorfinn bade him come to him if ever he wanted any help.

Grettir then travelled to Vagar, which was crowded with people. Many whom he had never set eyes on before greeted him warmly because of his exploit in killing the vikings, and several of the leading men invited him to stay with them, but he preferred to return to his friend Thorfinn. So he took his passage in a trading ship belonging to one Thorkell, a man of some consideration in Salfti in Halogaland. Grettir went to visit Thorkell in his home, where he received a hearty welcome and a very pressing invitation to stay there for the winter. Grettir accepted the invitation and stayed the winter with Thorkell, who treated him with great honour.

Chapter XXI
Adventure With A Bear

There was a man named Bjorn who was then on a visit to Thorkell. He was of a somewhat violent character of good family and related in some way to Thorkell. He was not generally liked, because he was too much given to talking against the men who were about Thorkell and drove many away from him. He and Grettir did not get on at all. Bjorn thought him of small account compared to himself; Grettir paid him little deference, and it became an open feud. Bjorn was a boisterous swaggering man, and many of the younger men imitated him, loitering about outside in the evenings.

It happened at the beginning of the winter that a savage brown bear broke out of its den and raged about destroying men and cattle. Every one declared that it had been provoked by the noise which Bjorn and his company made. The beast became most mischievous, attacking the flocks in the very face of the men themselves. Thorkell, being the wealthiest man of that part, suffered most. One day he called up his men to come with him and search out the bear's den. They found it in a cliff by the sea where there was a cave under an overhanging rock, with a narrow path leading to the entrance. Below was a sheer precipice down to the beach, threatening certain death to any one who stumbled. In this den the bear lay in the daytime, going abroad at night. Fences were of no avail against him, nor could the dogs do anything, so that all were in the utmost distress. Thorkell's kinsman Bjorn declared that the main thing was gained now that they had found the den. "Now we shall see," he said, "how the game will go with me and my namesake." Grettir pretended not to hear what he said.

In the evenings when the others retired to bed, Bjorn used generally to go out. One night he went to the bear's den and found the creature inside, growling horribly. He lay down in the path, placing his shield over him, intending to wait until the beast came out as usual. Bruin, however, got wind of him and was rather slow in coming out. Bjorn got very sleepy where he was lying and could not keep awake; in the meantime out came the bear from his den and saw a man lying there. He clawed at him, dragged off his shield and threw it down the cliff. Bjorn woke up, not a little startled, took to his heels and ran off home, narrowly escaping the bear's clutches. His friends knew all about it, having watched his movements; on the next morning they found the shield and made great game of his adventure.

At Yule-time Thorkell himself went out to the den with Bjorn, Grettir and others of his men, a party of eight in all. Grettir had on a fur cape which he put off when they were attacking the bear. It was rather difficult to get at him, since they could only reach him with spear-thrusts, which he parried with his teeth. Bjorn kept urging them on to tackle him, but himself did not go near enough to be in any danger. At last, when no one was looking out, he took Grettir's fur cloak and threw it in to the bear. They did not succeed in getting the bear out, and when night came on turned to go home. Grettir then missed his cloak and saw that the bear had got it into his grip.

"Who has been playing tricks on me?" he cried. "Who threw my cloak into the cave?"

Bjorn answered: "He who did it will not be afraid to say so."

"Things of that sort do not trouble me much," said Grettir.

Then they started on their way home. After they had gone a little way Grettir's garter broke. Thorkell told them to wait for him, but Grettir said it was not necessary. Then Bjorn said: "There is no need to suppose that Grettir will run away from his cloak. He wants to have the honour of killing the beast all alone, and he will say that we eight men went away. Then he would appear to be what he is said to be. He has been backward enough all day."

"I don't know how you stand in that matter," said Thorkell. "You and he are not equal in valour; do not make any to-do about him."

Bjorn said that neither he nor Grettir should choose the words out of his mouth.

There was a hill between them and Grettir, who had turned back along the footpath. Now he had no others to reckon with in making the attack. He drew his sword Jokulsnaut and tied a loop round the handle which he passed over his wrist, because he thought that he could carry out his plans better if his hand were free. He went along the path. When the bear saw a man coming, he charged savagely, and struck at him with the paw that was on the side away from the precipice. Grettir aimed a blow at him with his sword and cut off his paw just above the claws. Then the creature tried to strike him with his sound paw, but to do so he had to drop on the stump, which was shorter than he expected, and over he fell into Grettir's embraces. Grettir seized the beast by the ears and held him off so that he could not bite. He always said that he considered this holding back the bear the greatest feat of strength that he ever performed. The beast struggled violently; the space was very narrow, and they both fell over the precipice. The bear being the heavier came down first on the beach; Grettir fell on the top of him, and the bear was badly mauled on the side that was down. Grettir got his sword, ran it into the heart of the bear and killed him. Then he went home, after fetching his cloak which was torn to pieces. He also took with him the bit of the paw which he had cut off.

Thorkell was sitting and drinking when Grettir entered. They all laughed at the ragged cloak which he was wearing. Then he laid the piece of the paw upon the table. Thorkell said: "Where is my kinsman Bjorn? I never saw iron bite like that in your hands. Now I would like you to show Grettir some honour to make up for the shame which you cast upon him."

Bjorn said that could wait, and that it mattered little to him whether Grettir was pleased or not. Grettir then spoke a verse:

"Oft returned the watcher at night
trembling home, but sound in limb.
None ever saw me sit in the dusk
at the cave; yet now I am home returned."

"It is true," said Bjorn, "that you have fought well; and also true that our opinions differ. I suppose you think that your taunts hurt me."

Thorkell said: "I should be glad, Grettir, if you would not revenge yourself upon Bjorn. I will pay the full weregild of a man for you to be reconciled."

Bjorn said he might invest his money better than in paying for that; and that it would be better for him and Grettir to go on bickering since "each oak has that which it scrapes from the other." Thorkell said: "But I ask you, Grettir, to do so much for my sake as not to attack Bjorn while you are both with me."

"That I promise," said Grettir.

Bjorn said that he would walk without fear of Grettir wherever they met. Grettir grinned, and would accept no money on account of Bjorn. They stayed there the winter.

Chapter XXII
Grettir Kills Bjorn And Is Summoned Before Jarl Sveinn

In the spring Grettir went North to Vagar with Thorkell's men. They parted with friendship. Bjorn went West to England in Thorkell's ship, of which he was master, staying there for the summer and transacting the business which Thorkell had entrusted to him. In the end of the autumn he returned from the western parts. Grettir stayed in Vagar till the trading ships left, and then sailed South with some of the traders, as far as the part of Gartar at the mouth of the Thrandheim's Fjord, where he set up the awnings to make a stay. When they were settled down a ship came up along the coast from the South, which they at once recognised as one of the ships from England. She made fast further out off the coast and her crew landed. Grettir went out with his companions to visit them. On their meeting Grettir found Bjorn amongst the company and said: "It is well that we meet here, for now we can continue our former quarrel. I should like to try which of us is the better man."

Bjorn said that was all past now, as far as he was concerned. "But," he said, "if there has been anything between us I will pay you such compensation that you shall be satisfied." Grettir spoke a verse:

"Time was when the bear was slain by my hand;
my cloak in tatters was torn.
A rascally knave was the cause of it all
but now he shall make me amends."

Bjorn said that weightier matters than this had been settled by payment. Grettir said that few men had any reason to act maliciously towards him; he had accepted no money-atonement, nor would he do so now; that if he had his way they should not both go away unhurt, and that if Bjorn refused to fight he would brand him as a coward. Bjorn saw that excuses would not avail him, so he took his arms and went out. They rushed at each other and fought; soon Bjorn was wounded and then he fell dead to the ground. On seeing that, his men went on board their ship, sailed away to the North along the coast to Thorkell's place and told him what had happened. He said it had not come sooner than he expected. Directly afterwards he sailed to the South to Thrandheim where he found jarl Sveinn.

Grettir, after slaying Bjorn, went to More to his friend Thorfinn and told him exactly what had happened. Thorfinn received him in a most friendly way. "I am glad," he said, "that you will now have need of a friend. You must stay with me until this affair is finished." Grettir thanked him for his invitation and said he would accept it. Jarl Sveinn was staying at Steinker in Thrandheim when he heard of the slaying of Bjorn. With him was a brother of Bjorn named Hjarrandi, as one of his bodyguard. On hearing of Bjorn's death he became very angry and begged the jarl for his support in the matter, which the jarl promised that he should have. He sent messengers to Thorfinn to summon both him and Grettir to appear before him. Immediately on receiving the jarl's commands they both made ready and came to Thrandheim. The jarl held a council on the matter and ordered Hjarrandi to be present. Hjarrandi said he was not going to weigh his brother against his purse, and that he must either follow him or avenge him.

When the case was looked into, it became evident that Bjorn had given Grettir many provocations. Thorfinn offered to pay a fine such as the jarl thought suitable to the position of his kinsman, and dwelt at length upon Grettir's achievement in killing the berserks, and how he had delivered the men in the North from them.

The jarl answered: "Truth do you speak, Thorfinn! That was indeed a cleansing! It would befit us well to accept the compensation for your sake. Grettir, too, is a fine fellow, and noted for his strength and valour."

Hjarrandi, however, would accept no compensation, and the meeting came to an end. Thorfinn appointed one of his kinsmen, Arnbjorn, to accompany Grettir every day, for he knew that Hjarrandi was plotting against his life.

Chapter XXIII
Grettir Kills Hjarrandi

One day Grettir and Arnbjorn were walking along the road for their diversion when they passed a gate, whence a man rushed out holding an axe aloft with both hands and struck at Grettir, who was not on his guard and was moving slowly. Arnbjorn, however, saw the man coming, seized Grettir and pushed him aside with such force that he fell on his knee. The axe struck him in the shoulder-blade and cut down to below the arm, inflicting a severe wound. Grettir turned quickly and drew his sword; he saw that it was Hjarrandi who had attacked him. The axe had stuck fast in the road, and Hjarrandi was slow in recovering it. Grettir struck at him and cut off his arm at the shoulder. Then there came running up five of Hjarrandi's followers and a battle began with them. They were soon routed; Grettir and Arnbjorn killed the five who were with Hjarrandi; one man escaped and bore the tale to the jarl forthwith. The jarl was very angry indeed, and summoned the assembly for the next day. Thorfinn and his party appeared thereat. The jarl brought a charge of manslaughter against Grettir, who admitted it and said that he had been obliged to defend himself. "I bear the marks of it," he said. "I should have been killed if Arnbjorn had not defended me."

The jarl said it was a pity he had not been killed, for this affair would lead to many a man being slain if he lived.

There had come to the jarl's court Bersi the son of Skaldtorfa, Grettir's comrade and friend. He and Thorfinn stepped before the jarl and begged for pardon for Grettir. They asked that the jarl should decide the matter himself as he thought best, only that Grettir should have his life and the freedom of the country. The jarl was averse to any terms being granted to him, but gave way to their entreaties. He granted immunity to Grettir until the spring, but not absolutely until Gunnar the brother of Bjorn and Hjarrandi should be present. Gunnar was a landed proprietor in Tunsberg.

In the spring the jarl ordered Grettir and Thorfinn to appear at Tunsberg, where he himself intended to be while the shipping was assembled. So thither they went, and found the jarl was already in the town. There Grettir met his brother Thorsteinn Dromund, who greeted him joyfully and invited him to be his guest. He was a landowner in the town. Grettir told him all about his case, and Thorsteinn took his view of it, but told him to beware of Gunnar. So the spring passed.

Chapter XXIV
Grettir Kills Gunnar. His Friends Rally Round Him And Save Him From The Vengeance Of The Jarl

Gunnar was in the town and was plotting against Grettir's life. Wherever he went Gunnar dogged his steps wherever he found a chance of getting near him. One day Grettir was sitting in a booth and drinking, because he wanted to keep out of Gunnar's way. Suddenly there was a bang at the door, so hard that it broke in pieces, and in rushed four men armed and attacked Grettir. They were Gunnar with his followers. Grettir seized his arms which were hanging above his head and ran into a corner, where he defended himself, holding his shield before him, and hewing with his sword. They made little way against him. One blow he succeeded in delivering upon one of Gunnar's followers, who needed nothing more. Then Grettir advanced, driving them before him out of the booth, and killing another of them. Gunnar would fain have got away with his men, but on reaching the door he caught his foot on the doorstep, fell over and was not able to recover himself at once. He held his shield before him and retreated as Grettir pressed him hard. Then Grettir sprang on to the crossbenches near the door. Gunnar's hands and the shield were still inside the door, and Grettir struck down between him and the shield, cutting off both his hands at the wrist. He fell backwards out of the door, and Grettir gave him his death-blow. Then the man who was behind him got on his feet and ran off at once to tell the jarl what had happened. Sveinn was furious, and called the assembly to meet there and then in the town. When Thorfinn and Thorsteinn Dromund heard the news, they called all their followers and friends together and went to the meeting in force. The jarl was very wroth, and it was no easy matter to get speech with him. Thorfinn was the first to come before the jarl, and he said: "I have come to offer an honourable atonement for the man who has been slain by Grettir. The judgment shall remain with you alone if you but spare his life."

The jarl replied in great wrath: "It is too late to beg for Grettir's life, and you have no case that I can see. He has killed three brothers, one at the feet of the other; men of noble minds who would not weigh each other against their purses. Now, Thorfinn, it will not avail you to beg for Grettir; I will not do such a wrong in the land as to accept atonement for such a crime as this."

Then Bersi the son of Skaldtorfa came up and begged the jarl to accept blood-money. "Grettir," he said, "is a man of high birth and is my good friend. I offer you what I possess. May you see, my lord, that it is better by sparing one man to earn the goodwill of many and to fix the penalty yourself than to refuse honourable terms and risk whether you can arrest the man or not."

The jarl replied: "You do right, Bersi; and herein as ever you show your worth. But I do not mean to break the laws of the land by granting life to a man who has forfeited it."

Then Thorsteinn Dromund came forward, and he, too, offered blood-money on behalf of Grettir, adding many fair words thereto.

The jarl asked what moved him to offer blood-money for the man. Thorsteinn said Grettir was his brother. The jarl said he had not known that.

"It shows a manly spirit in you," he said, "that you want to help him. But as I am determined not to accept blood-money in this case, I must treat the requests of all of you alike. I must have Grettir's life whatever it cost, directly I can get him."

Then the jarl rose quickly up and refused to hear any more about atonement. They all went home with Thorsteinn and made their preparations, whereupon the jarl ordered all the men of his guard under arms and went forth with a large force. Before they came up, Grettir's friends had made ready to defend the house. Thorfinn, Thorsteinn, Grettir himself, and Bersi were in the forefront, each with a large force of followers behind him. The jarl summoned them to give up Grettir, and not to bring trouble on themselves. They repeated their former offers, but the jarl would not listen to them. Thorfinn and Thorsteinn said that more was at stake for the jarl than the taking of Grettir's life.

"One fate shall fall upon us all," they cried, "and men shall say that you have given much for the life of one man when we are all laid low with the ground."

The jarl said he would spare none of them, and they were on the very verge of a battle when many of the well-disposed men came up to him and begged him not to land himself in such a difficulty. He should bear in mind that these men would work great havoc among his own followers before they fell. The jarl thought this counsel was wise and let himself be somewhat appeased. Then the terms of atonement were settled. Thorfinn and Thorsteinn were ready to pay so long as Grettir's life was spared. The jarl said: "You must know that although I agree to this compromise, I do not consider it a full amnesty. Only I have no mind to fight against my own men, although they appear to hold me of little account in the matter."

Thorfinn said: "Yours is all the greater honour, my lord, that you will have the fixing of the penalty yourself."

The jarl said that Grettir should have leave from him to depart from the country in peace for Iceland, directly there was a ship leaving, if so it seemed good to them. They agreed and paid the money to the jarl to his satisfaction. They parted with little friendship. Grettir went with Thorfinn after bidding an affectionate farewell to his brother Thorsteinn.

Thorfinn earned great honour for the support which he had given Grettir against such odds as he had to deal with. Not one of the men who had helped Grettir was ever received into favour again with the jarl, excepting Bersi.

Grettir then spoke:

"Comrade of Odin, Thorfinn was born
to rescue my life from the fangs of Hel.
No less was Thorsteinn Dromund's aid
when I was doomed to the realm of the dead."

And again:

"The prince's retainers withdrew in fear
when Bersi threatened their hearts to pierce."

Grettir returned with Thorfinn to the North and stayed with him until he found a ship with some traders who were bound for Iceland. Thorfinn gave him many valuable garments and a colouredsaddle with a bridle. They parted with friendship, and Thorfinn invited him to come and see him if ever he returned to Norway.

Chapter XXV
Events In Iceland. Thorgils Maksson Attacked By The Foster-Brothers And Slain

smund Longhair was in Bjarg whilst Grettir was away, and was much respected as a bondi in Midfjord. Thorkell Krafla had died during Grettir's absence. Thorvald Asgeirsson dwelt in Ass in Vatnsdal and was a great chief. He was the father of Dalla who married Isleif, afterwards bishop in Skalaholt. Asmund had great support from Thorvald in legal suits and in other matters.

There grew up in Asmund's household a youth named Thorgils Maksson, a near kinsman of his. Thorgils was a strong man of his body and made much money under Asmund's guidance; he dwelt at Laekjamot, on a property which Asmund had bought for him. Thorgils was a good manager and went to Strandir every year, where he obtained whales and other things.

He was a man of great courage, and went as far as the eastern Almenningar. At that time the two foster-brothers Thorgeir Havarsson and Thormod Coalbrow-Skald were very much to the front; they kept a boat, gathering what they wanted from the country around, and had not the reputation of dealing fairly.

One summer Thorgils Maksson found a whale at the Almenningar and went out at once with his men to cut it up. When the two foster-brothers heard of it they went there too, and at first it seemed as if matters would be settled peaceably. Thorgils proposed that they should share equally that part of the whale which was yet uncut, but they wanted to have all the uncut part or else to share the entire whale. Thorgils positively refused to give up any portion of what had already been cut. They began to use threats and at last took to their arms and fought. Thorgeir and Thorgils fought each of them desperately together without either prevailing. After a long and furious battle Thorgils fell slain by Thorgeir. In another place Thormod was fighting with the followers of Thorgils, and he overcame them, killing three. Those who remained of Thorgils' party went off after he fell to Midfjord, taking his body with them and feeling that they had suffered a great loss. The foster-brothers took possession of the whole whale. The affair is referred to in the memorial poem which Thormod composed upon Thorgeir.

News of the death of his kinsman was brought to Asmund Longhair, on whom as nearest of kin the blood-feud devolved. He went to the spot, called witnesses to testify to the wounds and brought the case before the All-Thing, which appeared to be the proper course in this case where the act had been committed in another quarter. Some time was passed over this.

Chapter XXVI
The Feud With The Foster-Brothers Is Taken Up By Asmund And Thorsteinn Kuggason

There was a man named Thorsteinn; he was the son of Thorkell Kuggi, the son of Thord Yeller, the son of Olaf Feilan, the son of Thorsteinn the Red, the son of Aud the Deep-Minded. Thorsteinn Kuggason's mother was Thurid, daughter of Asgeir Hothead. Asgeir was the brother of Asmund Longhair's father. Thorsteinn Kuggason was equally responsible in the blood-feud over Thorgils' death with Asmund Longhair, who now sent for him. Thorsteinn was a great warrior and very masterful. He came at once to his kinsman Asmund and they had a talk together about the suit. Thorsteinn was for extreme measures. He said that no blood-money should be accepted; that with their connections they were powerful enough to carry through a sentence of either banishment or death on the slayer. Asmund said he would support any measures whatever that he chose to adopt. They rode then North to Thorvald their kinsman and asked for his support, which he at once promised them. So the suit was begun against Thorgeir and Thormod. Thorsteinn then rode home to his dwelling at Ljarskogar in the Hvamm district. Skeggi in Hvamm also joined Thorsteinn. He was a son of Thorarin Fylsenni, a son of Thord the Yeller. His mother was Fridgerd, a daughter of Thord from Hofdi. They had a large following at the All-Thing and pressed their suit valiantly. Asmund and Thorvald rode from the North with sixty men, halting several days at Ljarskogar.

Chapter XXVII
Sentences On The Foster-Brothers

There dwelt at Reykjaholar a man named Thorgils, the son of Ari, the son of Mar, the son of Atli the Red, the son of Ulf Squint-Eye, the first settler at Reykjanes. Thorgils' mother was Thorgerd the daughter of Alf of Dalir. Alf had another daughter named Thorelf, who was the mother of Thorgeir the son of Havar. Thorgeir, therefore, had a very strong backing through his connections, for Thorgils was the most powerful chief in the Vestfirding quarter. He was very open-handed and gave hospitality to any free-man for as long as he would. There was consequently always a crowd at Reykjaholar, and he lived in great grandeur. He was both kindly and wise. Thorgeir stayed with him in the winter and went to Strandir in the summer.

After slaying Thorgils the son of Mak, Thorgeir went to Reykjaholar and told Thorgils Arason what had happened. Thorgils told him his house was open to him. "But," he said, "they will press the matter vigorously, and I am most unwilling to involve myself in difficulties. I will send a man now to Thorsteinn and offer him blood-money for the Thorgils affair; if he will not accept it I will not adopt any violent measures."

Thorgeir declared that he would submit to his wisdom. In the autumn Thorgils sent a messenger to Thorsteinn Kuggason to try and arrange a settlement.   Thorsteinn was very disinclined to accept any money in atonement for the slaying of Thorgils, although for the others he was willing to follow the advice of men of counsel.   Thorgils on receiving the report of his messenger called Thorgeir to a consultation with him and asked him what support he thought was proper.   Thorgeir said that if a sentence of banishment were passed upon him he would go.   Thorgils said that his resolve would be put to the trial.

There came a ship into the Nordra river in Borgarfjord, and Thorgils secretly took a passage in her for the two foster-brothers. The winter now passed, and Thorgils heard that Thorsteinn and his party had assembled in great force for the All-Thing and were then in Ljarskogar. So he put off his departure, intending that they should arrive from the North before he came up from the West. So it came to pass. Thorgils and Thorgeir then rode towards the South, Thorgeir killing one Boggul-Torfi on the way at Marskelda and two other men named Skuf and Bjarni at Hundadal. Thormod sings about this affair in his Thorgeir's drapa:

> "The hem slew the son of Mak;
> there was storm of swords and raven's food.
> Skuf and Bjarni he also felled;
> gladly he bathed his hands in blood."

Thorgils settled for the slaying of Skuf and Bjarni there and then in the dale, and was delayed by the affair longer than he intended. Thorgeir embarked on the ship and Thorgils went to the Thing, where he did not arrive before they were proceeding to judgment in Thorgils Maksson's case. Asmund Longhair then called for the defence. Thorgils appeared before the court and offered blood-money in atonement on condition of Thorgeir not being sentenced to banishment. He endeavoured to meet the charge by pleading that finds in the Almenningar were free to all. The question whether this was a valid defence or not was referred to the Lawman, who at that time was Skapti. He upheld Asmund's view on account of their kinship together. He declared that this was indeed the law in the case of men equal in position, but that a bondi had precedence over a vagrant. Asmund further urged that Thorgils had offered to share the uncut portion of the whale with the foster-brothers when they arrived. The defendants were non-suited on that point. Then Thorsteinn and his party pressed their suit resolutely and said they would not be satisfied with any sentence short of banishment upon Thorgeir. Thorgils saw that no choice was left to him but either to call up his men and try to carry his case with violence, the issue of which would be uncertain, or else to submit to the sentence demanded by the opposite party, and since Thorgeir was already on board his ship Thorgils had no desire to press the case further. Thorgeir was banished, but Thormod was discharged upon payment of blood-money.

Asmund and Thorsteinn gained great glory by this case. The men rode home from the Thing. There were some who said that Thorgils had not taken much trouble in the case, but he paid little attention and let them say what they pleased.

When Thorgeir heard that he was banished, he said that if he had his way, those who had brought it about should be repayed in full before it was over.

There was a man named Gaut, called the son of Sleita, a kinsman of Thorgils Maksson. He was intending to travel in the same ship with Thorgeir, with whom he was on very bad terms, and frowned on him. The traders thought it would never do to have them both together in the ship. Thorgeir said he did not care what Gaut did with his eyebrows. Nevertheless they decided that Gaut should leave the ship. He went into the northern districts and for that time nothing happened, but the affair brought about a feud between them which broke out later.

Chapter XXVIII
Grettir's Visit To Audun In Vididal; Offers His Services To Bardi

In the course of that summer Grettir Asmundsson returned to Skagafjord. He had such a reputation for strength that none of the younger men was supposed to be his equal. He soon came to his home in Bjarg, and Asmund gave him a fitting welcome. Atli was then managing the property and the brothers agreed well together, but Grettir became so over-weening that he thought nothing was beyond his powers.

Many of the youths with whom Grettir had played at Midfjordsvatn before he left were now grown up. Audun, the son of Asgeir, the son of Audun, was now living at Audunarstad in Vididal. He was a good bondi and a kindly man, and was the strongest of all the men in the northern parts, as well as the most modest.

Grettir had not forgotten how he had seemingly been worsted by Audun at the ball-play, as related above, and he was anxious to try which of them had gained most since. With this object he went at the beginning of the hay-harvest to Audunarstad. Grettir put on all his finery and rode with the coloured and richly ornamented saddle which Thorfinn had given him, on a splendid horse and in his best armour to Audun's place, where he arrived early in the day and knocked at the door. Few of the men were in the house, and to Grettir's question whether Audun was at home, they replied that he had gone to the hill-dairy to bring home some produce. Grettir took the bridle off his horse. The hay had not been mown in the meadow and the horse went for the part where the grass was thickest. Grettir entered the room and sat down on the bench, where he fell asleep. Soon Audun returned home and saw a horse in the meadow with a coloured saddle on its back. He was bringing two horses loaded with curds in skins tied at the mouth—so-called "curd-bags." Audun took the skins off the horses and was carrying them in his arms so that he could not see in front of him. Grettir's leg was stretched out before him and Audun stumbled over it, falling on the curd-bags which broke at the neck. Audun sprang up and asked what rascal that was in his house. Grettir told him his name.

"That was very awkward of you," said Audun. "But what do you want here?"

"I want to fight with you."

"First I must look after my dairy produce," Audun said.

"You can do that," answered Grettir, "if you have no one else to do it for you."

Audun bent down, gathered up the skin and threw it right into Grettir's breast, telling him to take what he sent him. Grettir was all covered with curds, and felt more disgusted than at any wound which Audun could have given him. Then they went for each other and wrestled pretty smartly. Grettir rushed at him, but Audun escaped his grasp. He saw, however, that Grettir had gained upon him. They drove up and down the room, overthrowing everything that was near them. Neither of them spared himself, but Grettir had the advantage, and at last Audun fell, after tearing off all Grettir's weapons. They struggled hard and the din was terrific.

Then there was a loud noise below. Grettir heard a man ride up to the house, get off his horse and come quickly inside. He saw a handsome man in a red jacket wearing a helmet. Hearing the commotion going on in the room where they were wrestling, he came in and asked what was in the room. Grettir told him his name; "but who is it that wants to know?" he asked.

"My name is Bardi," answered the stranger.

"Are you Bardi the son of Gudmund from Asbjarnarnes?"

"The same," he replied. "But what are you after?"

Grettir said: "I and Audun are playing here."

"I don't know about your play," said Bardi. "But you are not alike. You are overbearing and insolent, while he is modest and good-natured. Let him get up at once."

Grettir said: "Many a man seizes the lock for the door. You would do better to avenge your brother Hall than to come between me and Audun when we are contending."

"I am always hearing that," said Bardi, "and I don't know whether I shall ever obtain my vengeance. But I want you to leave Audun in peace, for he is a quiet man."

Grettir said he was willing to do so because of Bardi's intercession, though he did not like it much. Bardi asked what they were contending about. Grettir replied in a verse:

"I know not if for all your pride
he may not try your throat to squeeze.
Thus when within my home I dwelt
did he once belabour me."

Bardi said there was certainly some excuse if he was taking revenge. "Let me now settle it between you," he said. "Let matters remain as they are and cease your strife."

So they consented, for they were kinsmen. But Grettir had little liking for Bardi or his brothers. They all rode away together. On the way Grettir said: "I hear, Bardi, that you intend to go South to Borgarfjord this summer; I propose that I shall go with you, which I think is more than you deserve."

Bardi was very pleased with this offer, and at once accepted it most thankfully. Then they parted. Bardi then turned back and said to Grettir: "I would like it to be understood that you only come with me if it meets with Thorarin's approval, since all the arrangements for the expedition are with him."

"I thought," said Grettir, "you were competent to make your arrangements for yourself. I do not leave my affairs to other people to settle. I shall take it very ill if you refuse me."

Then each went his own way. Bardi promised to send Grettir word "if Thorarin wished him to go." Otherwise he could remain quietly at home. Grettir then rode to Bjarg and Bardi to his own home.

Chapter XXIX
Horse-Fight At Langafit

That summer there was a great horse-fight at Langafit below Reykir, whither a great many people came together. Atli of Bjarg had a good stallion of Keingala's race; grey with a dark stripe down his back. Both father and son valued the horse highly. The two brothers Kormak and Thorgils in Mel had a very mettlesome brown stallion, and they arranged to match it against that of Atli from Bjarg. Many other excellent stallions were brought. Odd the Needy-Skald, Kormak's kinsman, had the charge of their horse on the day. He had grown into a strong man and had a high opinion of himself; he was surly and reckless. Grettir asked Atli who should have charge of his stallion.

"That is not so clear to me," said Atli.

"Would you like me to back him?"

"Then you must keep very cool, kinsman," he said. "We have men to deal with who are rather overbearing."

"Let them pay for their bluster," he said, "if they cannot control it."

The stallions were led out and the mares tethered together in the front on the bank of the river. There was a large pool just beyond the bank. The horses fought vigorously and there was excellent sport. Odd managed his horse pluckily and Grettir gave way before him, holding the tail of his horse with one hand and with the other the stick with which he pricked it on. Odd stood in the front by his horse, and one could not be sure that he was not pricking off Atli's horse from his own. Grettir pretended not to notice it. The horses then came near the river. Then Odd thrust with his pointed stick at Grettir and caught him in the shoulder-blade which Grettir was turning towards him. He struck pretty hard, and the flesh swelled up, but Grettir was little hurt. At the same moment the horses reared. Grettir ducked beneath the flank of his horse and drove his stick into Odd's side with such violence that three of his ribs were broken and Odd fell into the pool with his horse and all the mares that were tethered there by the bank. Some people swam out and rescued them. There was great excitement about it. Kormak's men on one side and those of Bjarg on the other seized their arms, but the men of Hrutafjord and Vatnsnes came between them and parted them.

They all went home in great wrath, but kept quiet for a time. Atli said very little, but Grettir rather swaggered and said that they should meet again if he had his way.

Chapter XXX
Thorbjorn Oxmain And The Fray At Hrutafjardarhals

There was living in Thoroddsstad in Hrutafjord a man named Thorbjorn. He was the son of Arnor Downy-Nose, the son of Thorodd who had settled in that side of Hrutafjord which lies opposite to Bakki. Thorbjorn was of all men the strongest, and was called Oxmain. He had a brother named Thorodd, called Drapustuf. Their mother was Gerd, daughter of Bodvar from Bodvarsholar. Thorbjorn was a great swashbuckler and kept a large troop of followers. He was noted for being worse at getting servants than other men, and scarcely paid them any wages. He was not a man easy to deal with. There was a kinsman of his, also named Thorbjorn, called Slowcoach. He was a mariner, and the two namesakes were in partnership together. He was always at Thoroddsstad and people did not think he made Thorbjorn any better. He liked to talk scandal and spoke offensively of several men.

There was a man named Thorir, a son of Thorkell, at Bordeyr. He first lived at Melar in Hrutafjord, and had a daughter named Helga who married Sleitu-Helgi. After the Fagrabrekka affair Thorir went South to Haukadal and lived in Skard, selling the property at Melar to Thorhall the Winelander, the son of Gamli. Thorhall's son Gamli married Rannveig, the daughter of Asmund Longhair, Grettir's sister. They lived at that time in Melar and had a good establishment. Thorir of Skard had two sons, Gunnar and Thorgeir, both promising men, who took over the property from their father, but were always with Thorbjorn Oxmain, and became very overbearing.

In the summer of that year Kormak and Thorgils rode with a kinsman of theirs named Narfi South to Nordrardal on some business. Odd the Needy-Skald had recovered from the hurts which he had received at the horse-fight and was of the party. While they were south of the heath Grettir was journeying from his home at Bjarg with two of Atli's men. They rode to Burfell and then across the neck to Hrutafjord, reaching Melar in the evening, where they spent three nights. Rannveig and Gamli gave Grettir a friendly reception and invited him to stay, but he wanted to return home. Then Grettir learned of Kormak's company having come from the South, and that they were staying at Tunga at night. He prepared to leave Melar at once, and Gamli offered to send some of his men with him. Gamli's brother Grim, who was very smart and active, and another rode with Grettir. The party, five in number, came to Hrutafjardarhals to the west of Burfell, where the great stone called Grettishaf lies; he struggled a long time with that stone, trying to lift it, and delayed his journey thereby until Kormak's party came up. Grettir went towards them and both alighted from their horses. Grettir said it would be more seemly for free men to set to work with all their might instead of fighting with sticks like tramps. Kormak told them to take up the challenge like men and to do their best. So they went for each other. Grettir was in front of his men and told them to see that nobody got behind him. They fought for a time and both were hurt.

On the same day Thorbjorn Oxmain had ridden across the neck to Burfell, and as he returned with Thorbjorn Slowcoach, Gunnar and Thorgeir, the sons of Thorir, and Thorodd Drapustuf, he saw the fight going on. On coming up, Thorbjorn called upon his men to go between them, but they were struggling so furiously that nobody could get at them. Grettir was making a clean sweep of everything round him. Before him were the sons of Thorir. He pushed them back and they both fell over. This made them furious, and the consequence was that Gunnar gave a blow to one of Atli's men which killed him. Thorbjorn on seeing that ordered them to separate, saying that he would give his support to whichever side obeyed him. By then two of Kormak's men had fallen. Grettir saw that it would scarcely do if Thorbjorn joined the opposite side, so he gave up the battle. All those who had fought were wounded. Grettir was much disgusted at their being separated, but both parties rode home and were not reconciled on this occasion.

Thorbjorn Slowcoach made great game of all this, and the relations between the men of Bjarg and Thorbjorn Oxmain became strained in consequence, until at last there was a regular feud, which however broke out later. No compensation was offered to Atli for his man, and he went on as if he knew nothing of it. Grettir stayed at Bjarg till the Tvi-month. It is not known that he and Kormak ever met again; at least it is not mentioned anywhere.

Chapter XXXI
Grettir's Vain Endeavour To Provoke Bardi

Bardi the son of Gudmund and his brothers rode home to Asbjarnarnes when they left Grettir. They were the sons of Gudmund the son of Solmund. Solmund's mother was Thorlaug, daughter of Saemund the Southerner, the foster-brother of Ingimund the Old. Bardi was a man of great distinction. Soon he went to see his foster-father Thorarin the Wise, who welcomed him and asked what help he had been able to obtain, for Bardi's journey had been arranged beforehand by them both. Bardi answered that he had engaged a man whose help he thought worth more than that of two others. Thorarin was silent for a moment and then said: "That must be Grettir the son of Asmund."

"The guess of the wise is truth," said Bardi. "That is the very man, my foster-father."

Thorarin answered: "It is true that Grettir is beyond all other men of whom there is now choice in the country; nor will he be easily subdued by arms so long as he is sound. But great arrogance is in him now, and I have misgivings as to his luck. It is important for you that all your men on your expedition are not men of an evil star. It is enough if he does not fare with you. He shall not come if my counsel is followed."

"I did not expect, my foster-father," said he, "that you would deny me the man who is bravest in all that he undertakes. A man in such straits as I seem to be in cannot provide against everything."

"It will be better for you," he replied, "to let me provide."

So it came about that as Thorarin desired, word was not sent to Grettir. Bardi went to the South and the battle of the Heath was fought.

Grettir was at Bjarg when he received the news that Bardi had started on his expedition. He was very angry that word had not been sent to him, and said it should not end there. He found out when they were expected back from the South, and rode off to Thoreyjargnup, where he meant to lie in wait for Bardi and his men as they rode back. He left the homestead behind and remained at the cliffs. On that day rode Bardi back from the battle of the Heath from Tvidaegra; there were six of them in his party, all sorely wounded. When they came to the homestead Bardi said: "There is a man up there on the cliff, very tall and armed. Whom do you take him for?"

They could not say who he was. Bardi said: "I believe it is Grettir the son of Asmund. If it is, he will be wanting to meet us, for I expect he is little pleased at not having been with us. It seems to me that we are not in a very fit condition if he wants to annoy us. I will send home to Thoreyjargnup for some men and not allow myself to be put out by his evil intentions."

They said that was the best thing he could do, and it was done. Bardi's party rode on; Grettir watched where they were going and went there too. They met and greeted each other. Grettir asked what the news was, and Bardi told him without hesitation. Grettir asked who had been with them. Bardi answered that his brothers and Eyjvolf his brother-in-law had been with him.

"You have wiped out your disgrace," said Grettir. "Now the next thing is for us two here to try which is the stronger."

"I have more urgent business," said Bardi, "than to fight with you about nothing. I think I may be excused that now."

"It seems to me that you are afraid, Bardi; that is the reason why you dare not fight me."

"Call it what you please. If you wish to bully, find some one else; that seems to be what you want, for your insolence passes all bounds."

Grettir thought luck was against him. He hesitated now whether he should attack any of them; it seemed rather rash as they were six and he was only one. Then the men from Thoreyjargnup came up and joined Bardi's party, so he left them and went back to his horse. Bardi and his men went on, and there was no greeting between them when they parted. We are not told that any strife arose between Bardi and Grettir after this.

Grettir once said that he would trust himself to fight with most men if there were not more than three against him. Even with four he would not give way without trying, but more he would not attempt, except in self-defence. Thus he says in a verse:

"Oh skilled in war! When three are before me
I yet will endeavour to fight with them all.
But more than four I dare not encounter
in the clashing of arms, if the choice is with me."

On leaving Bardi, Grettir returned to Bjarg, and was much aggrieved at finding nothing to try his strength on. He sought everywhere for something to fight with.

Chapter XXXXII
The Spook At Thorhallsstad. Glam The Shepherd Killed By A Fiend. His Ghost Walks

There was a man named Thorhall living in Thorhallsstad in Forsaeludal, up from Vatnsdal. He was the son of Grim, the son of Thorhall, the son of Fridmund, who was the first settler in Forsaeludal. Thorhall's wife was named Gudrun; they had a son named Grim and a daughter named Thurid who were just grown up. Thorhall was fairly wealthy, especially in live-stock. His property in cattle exceeded that of any other man. He was not a chief, but an honest bondi nevertheless. He had great difficulty in getting a shepherd to suit him because the place was haunted. He consulted many men of experience as to what he should do, but nobody gave him any advice which was of any use. Thorhall had good horses, and went every summer to the Thing. On one occasion at the All-Thing he went to the booth of the Lawman Skapti the son of Thorodd, who was a man of great knowledge and gave good counsel to those who consulted him. There was a great difference between Thorodd the father and Skapti the son in one respect. Thorodd possessed second sight, but was thought by some not to be straight, whereas Skapti gave to every man the advice which he thought would avail him, if he followed it exactly, and so earned the name of Father-betterer.

So Thorhall went to Skapti's booth, where Skapti, knowing that he was a man of wealth, received him graciously, and asked what the news was.

"I want some good counsel from you," said Thorhall.

"I am little fit to give you counsel," he replied; "but what is it that you need?"

"It is this: I have great difficulty in keeping my shepherds. Some get injured and others cannot finish their work. No one will come to me if he knows what he has to expect."

Skapti answered: "There must be some evil spirit abroad if men are less willing to tend your flocks than those of other men. Now since you have come to me for counsel, I will get you a shepherd. His name is Glam, and he came from Sylgsdale in Sweden last summer. He is a big strong man, but not to everybody's mind."

Thorhall said that did not matter so long as he looked after the sheep properly. Skapti said there was not much chance of getting another if this man with all his strength and boldness should fail. Then Thorhall departed. This happened towards the end of the Thing.

Two of Thorhall's horses were missing, and he went himself to look for them, which made people think he was not much of a man. He went up under Sledaass and south along the hill called Armannsfell. Then he saw a man coming down from Godaskog bringing some brushwood with a horse. They met and Thorhall asked him his name. He said it was Glam. He was a big man with an extraordinary expression of countenance, large grey eyes and wolfgrey hair. Thorhall was a little startled when he saw him, but soon found out that this was the man who had been sent to him.

"What work can you do best?" he asked.

Glam said it would suit him very well to mind sheep in the winter.

"Will you mind my sheep?" Thorhall asked. "Skapti has given you over to me."

"My service will only be of use to you if I am free to do as I please," he said. "I am rather crossgrained when I am not well pleased."

"That will not hurt me," said Thorhall. "I shall be glad if you will come to me."

"I can do so," he said. "Are there any special difficulties?"

"The place seems to be haunted."

"I am not afraid of ghosts. It will be the less dull."

"You will have to risk it," said Thorhall. "It will be best to meet it with a bold face."

Terms were arranged and Glam was to come in the autumn. Then they parted. Thorhall found his horses in the very place where he had just been looking for them. He rode home and thanked Skapti for his service.

The summer passed. Thorhall heard nothing of his shepherd and no one knew anything about him, but at the appointed time he appeared at Thorhallsstad. Thorhall treated him kindly, but all the rest of the household disliked him, especially the mistress. He commenced his work as shepherd, which gave him little trouble.

He had a loud hoarse voice. The beasts all flocked together whenever he shouted at them. There was a church in the place, but Glam never went to it. He abstained from mass, had no religion, and was stubborn and surly. Every one hated him.

So the time passed till the eve of Yule-tide. Glam rose early and called for his meal. The mistress said: "It is not proper for Christian men to eat on this day, because to-morrow is the first day of Yule and it is our duty to fast to-day."

"You have many superstitions," he said; "but I do not see that much comes of them. I do not know that men are any better off than when there was nothing of that kind. The ways of men seemed to me better when they were called heathen. I want my food and no foolery."

"I am certain," she said, "that it will fare ill with you to-day if you commit this sin."

Glam told her that she should bring his food, or that it would be the worse for her. She did not dare to do otherwise than as he bade her. When he had eaten he went out, his breath smelling abominably. It was very dark; there was driving snow, the wind was howling and it became worse as the day advanced. The shepherd's voice was heard in the early part of the day, but less later on. Blizzards set in and a terrific storm in the evening. People went to mass and so the time passed. In the evening Glam did not return. They talked about going out to look for him, but the storm was so violent and the night so dark that no one went. The night passed and still he had not returned; they waited till the time for mass came. When it was full day some of the men set forth to search. They found the animals scattered everywhere in the snow and injured by the weather; some had strayed into the mountains. Then they came upon some well-marked tracks up above in the valley. The stones and earth were torn up all about as if there had been a violent tussle. On searching further they came upon Glam lying on the ground a short distance off. He was dead; his body was as black as Hel and swollen to the size of an ox. They were overcome with horror and their hearts shuddered within them. Nevertheless they tried to carry him to the church, but could not get him any further than the edge of a gully a short way off. So they left him there and went home to report to the bondi what had happened. He asked what could have caused Glam's death. They said they had tracked him to a big place like a hole made by the bottom of a cask thrown down and dragged along up below the mountains which were at the top of the valley, and all along the track were great drops of blood. They concluded that the evil spirit which had been about before must have killed Glam, but that he had inflicted wounds upon it which were enough, for that spook was never heard of again. On the second day of the festival they went out again to bring in Glam's body to the church. They yoked oxen to him, but directly the downward incline ceased and they came to level ground, they could not move him; so they went home again and left him. On the third day they took a priest with them, but after searching the whole day they failed to find him. The priest refused to go again, and when he was not with them they found Glam. So they gave up the attempt to bring him to the church and buried him where he was under a cairn of stones.

It was not long before men became aware that Glam was not easy in his grave. Many men suffered severe injuries; some who saw him were struck senseless and some lost their wits. Soon after the festival was over, men began to think they saw him about their houses. The panic was great and many left the neighbourhood. Next he began to ride on the house-tops by night, and nearly broke them to pieces. Almost night and day he walked, and people would scarcely venture up the valley, however pressing their business. The district was in a grievous condition.

Chapter XXXIII
Doings Of Glam's Ghost. Awful Condition Of Vatnsdal

In the spring Thorhall procured servants and built a house on his lands. As the days lengthened out the apparitions became less, until at midsummer a ship sailed up the Hunavatn in which was a man named Thorgaut. He was a foreigner, very tall and powerful; he had the strength of two men. He was travelling on his own account, unattached, and being without money was looking out for employment. Thorhall rode to the ship, saw him and asked if he would take service with him. Thorgaut said he would indeed, and that there would be no difficulties.

"You must be prepared," said Thorhall, "for work which would not be fitting for a weak-minded person, because of the apparitions which have been there lately. I will not deceive you about it."

"I shall not give myself up as lost for the ghostlings," he said.

"Before I am scared some others will not be easy. I shall not change my quarters on that account."

The terms were easily arranged and Thorgaut was engaged for the sheep during the winter. When the summer had passed away he took over charge of them, and was on good terms with everybody. Glam continued his rides on the roofs. Thorgaut thought it very amusing and said the thrall must come nearer if he wished to frighten him. Thorhall advised him not to say too much, and said it would be better if they did not come into conflict.

Thorgaut said: "Surely all the spirit has gone out of you. I shall not fall dead in the twilight for stories of that sort."

Yule was approaching. On the eve the shepherd went out with his sheep. The mistress said: "Now I hope that our former experiences will not be repeated."

"Have no fear for that, mistress," he said. "There will be something worth telling of if I come not back."

Then he went out to his sheep. The weather was rather cold and there was a heavy snowstorm. Thorgaut usually returned when it was getting dark, but this time he did not come. The people went to church as usual, but they thought matters looked very much as they did on the last occasion. The bondi wanted them to go out and search for the shepherd, but the churchgoers cried off, and said they were not going to trust themselves into the power of trolls in the night; the bondi would not venture out and there was no search. On Yule day after their meal they went out to look for the shepherd, and first went to Glam's cairn, feeling sure that the shepherd's disappearance must be due to him. On approaching the cairn they saw an awful sight; there was the shepherd, his neck broken, and every bone in his body torn from its place. They carried him to the church and no one was molested by Thorgaut.

Glam became more rampageous than ever. He was so riotous that at last everybody fled from Thorhallsstad, excepting the bondi and his wife.

Thorhall's cowherd had been a long time in his service and he had become attached to him; for this reason and because he was a careful herdsman he did not want to part with him. The man was very old and thought it would be very troublesome to have to leave; he saw, too, that everything the bondi possessed would be ruined if he did not stay to look after them. One morning after midwinter the mistress went to the cow-house to milk the cows as usual. It was then full day, for no one would venture out of doors till then, except the cowherd, who went directly it was light. She heard a great crash in the cow-house and tremendous bellowing. She rushed in, shouting that something awful, she knew not what, was going on in the cow-house. The bondi went out and found the cattle all goring each other. It seemed not canny there, so he went into the shed and there saw the cowherd lying on his back with his head in one stall and his feet in the other.

He went up and felt him, but saw at once that he was dead with his back broken. It had been broken over the flat stone which separated the two stalls. Evidently it was not safe to remain any longer on his estate, so he fled with everything that he could carry away. All the live-stock which he left behind was killed by Glam. After that Glam went right up the valley and raided every farm as far as Tunga, while Thorhall stayed with his friends during the rest of the winter. No one could venture up the valley with a horse or a dog, for it was killed at once. As the spring went on and the sun rose higher in the sky the spook diminished somewhat, and Thorhall wanted to return to his land, but found it not easy to get servants. Nevertheless, he went and took up his abode at Thorhallsstad. Directly the autumn set in, everything began again, and the disturbances increased. The person most attacked was the bondi's daughter, who at last died of it. Many things were tried but without success. It seemed likely that the whole of Vatnsdal would be devastated unless help could be found.

Chapter XXXIV
Grettir Visits His Uncle Jokull

W e have now to return to Grettir, who was at home in Bjarg during the autumn which followed his meeting with Warrior-Bardi at Thoreyjargnup. When the winter was approaching, he rode North across the neck to Vididal and stayed at Audunarstad. He and Audun made friends again; Grettir gave him a valuable battle-axe and they agreed to hold together in friendship. Audun had long lived there, and had many connections. He had a son named Egill, who married Ulfheid the daughter of Eyjolf, the son of Gudmund; their son Eyjolf, who was killed at the All-Thing, was the father of Orin the chaplain of Bishop Thorlak.

Grettir rode to the North to Vatnsdal and went on a visit to Tunga, where dwelt his mother's brother, Jokull the son of Bard, a big strong man and exceedingly haughty. He was a mariner, very cantankerous, but a person of much consideration. He welcomed Grettir, who stayed three nights with him. Nothing was talked about but Glam's walking, and Grettir inquired minutely about all the particulars. Jokull told him that no more was said than had really happened.

"Why, do you want to go there?" he asked.

Grettir said that it was so. Jokull told him not to do it.

"It would be a most hazardous undertaking," he said. "Your kinsmen incur a great risk with you as you are. There does not seem to be one of the younger men who is your equal. It is ill dealing with such a one as Glam. Much better fight with human men than with goblins of that sort."

Grettir said he had a mind to go to Thorhallsstad and see how things were. Jokull said: "I see there is no use in dissuading you. The saying is true that Luck is one thing, brave deeds another."

"Woe stands before the door of one but enters that of another," answered Grettir. "I am thinking how it may fare with you yourself before all is done."

"It may be," said Jokull, "that we both see what is before us, and yet we may not alter it."

Then they parted, neither of them well pleased with the other's prophetic saying.

Chapter XXXV
The Fight With Glam's Ghost

Grettir rode to Thorhallsstad where he was welcomed by the bondi.

He asked Grettir whither he was bound, and Grettir said he wished to spend the night there if the bondi permitted. Thorhall said he would indeed be thankful to him for staying there.

"Few," he said, "think it a gain to stay here for any time. You must have heard tell of the trouble that is here, and I do not want you to be inconvenienced on my account. Even if you escape unhurt yourself, I know for certain that you will lose your horse, for no one can keep his beast in safety who comes here."

Grettir said there were plenty more horses to be had if anything happened to this one.

Thorhall was delighted at Grettir's wishing to remain, and received him with both hands. Grettir's horse was placed securely under lock and key and they both went to bed. The night passed without Glam showing himself.

"Your being here has already done some good," said Thorhall. "Glam has always been in the habit of riding on the roof or breaking open the doors every night, as you can see from the marks."

"Then," Grettir said, "either he will not keep quiet much longer, or he will remain so more than one night. I will stay another night and see what happens."

Then they went to Grettir's horse and found it had not been touched. The bondi thought that all pointed to the same thing. Grettir stayed a second night and again the thrall did not appear. The bondi became hopeful and went to see the horse. There he found the stable broken open, the horse dragged outside and every bone in his body broken. Thorhall told Grettir what had occurred and advised him to look to himself, for he was a dead man if he waited for Glam.

Grettir answered: "I must not have less for my horse than a sight of the thrall."

The bondi said there was no pleasure to be had from seeing him: "He is not like any man. I count every hour a gain that you are here."

The day passed, and when the hour came for going to bed Grettir said he would not take off his clothes, and lay down on a seat opposite to Thorkell's sleeping apartment. He had a shaggy cloak covering him with one end of it fastened under his feet and the other drawn over his head so that he could see through the neck-hole. He set his feet against a strong bench which was in front of him. The frame-work of the outer door had been all broken away and some bits of wood had been rigged up roughly in its place. The partition which had once divided the hall from the entrance passage was all broken, both above the cross-beam and below, and all the bedding had been upset. The place looked rather desolate. There was a light burning in the hall by night.

When about a third part of the night had passed Grettir heard a loud noise. Something was going up on to the building, riding above the hall and kicking with its heels until the timbers cracked again. This went on for some time, and then it came down towards the door. The door opened and Grettir saw the thrall stretching in an enormously big and ugly head. Glam moved slowly in, and on passing the door stood upright, reaching to the roof. He turned to the hall, resting his arms on the cross-beam and peering along the hall. The bondi uttered no sound, having heard quite enough of what had gone on outside. Grettir lay quite still and did not move. Glam saw a heap of something in the seat, came farther into the hall and seized the cloak tightly with his hand. Grettir pressed his foot against the plank and the cloak held firm. Glam tugged at it again still more violently, but it did not give way. A third time be pulled, this time with both hands and with such force that he pulled Grettir up out of the seat, and between them the cloak was torn in two. Glam looked at the bit which he held in his hand and wondered much who could pull like that against him. Suddenly Grettir sprang under his arms, seized him round the waist and squeezed his back with all his might, intending in that way to bring him down, but the thrall wrenched his arms till he staggered from the violence. Then Grettir fell back to another bench. The benches flew about and everything was shattered around them. Glam wanted to get out, but Grettir tried to prevent him by stemming his foot against anything he could find. Nevertheless Glam succeeded in getting him outside the hall. Then a terrific struggle began, the thrall trying to drag him out of the house, and Grettir saw that however hard he was to deal with in the house, he would be worse outside, so he strove with all his might to keep him from getting out. Then Glam made a desperate effort and gripped Grettir tightly towards him, forcing him to the porch. Grettir saw that he could not put up any resistance, and with a sudden movement he dashed into the thrall's arms and set both his feet against a stone which was fastened in the ground at the door. For that Glam was not prepared, since he had been tugging to drag Grettir towards him; he reeled backwards and tumbled hind-foremost out of the door, tearing away the lintel with his shoulder and shattering the roof, the rafters and the frozen thatch. Head over heels he fell out of the house and Grettir fell on top of him. The moon was shining very brightly outside, with light clouds passing over it and hiding it now and again. At the moment when Glam fell the moon shone forth, and Glam turned his eyes up towards it. Grettir himself has related that that sight was the only one which ever made him tremble. What with fatigue and all else that he had endured, when he saw the horrible rolling of Glam's eyes his heart sank so utterly that he had not strength to draw his sword, but lay there well-nigh betwixt life and death. Glam possessed more malignant power than most fiends, for he now spoke in this wise:

"You have expended much energy, Grettir, in your search for me. Nor is that to be wondered at, if you should have little joy thereof. And now I tell you that you shall possess only half the strength and firmness of heart that were decreed to you if you had not striven with me. The might which was yours till now I am not able to take away, but it is in my power to ordain that never shall you grow stronger than you are now. Nevertheless your might is sufficient, as many shall find to their cost. Hitherto you have earned fame through your deeds, but henceforward there shall fall upon you exile and battle; your deeds shall turn to evil and your guardian-spirit shall forsake you. You will be outlawed and your lot shall be to dwell ever alone. And this I lay upon you, that these eyes of mine shall be ever before your vision. You will find it hard to live alone, and at last it shall drag you to death."

When the thrall had spoken the faintness which had come over Grettir left him. He drew his short sword, cut off Glam's head and laid it between his thighs. Then the bondi came out, having put on his clothes while Glam was speaking, but he did not venture to come near until he was dead. Thorhall praised God and thanked Grettir warmly for having laid this unclean spirit. Then they set to work and burned Glam to cold cinders, bound the ashes in a skin and buried them in a place far away from the haunts of man or beast. Then they went home, the day having nearly broken.

Grettir was very stiff and lay down to rest. Thorhall sent for some men from the next farms and let them know how things had fared. They all realised the importance of Grettir's deed when they heard of it; all agreed that in the whole country side for strength and courage and enterprise there was not the equal of Grettir the son of Asmund.

Thorhall bade a kindly farewell to Grettir and dismissed him with a present of a fine horse and proper clothes, for all that he had been wearing were torn to pieces. They parted in friendship. Grettir rode to Ass in Vatnsdal and was welcomed by Thorvald, who asked him all about his encounter with Glam. Grettir told him everything and said that never had his strength been put to trial as it had been in their long struggle. Thorvald told him to conduct himself discreetly; if he did so he might prosper, but otherwise he would surely come to disaster. Grettir said that his temper had not improved, that he had even less discretion than before, and was more impatient of being crossed. In one thing a great change had come over him; he had become so frightened of the dark that he dared not go anywhere alone at night. Apparitions of every kind came before him. It has since passed into an expression, and men speak of "Glam's eyes" or "Glam visions" when things appear otherwise than as they are.

Having accomplished his undertaking Grettir rode back to Bjarg and spent the winter at home.

Chapter XXXVI
Thorbjorn Slowcoach At Home

Thorbjorn Oxmain gave a great feast in the autumn at which many were assembled, whilst Grettir was in the North in Vatnsdal. Thorbjorn Slowcoach was there and many things were talked about. The Hrutafjord people inquired about Grettir's adventure on the ridge in the summer. Thorbjorn Oxmain praised Grettir's conduct, and said that Kormak would have had the worst of it if no one had come to part them. Then Thorbjorn Slowcoach said: "What I saw of Grettir's fighting was not famous; and he seemed inclined to shirk when we came up. He was very ready to leave off, nor did I see him make any attempt to avenge the death of Atli's man. I do not believe there is much heart in him, except when he has a sufficient force behind him."

Thorbjorn went on jeering at him in this way. Many of the others had something to say about it, and they thought that Grettir would not leave it to rest if he heard what Thorbjorn was saying.

Nothing more happened at the festivities; they all went home, and there was a good deal of ill-will between them all that winter, though no one took any action. Nothing more happened that winter.

Chapter XXXVII
Grettir Sails For Norway And Kills Thorbjorn Slowcoach

Early in the spring, before the meeting of the Thing, there arrived a ship from Norway. There was much news to tell, above all of the change of government. Olaf the son of Harald was now king, having driven away jarl Sveinn from the country in the spring which followed the battle of Nesjar. Many noteworthy things were told of King Olaf. Men said that he took into favour all men who were skilled in any way and made them his followers. This pleased many of the younger men in Iceland and made them all want to leave home. When Grettir heard of it he longed to go too, deeming that he merited the king's favour quite as much as any of the others. A ship came up to Gasar in Eyjafjord; Grettir engaged a passage in her and prepared to go abroad. He had not much outfit as yet.

Asmund was now becoming very infirm and scarcely left his bed. He and Asdis had a young son named Illugi, a youth of much promise. Atli had taken over all the management of the farm and the goods, and things went much better, for he was both obliging and provident.

Grettir embarked on his ship. Thorbjorn Slowcoach had arranged to travel in the same vessel without knowing that Grettir would be in her. Some of his friends tried to dissuade him from travelling in Grettir's company, but he insisted upon going. He was rather a long time over his preparations and did not get to Gasar before the ship was ready to sail. Before he left home Asmund Longhair was taken ill and was quite confined to his bed. Thorbjorn Slowcoach arrived on the beach late in the day, when the men were going on board and were washing their hands outside near their booths. When he rode up to the rows of booths they greeted him and asked what news there was.

"I have nothing to tell," he said, "except that the valorous Asmund at Bjarg is now dead."

Some of them said that a worthy bondi had left the world and asked how it happened.

"A poor lot befell his Valour," he replied. "He was suffocatedby the smoke from the hearth, like a dog. There is no great loss in him, for he was in his dotage."

"You talk strangely about such a man as he was," they said. "Grettir would not be much pleased if he heard you."

"I can endure Grettir's wrath," he said. "He must bear his axe higher than he did at Hrutafjardarhals if he wishes to frighten me."

Grettir heard every word that Thorbjorn said, but took no notice as long as he was speaking. When he had finished Grettir said:

"I prophesy, Slowcoach, that you will not die of the smoke from the hearth, and yet perhaps you will not die of old age either. It is strange conduct to say shameful things of innocent men."

Thorbjorn said: "I have nothing to unsay. I never thought you would fire up like this on the day when we got you out of the hands of the men of Mel who were belabouring you like an ox's head."

Then Grettir spoke a verse:

"Too long is the tongue of the spanner of bows.
Full often he suffers the vengeance due.
Slowcoach! I tell thee that many a man
has paid for less shameful speech with his life."

Thorbjorn said his life was neither more nor less in danger than it was before.

"My prophecies are not generally long-lived," said Grettir, "nor shall this one be. Defend yourself if you will; you never will have better occasion for it than now."

Grettir then struck at him. He tried to parry the blow with his arm, but it struck him above the wrist and glanced off on to his neck so that his head flew off. The sailors declared it was a splendid stroke, and that such were the men for the king. No one would grieve, they said, because a man so quarrelsome and scurrilous as Thorbjorn had been killed.

Soon after this they got under way and towards the end of the summer reached the south coast of Norway, about Hordland, where they learned that King Olaf was in the North at Thrandheim. Grettir took a passage thither with some traders intending to seek audience of the king.

Chapter XXXVIII
Grettir Fetches Fire — The Sons Of Thorir Are Burnt

There was a man named Thorir dwelling in Gard in Adaldal. He was a son of Skeggi Bodolfsson, who had settled in Kelduhverfi, on lands extending right up to Keldunes, and had married Helga the daughter of Thorgeir at Fiskilaek. Thorir was a great chief, and a mariner. He had two sons whose names were Thorgeir and Skeggi, both men of promise, and pretty well grown up at that time. Thorir had been in Norway in the summer in which Olaf came East from England, and had won great favour with the king as well as with Bishop Sigurd. In token of this it is related that Thorir asked the bishop to consecrate a large sea-going ship he had built in the forest, and the bishop did so. Later he came out to Iceland and had his ship broken up because he was tired of seafaring. He set up the figures from her head and stem over his doors, where they long remained foretelling the weather, one howling for a south, the other for a north wind.

When Thorir heard that Olaf had become sole ruler of Norway he thought he might expect favour from him, so he dispatched his sons to Norway to wait upon the king, hoping that they would be received into his service. They reached the south coast late in the autumn and engaged a rowing vessel to take them up the coast to the North, intending to go to the king. They reached a port to the south of Stad, where they put in for a few days. They were well provided with food and drink, and did not go out much because of the bad weather.

Grettir also sailed to the North along the coast, and as the winter was just beginning he often fell in with dirty weather. When they reached the neighbourhood of Stad the weather became worse, and at last one evening they were so exhausted with the snow and frost that they were compelled to put in and lie under a bank where they found shelter for their goods and belongings. The men were very much distressed at not being able to procure any fire; their safety and their lives seemed almost to depend upon their getting some. They lay there in a pitiful condition all the evening, and as night came on they saw a large fire on the other side of the channel which they were in. When Grettir's companions saw the fire they began talking and saying that he who could get some of it would be a happy man. They hesitated for some time whether they should put out, but all agreed that it would be too dangerous. Then they had a good deal of talk about whether there was any man living doughty enough to get the fire. Grettir kept very quiet, but said that there probably had been men who would not have let themselves be baulked. The men said that they were none the better for what had been if there were none now.

"But won't you venture, Grettir? The people of Iceland all talk so much about your prowess, and you know very well what we want."

Grettir said: "It does not seem to me such a great thing to get the fire, but I do not know whether you will reward it any better than he requires who does it."

"Why," they said, "should you take us to be men of so little honour that we shall not reward you well?"

"Well," said Grettir, "if you really think it so necessary I will try it; but my heart tells me that no good will come to me therefrom."

They said it would not be so, and told him that he should have their thanks.

Then Grettir threw off his clothes and got ready to go into the water. He went in a cloak and breeches of coarse stuff. He tucked up the cloak, tied a cord of bast round his waist, and took a barrel with him. Then he jumped overboard, swam across the channel and reached the land on the other side. There he saw a house standing and heard sounds of talking and merriment issuing from it. So he went towards the house.

We have now to tell of the people who were in the house. They were the sons of Thorir who have been mentioned. They had been there some days waiting for a change of weather and for a wind to carry them to the North. There were twelve of them and they were all sitting and drinking. They had made fast in the inner harbour where there was a place of shelter set up for men who were travelling about the country, and they had carried in a quantity of straw. There was a huge fire on the ground. Grettir rushed into the house, not knowing who was there. His cloak had all frozen directly he landed, and he was a portentous sight to behold; he looked like a troll. The people inside were much startled, thinking it was a fiend. They struck at him with anything they could get, and a tremendous uproar there was. Grettir pushed them back with his arms. Some of them struck at him with firebrands, and the fire spread all through the house. He got away with his fire and returned to his companions, who were loud in praise of his skill and daring, and said there was no one like him. The night passed and they were happy now that they had fire.

On the next morning the weather was fine. They all woke early and made ready to continue their journey. It was proposed that they should go and find out who the people were who had had the fire, so they cast off and sailed across the channel. They found no house there, nothing but a heap of ashes and a good many bones of men amongst them. Evidently the house with all who were in it had been burned. They asked whether Grettir had done it, and declared it was an abominable deed. Grettir said that what he expected had come to pass, and that he was ill rewarded for getting the fire for them. He said it was thankless work to help such miserable beings as they were. He suffered much annoyance in consequence, for wherever the traders went they told that Grettir had burned the men in the house. Soon it became known that it was the sons of Thorir of Gard and their followers who had been burned. The traders refused to have Grettir on board their ship any longer and drove him away. He was so abhorred that scarcely any one would do him a service. His case seemed hopeless, and his only desire was at any cost to appear before the king. So he went North to Thrandheim where the king was, and had heard the whole story before Grettir came, for many had been busy in slandering him. Grettir waited several days in the town before he was able to appear before the king.

Chapter XXXIX
Grettir Appears Before The King And Fails To Undergo The Ordeal

One day when the king was sitting in judgment Grettir came before him and saluted him respectfully. The king looked at him and said:

"Are you Grettir the Strong?"

"So I have been called," he replied, "and I have come here in the hope of obtaining deliverance from the slanders which are being spread about me, and to say that I did not do this deed."

The king said: "You are worthy enough; but I know not what fortune you will have in defending yourself. It is quite possible that you did not intend to burn the men in the house."

Grettir said that he was most anxious to prove his innocence if the king would permit him. Then the king bade him relate faithfully all that had happened. Grettir told him everything exactly as it was, and declared that they were all alive when he escaped with his fire; he was ready to undergo any ordeal which the king considered that the law required.

King Olaf said: "I decree that you shall bear iron, if your fate so wills it."

Grettir was quite content with that, and began his fast for the ordeal. When the day for the ceremony arrived the king and the bishop went to the church together with a multitude of people who came out of curiosity to see a man so much talked about as Grettir. At last Grettir himself was led to the church. When he entered many looked at him and remarked that he excelled most men in strength and stature. As he passed down the aisle there started up a very ill-favoured, overgrown boy and cried to him:

"Wondrous are now the ways in a land where men should call themselves Christians, when evil-doers and robbers and thieves walk in peace to purge themselves. What should a wicked man find better to do than to preserve his life so long as he may? Here is now a malefactor convicted of guilt, one who has burnt innocent men in their houses, and yet is allowed to undergo purgation. Such a thing is most unrighteous."

Then he went at Grettir, pointing at him with his finger, making grimaces and calling him son of a sea-ogress, with many other bad names. Then Grettir lost his temper and his self-control. He raised his hand and gave him a box on the ear so that he fell senseless, and some thought he was dead. No one seemed to know whence the boy had come nor what became of him afterwards, but it was generally believed that he was some unclean spirit sent forth for the destruction of Grettir.

There arose an uproar in the church; people told the king that the man who had come to purge himself was fighting with those around him. King Olaf came forward into the church to see what was going on, and said:

"You are a man of ill luck, Grettir. All was prepared for the ordeal, but it cannot take place now. It is not possible to contend against your ill-fortune."

Grettir said: "I expected, oh king, more honour from you for the sake of my family than I now seem likely to obtain."

Then he told again the story as he had done before of what had taken place with the men. "Gladly," he said, "would I enter your service; there is many a man with you who is not my better as a warrior."

"I know," said the king, "that few are your equals in strength and courage, but your luck is too bad for you to remain with me. You have my leave to depart in peace whithersoever you will for the winter, and then in the summer you may return to Iceland, where you are destined to lay your bones."

"First I should like to clear myself of the charge of burning, if I may," said Grettir; "for I did not do it intentionally."

"Very likely it is so," said the king; "but since the purgation has come to naught through your impatience you cannot clear yourself further than you have done. Impetuosity always leads to evil. If ever a man was doomed to misfortune you are."

After that Grettir remained for a time in the town, but he got nothing more out of Olaf. Then he went to the South, intending after that to go East to Tunsberg to find his brother Thorsteinn Dromund. Nothing is told of his journey till he came to Jadar.

Chapter XL
Adventure With The Berserk Snaekoll

At Yule Grettir came to a bondi named Einar, a man of wealth who had a wife and a marriageable daughter named Gyrid. She was a beautiful maiden and was considered an excellent match. Einar invited Grettir to stay over Yule, and he accepted.

It was no uncommon thing throughout Norway that robbers and other ruffians came down from the forest and challenged men to fight for their women, or carried off their property with violence if there was not sufficient force in the house to protect them. One day at Yule-tide there came a whole party of these miscreants to Einar's house. Their leader was a great berserk named Snaekoll. He challenged Einar to hand over his daughter to him or else to defend her, if he felt himself man enough to do so. Now the bondi was no longer young, and no fighter. He felt that he was in a great difficulty, and asked Grettir privately what help he would give him, seeing that he was held to be so famous a man. Grettir advised him to consent only to what was not dishonourable. The berserk was sitting on his horse wearing his helmet, the chin-piece of which was not fastened. He held before him a shield bound with iron and looked terribly threatening. He said to the bondi:

"You had better choose quickly: either one thing or the other. What does that big fellow standing beside you say? Would he not like to play with me himself?"

"One of us is as good as the other," said Grettir, "neither of us is very active."

"All the more afraid will you be to fight with me if I get angry."

"That will be seen when it is tried," said Grettir.

The berserk thought they were trying to get off by talking. He began to howl and to bite the rim of his shield. He held the shield up to his mouth and scowled over its upper edge like a madman. Grettir stepped quickly across the ground, and when he got even with the berserk's horse he kicked the shield with his foot from below with such force that it struck his mouth, breaking the upper jaw, and the lower jaw fell down on to his chest. With the same movement he seized the viking's helmet with his left hand and dragged him from his horse, while with his right hand he raised his axe and cut off the berserk's head. Snaekoll's followers when they saw what had happened fled, every man of them. Grettir did not care to pursue them for he saw that there was no heart in them. The bondi thanked him for what he had done, as did many other men, for the quickness and boldness of his deed had impressed them much. Grettir stayed there for Yule and was well taken care of till he left, when the bondi dismissed him handsomely. Then Grettir went East to Tunsberg to visit his brother Thorsteinn, who received him joyfully and asked him about his adventures. Grettir told him how he had killed the berserk, and composed a verse:

> "The warrior's shield by my foot propelled
> in conflict came with Snaekoll's mouth.
> His nether jaw hung down on his chest,
> wide gaped his mouth from the iron ring."

"You would be very handy at many things," said Thorsteinn, "if misfortune did not follow you."

"Men will tell of deeds that are done," said Grettir.

Chapter XLI
Thorsteinn Dromund's Arms

Grettir stayed with Thorsteinn for the rest of the winter and on into the spring. One morning when Thorsteinn and Grettir were above in their sleeping room Grettir put out his arm from the bed-clothes and Thorsteinn noticed it when he awoke. Soon after Grettir woke too, and Thorsteinn said: "I have been looking at your arms, kinsman, and think it is not wonderful that your blows fall heavily upon some. Never have I seen any man's arms that were like yours."

"You may know," said Grettir, "that I should not have done the deeds I have if I had not been very mighty."

"Yet methinks it would be of advantage," said Thorsteinn, "if your arm were more slender and your fortune better."

"True," said Grettir, "is the saying that no man shapes his own fortune. Let me see your arm."

Thorsteinn showed it to him. He was a tall lanky man. Grettir smiled and said:

"There is no need to look long at that; all your ribs are run together. I never saw such a pair of tongs as you carry about! Why, you are scarcely as strong as a woman!"

"It may be so," said Thorsteinn, "and yet you may know that these thin arms of mine and no others will avenge you some day—if you are avenged."

"Who shall know how it will be when the end comes?" said Grettir; "but that seems unlikely."

No more is related of their conversation. The spring came and Grettir took a ship for Iceland in the summer. The brothers parted with friendship and never saw one another again.

Chapter XLII
Death Of Asmund Longhair

We have now to return to where we broke off before. Thorbjorn Oxmain when he heard of the death of Thorbjorn Slowcoach flew into a violent passion and said he wished that more men might deal blows in other people's houses. Asmund Longhair lay sick for some time in the summer. When he thought his end was nigh he called his kinsmen round him and said his will was that Atli should take over all the property after his day. "I fear," he said, "that the wicked will scarce leave you in peace. And I wish all my kinsmen to support him to the best of their power. Of Grettir I can say nothing, for his condition seems to me like a rolling wheel. Strong though he is, I fear he will have more dealing with trouble than with kinsmen's support. And Illugi, though young now, shall become a man of valiant deeds if he remain unscathed."

When Asmund had settled everything with his sons according to his wish his sickness grew upon him. He died soon after and was buried at Bjarg, where he had had a church built. All felt his loss deeply.

Atli became a great bondi and kept a large establishment. He was a great dealer in household provisions. Towards the end of the summer he went to Snaefellsnes to get dried fish. He drove several horses with him and rode from home to Melar in Hrutafjord to his brother-in-law, Gamli. Then Grim, the son of Thorhall, Gamli's brother, made ready to accompany him along with another man. They rode West by way of Haukadalsskard and the road which leads out to the Ness, where they bought much fish and carried it away on seven horses; when all was ready they turned homewards.

Chapter XLIII
The Sons Of Thorir Of Skard Are Slain By Atli And Grim

Thorbjorn Oxmain heard of Atli and Grim having left home just when Gunnar and Thorgeir, the sons of Thorir of Skard, were with him. Thorbjorn was jealous of Atli's popularity and egged on the two brothers, the sons of Thorir, to lie in wait for him as he returned from Snaefellsnes. They rode home to Skard and waited there for Atli returning with his loads. They could see the party from their house as they passed Skard, and made ready quickly to pursue them with their servants. Atli on seeing them ordered his horses to be unloaded.

"Perhaps," he said, "they want to offer me compensation for my man whom Gunnar slew last summer. We will not be the first to attack, but if they begin fighting us we will defend ourselves."

Then they came up and at once sprang off their horses. Atli greeted them and asked what news there was, and whether Gunnar desired to offer him some compensation for his servant. Gunnar answered:

"You men of Bjarg, you deserve something else than that I should pay compensation for him with my goods. Thorbjorn whom Grettir slew is worth a higher atonement than he."

"I have not to answer for that," said Atli, "nor are you the representative of Thorbjorn."

Gunnar said it would have to be so nevertheless. "And now," he cried, "let us go for them and profit by Grettir being away."

There were eight of them, and they set upon Atli's six. Atli led on his men and drew the sword Jokulsnaut which Grettir had given him. Thorgeir cried: "Good men are alike in many things. High did Grettir bear his sword last summer on Hrutafjardarhals."

Atli answered: "He is more accustomed to deeds of strength than I am."

Then they fought. Gunnar made a resolute attack on Atli, and fought fiercely. After they had battled for a time Atli said:

"There is nothing to be gained by each of us killing the other's followers. The simplest course would be for us to play together, for I have never fought with weapons before."

Gunnar, however, would not have it. Atli bade his servants look to the packs, and he would see what the others would do. He made such a vigorous onslaught that Gunnar's men fell back, and he killed two of them. Then he turned upon Gunnar himself and struck a blow that severed his shield right across below the handle, and the sword struck his leg below the knee. Then with another rapid blow he killed him.

In the meantime Grim, the son of Thorhall, was engaging Thorgeir, and a long tussle there was, both of them being men of great valour. When Thorgeir saw his brother Gunnar fall he wanted to get away, but Grim pressed upon him and pursued him until at last his foot tripped and he fell forward. Then Grim struck him with an axe between the shoulders, inflicting a deep wound. To the three followers who were left they gave quarter. Then they bound up their wounds, reloaded the packs on to the horses and went home, giving information of the battle. Atli stayed at home with a strong guard of men that autumn. Thorbjorn Oxmain was not at all pleased, but could do nothing, because Atli was very wary. Grim was with him for the winter, and his brother-in-law Gamli. Another brother-in-law, Glum the son of Ospak from Eyr in Bitra, was with them too. They had a goodly array of men settled at Bjarg, and there was much merriment there during the winter.

Chapter XLIV
Settlement Of The Feud At The Hunavatn Thing

Thorbfron Oxmain took up the suit arising from the death of Thorir's sons. He prepared his case against Grim and Atli, and they prepared their defence on the grounds that the brothers had attacked them wrongfully and were, therefore, "ohelgir." The case was brought before the Hunavatn Thing and both sides appeared in force. Atli had many connections, and was, therefore, strongly supported. Then those who were friends of both came forward and tried to effect a reconciliation; they urged that Atli was a man of good position and peacefully disposed, though fearless enough when driven into a strait. Thorbjorn felt that no other honourable course was open to him but to agree to a reconciliation. Atli made it a condition that there should be no sentence of banishment either from the district or the country. Then men were appointed to arbitrate: Thorvald Asgeirsson on behalf of Atli, and Solvi the Proud on behalf of Thorbjorn. This Solvi was a son of Asbrand, the son of Thorbrand, the son of Harald Ring who had settled in Vatnsnes, taking land as far as Ambattara to the West, and to the East up to the Thvera and across to Bjargaoss and the whole side of Bjorg as far as the sea. Solvi was a person of much display, but a man of sense, and therefore Thorbjorn chose him as his arbitrator.

The decree of the arbitrators was that half penalties should be paid for Thorir's sons and half should be remitted on account of the wrongful attack which they made and their designs on Atli's life. The slaying of Atli's man at Hrutafjardarhals should be set off against the two of theirs who had been killed. Grim the son of Thorhall was banished from his district and the penalties were to be paid by Atli. Atli was satisfied with this award, but Thorbjorn was not; they parted nominally reconciled, but Thorbjorn let drop some words to the effect that it was not over yet if all happened as he desired.

Atli rode home from the Thing after thanking Thorvald for his assistance. Grim the son of Thorhall betook himself to the South to Borgarfjord and dwelt at Gilsbakki, where he was known as a worthy bondi.

Chapter XLV
Atli Murdered By Thorbjorn Oxmain

There was dwelling with Thorbjorn Oxmain a man whose name was Ali, a servant, rather stubborn and lazy. Thorbjorn told him he must work better or he would be beaten. Ali said he had no mind for work and became abusive. Thorbjorn was not going to endure that, and got him down and handled him roughly. After that Ali ran away and went to the North across the neck to Midfjord; he did not stop till he reached Bjarg. Atli was at home and asked whither he was going. He said he was seeking an engagement.

"Are you not a servant of Thorbjorn?" Atli asked.

"We did not get on with our bargain. I was not there long, but it seemed to me a bad place while I was there. Our parting was in such a way that his song on my throat did not please me. I will never go back there, whatever becomes of me. And it is true that there is a great difference between you two in the way you treat your servants. I would be glad to take service with you if there is a place, for me."

Atli said: "I have servants enough without stretching forth my hands for those whom Thorbjorn has hired. You seem an impatient man and had better go back to him."

"I am not going there of my own free will," said Ali.

He stayed there for the night, and in the morning went out to work with Atli's men, and toiled as if he had hands everywhere. So he continued all the summer; Atli took no notice of him, but allowed him his food, for he was pleased with the man's work. Soon Thorbjorn learned that Ali was at Bjarg. He rode thither with two others and called to Atli to come out and speak with him. Atli went out and greeted him.

"You want to begin again provoking me to attack you, Atli," he said. "Why have you taken away my workman? It is a most improper thing to do."

Atli replied: "It is not very clear to me that he is your workman. I do not want to keep him if you can prove that he belongs to your household; but I cannot drive him out of my house."

"You must have your way now," said Thorbjorn; "but I claim the man and protest against his working for you. I shall come again, and it is not certain that we shall then part any better friends than we are now."

Atli rejoined: "I shall stay at home and abide whatever comes to hand."

Thorbjorn then went off home. When the workmen came back in the evening Atli told them of his conversation with Thorbjorn and said to Ali that he must go his own ways, for he was not going to be drawn into a quarrel for employing him.

Ali said: "True is the ancient saying: The over-praised are the worst deceivers. I did not think that you would have turned me off now after I had worked here till I broke in the summer. I thought that you would have given me protection. Such is your way, however you play the beneficent. Now I shall be beaten before your very eyes if you refuse to stand by me."

Atli's mind was changed after the man had spoken; he no longer wanted to drive him away.

So the time passed until the hay-harvest began. One day a little before midsummer Thorbjorn Oxmain rode to Bjarg. He wore a helmet on his head, a sword was girt at his side, and in his hand was a spear which had a very broad blade. The weather was rainy; Atli had sent his men to mow the hay, and some were in the North at Horn on some work. Atli was at home with a few men only. Thorbjorn arrived alone towards midday and rode up to the door. The door was shut and no one outside. Thorbjorn knocked at the door and then went to the back of the house so that he could not be seen from the door. The people in the house heard some one knocking and one of the women went out. Thorbjorn got a glimpse of the woman, but did not let himself be seen, for he was seeking another person. She went back into the room and Atli asked her who had come. She said she could see nobody outside. As they were speaking Thorbjorn struck a violent blow on the door. Atli said:

"He wants to see me; perhaps he has some business with me, for he seems very pressing."

Then he went to the outer door and saw nobody there. It was raining hard, so he did not go outside, but stood holding both the door-posts with his hands and peering round. At that moment Thorbjorn sidled round to the front of the door and thrust his spear with both hands into Atli's middle, so that it pierced him through. Atli said when he received the thrust: "They use broad spear-blades nowadays."

Then he fell forward on the threshold. The women who were inside came out and saw that he was dead. Thorbjorn had then mounted his horse; he proclaimed the slaying and rode home. Asdis, the mistress of the house, sent for men; Atli's body was laid out and he was buried beside his father. There was much lamentation over his death, for he was both wise and beloved. No blood-money was paid for his death, nor was any demanded, for his representative was Grettir, if he should ever return to Iceland. The matter rested there during the summer. Thorbjorn gained little credit by this deed, but remained quietly at home.

Chapter XLVI
Sentence Of Outlawry Passed Upon Grettir At The All-Thing

In that same summer before the assembly of the Thing there came a ship out to Gasar bringing news of Grettir and of his house-burning adventure. Thorir of Gard was very angry when he heard of it and bethought himself of vengeance for his sons upon Grettir. Thorir rode with a large retinue to the Thing and laid a complaint in respect of the burning, but men thought nothing could be done as long as there was no one to answer the charge. Thorir insisted that he would be content with nothing short of banishment for Grettir from the whole country after such a crime.

Then Skapti the Lawman said: "It certainly was an evil deed if all really happened as has been told. But one man's tale is but half a tale. Most people try and manage not to improve a story if there is more than one version of it. I hold that no judgment should be passed for Grettir's banishment without further proceedings."

Thorir was a notable person and possessed great influence in the district; many powerful men were his friends. He pressed his suit so strongly that nothing could be done to save Grettir. Thorir had him proclaimed an outlaw throughout the country, and was ever afterwards the most bitter of his opponents, as he often found. Having put a price upon his head, as it was usual to do with other outlaws, he rode home. Many said that the decree was carried more by violence than by law, but it remained in force. Nothing more happened until after midsummer.

Chapter XLVII
Grettir Returns To Bjarg—Sveinn And His Horse Saddle-Head

Later in the summer Grettir the son of Asmund came back to Iceland, landing in the Hvita in Borgarfjord. People about the district went down to the ship and all the news came at once upon Grettir, first that his father was dead, then that his brother was slain, and third that he was declared outlaw throughout the land. Then he spoke this verse:

> "All fell at once upon the bard,
> exile, father dead and brother.
> Oh man of battle! Many an one
> who breaks the swords shall smart for this."

It is told that Grettir changed his manner no whit for these tidings, but was just as merry as before. He remained on board his ship for a time because he could not get a horse to suit him.

There was a man named Sveinn who dwelt at Bakki up from Thingnes.

He was a good bondi and a merry companion; he often composed verses which it was a delight to listen to. He had a brown mare, the swiftest of horses, which he called Saddle-head. Once Grettir left Vellir in the night because he did not wish the traders to know of it. He got a black cape and put it over his clothes to conceal himself. He went up past Thingnes to Bakki, by which time it was light. Seeing a brown horse in the meadow he went up and put a bridle on it, mounted on its back and rode up along the Hvita river below Baer on to the river Flokadalsa and up to the road above Kalfanes. The men working at Bakki were up by then, and told the bondi that a man was riding his horse. He got up and laughed and spoke a verse:

"There rode a man upon Saddle-head's back;
close to the garth the thief has come.
Frey of the Odin's cloud, dreadful of aspect,
appears from his strength to be busy with mischief."

Then he took a horse and rode after him. Grettir rode on till he came to
the settlement at Kropp, where he met a man named Halli who said he was
going down to the ship at Vellir. Grettir then spoke a verse:

"Tell, oh tell in the dwellings abroad
tell thou hast met with Saddle-head.
The handler of dice in sable cowl
sat on his back; hasten, oh Halli!"

Then they parted. Halli went along the road as far as Kalfanes before he
met Sveinn. They greeted each other hurriedly and Sveinn said:

"Saw you that loafer ride from the dwellings?
Sorely he means my patience to try.
The people about shall deal with him roughly;
blue shall his body be if I meet him."

"You can know from what I tell you," said Halli, "that I met the man
who said he was riding Saddle-head, and he told me to spread it abroad in
the dwellings and the district. He was a huge man in a black cloak."

"Well, he seems to think something of himself," said the bondi. "I mean
to know who he is."

Then he went on after him. Grettir came to Deildartunga and found a
woman outside. He began to talk to her and spoke a verse:

"Mistress august! Go tell of the jest
that the serpent of earth has past on his way.
The garrulous brewer of Odin's mead
will come to Gilsbakki before he will rest."

The woman learned the verse and Grettir rode on. Soon after Sveinn
rode up; she was still outside, and when he came he spoke the verse:

"Who was the man who a moment ago
rode past on a dusky horse in the storm?
The hound-eyed rascal, practised in mischief.
This day I will follow his steps to the end."

She told him as she had been taught. He considered the lines and said: "It is not unlikely that this man is no play-fellow for me. But I mean to catch him."

He then rode along the cultivated country. Each could see the other's path. The weather was stormy and wet. Grettir reached Gilsbakki that day, where Grim the son of Thorhall welcomed him warmly and begged him to stay, which he did. He let Saddle-head run loose and told Grim how he had come by her. Then Sveinn came up, dismounted and saw his horse. Then he said:

> "Who has ridden on my mare?
> Who will pay me for her hire?
> Who ever saw such an arrant thief?
> What next will be the cowl-man's game?"

Grettir had then put off his wet clothes, and heard the ditty. He said:

> "Home I rode the mare to Grim's,
> a better man than the hovel-dweller!
> Nothing will I pay for hire!
> Now we may be friends again."

"Just so shall it be," said the bondi. "Your ride on the horse is fully paid for."

Then they each began repeating verses, and Grettir said he could not blame him for looking after his property. The bondi stayed there the night and they had great jokes about the matter. The verses they made were called "Saddle-head verses." In the morning the bondi rode home, parting good friends with Grettir. Grim told Grettir of many things that had been done in Midfjord in the North during his absence, and that no blood-money had been paid for Atli. Thorbjorn Oxmain's interest, he said, was so great that there was no certainty of Grettir's mother, Asdis, being allowed to remain at Bjarg if the feud continued.

Grettir stayed but a few nights with Grim, for he did not want it to become known that he was about to travel North across the Heath. Grim told him to come back to visit him if he needed protection. "Yet," he said, "I would gladly avoid the penalty of being outlawed for harbouring you."

Grettir bade him farewell and said: "It is more likely that I shall need your good services still more later on."

Then Grettir rode North over the Tvidaegra Heath to Bjarg, where he arrived at midnight. All were asleep except his mother. He went to the back of the house and entered by a door which was there, for he knew all the ways about. He entered the hall and went to his mother's bed, groping his way. She asked who was there. Grettir told her. She sat up and turned to him, heaving a weary sigh as she spoke:

"Welcome, my kinsman! My hoard of sons has quickly passed away. He is killed who was most needful to me; you have been declared an outlaw and a criminal; my third is so young that he can do nothing."

"It is an ancient saying," said Grettir, "that one evil is mended by a worse one. There is more in the heart of man than money can buy; Atli may yet be avenged. As for me, there will be some who think they have had enough in their dealings with me."

She said that was not unlikely. Grettir stayed there for a time, but few knew of it, and he obtained news of the movements of the men of the district. It was not known then that he had come to Midfjord. He learned that Thorbjorn Oxmain was at home with few men. This was after the hay-harvest.

Chapter XLVIII
Death Of Thorbjorn Oxmain

One fine day Grettir rode to the West across the ridge to Thoroddsstad, where he arrived about noon and knocked at the door. Some women came out and greeted him, not knowing who he was. He asked for Thorbjorn, and they told him that he was gone out into the fields to bind hay with his sixteen-year-old son Arnor. Thorbjorn was a hard worker and was scarcely ever idle. Grettir on hearing that bade them farewell and rode off North on the road to Reykir. There is some marsh-land stretching away from the ridge with much grass-land, where Thorbjorn had made a quantity of hay which was just dry. He was just about to bind it up for bringing in with the help of his son, while a woman gathered up what was left. Grettir rode to the field from below, Thorbjorn and his son being above him; they had finished one load and were beginning a second. Thorbjorn had laid down his shield and sword against the load, and his son had his hand-axe near him.

Thorbjorn saw a man coming and said to his son: "There is a man riding towards us; we had better stop binding the hay and see what he wants."

They did so; Grettir got off his horse. He had a helmet on his head, a short sword by his side, and a great spear in his hand without barbs and inlaid with silver at the socket. He sat down and knocked out the rivet which fastened the head in order to prevent Thorbjorn from returning the spear upon him.

Thorbjorn said: "This is a big man. I am no good at judging men if that is not Grettir the son of Asmund. No doubt he thinks that he has sufficient business with us. We will meet him boldly and show him no signs of fear. We must act with a plan. I will go on ahead towards him and see how we get on together, for I will trust myself against any man if I can meet him alone. Do you go round and get behind him; take your axe with both hands and strike him between the shoulders. You need not fear that he will hurt you, for his back will be turned towards you."

Neither of them had a helmet. Grettir went along the marsh and when he was within range launched his spear at Thorbjorn. The head was not so firm as he had intended it to be, so it got loose in its flight and fell off on to the ground. Thorbjorn took his shield, held it before him, drew his sword and turned against Grettir directly he recognised him. Grettir drew his sword, and, turning round a little, saw the boy behind him; so he kept continually on the move. When he saw that the boy was within reach he raised his sword aloft and struck Arnor's head with the back of it such a blow that the skull broke and he died. Then Thorbjorn rushed upon Grettir and struck at him, but he parried it with the buckler in his left hand and struck with his sword a blow which severed Thorbjorn's shield in two and went into his head, reaching the brain. Thorbjorn fell dead. Grettir gave him no more wounds; he searched for the spear-head but could not find it. He got on to his horse, rode to Reykir and proclaimed the slaying.

The woman who was out in the field with them witnessed the battle. She ran home terrified and told the news that Thorbjorn and his son were killed. The people at home were much taken aback, for no one was aware of Grettir's arrival. They sent to the next homestead for men, who came in plenty and carried the body to the church. The blood-feud then fell to Thorodd Drapustuf, who at once called out his men.

Grettir rode home to Bjarg and told his mother what had happened.

She was very glad and said he had now shown his kinship to the Vatnsdal race. "And yet," she said, "this is the root and the beginning of your outlawry; for certain I know that your dwelling here will not be for long by reason of Thorbjorn's kinsmen, and now they may know that they have the means of annoying you."

Grettir then spoke a verse:

"Atli's death was unatoned;
fully now the debt is paid."

Asdis said it was true: "but I know not what counsel you now mean to take."

Grettir said he meant now to visit his friends and kinsmen in the western regions, and that she should have no unpleasantness on his account. Then he made ready to go, and parted with much affection from his mother. First he went to Melar in Hrutafjord and recounted to his brother-in-law Gamli all his adventure with Thorbjorn. Gamli begged him to betake himself away from Hrutafjord while the kinsmen of Thorbjorn were abroad with their men, and said they would support him in the suit about Atli's slaying to the best of their power. Then Grettir rode to the West across the Laxardal Heath and did not stop before he reached Ljarskogar, where he stayed some time in the autumn with Thorsteinn Kuggason.

Chapter XLIX
Grettir Visits Thorsteinn Kuggason And Snorri Godi

Thorodd Drapustuf now made inquiries who it was who had killed Thorbjorn and his son. They went to Reykir, where they were told that Grettir had proclaimed the slaying. Thorodd then saw how matters stood and went to Bjarg, where he found many people and asked whether Grettir was there. Asdis said that he was gone, and that he would not hide if he were at home.

"You can be well content to leave things as they are. The vengeance for Atli was not excessive, if it be reckoned up. No one asked what I had to suffer then, and now it were well for it to rest."

Then they rode home, and it seemed as if there were nothing to be done. The spear which Grettir had lost was never found until within the memory of men now living. It was found in the later days of Sturla the Lawman, the son of Thord, in the very marsh where Thorbjorn fell, now called Spearmarsh. This is the proof that he was killed there and not in Midfitjar, as has been elsewhere asserted.

Thorbjorn's kinsmen learned of Grettir's being in Ljarskogar and called together their men with the purpose of going there. Gamli heard of this at Melar and sent word to Thorsteinn and Grettir of their approach. Thorsteinn sent Grettir on to Tunga to Snorri the Godi, with whom he was then at peace, and advised Grettir to ask for his protection, and if it were refused to go West to Thorgils the son of Ari in Reykjaholar, "who will surely take you in for the winter. Stay there in the Western fjords until the affair is settled."

Grettir said he would follow his counsel. He rode to Tunga where he found Snorri and asked to be taken in. Snorri answered: "I am now an old man, and have no mind to harbour outlaws, unless in a case of necessity. But what has happened that the old man should have turned you out?"

Grettir said that Thorsteinn had often shown him kindness; "but we shall need more than him alone to do any good."

Snorri said: "I will put in my word on your behalf, if it will be of any use to you. But you must seek your quarters elsewhere than with me."

So they parted. Grettir then went West to Reykjanes. The men of Hrutafjord came with their followers to Samsstad, where they heard that Grettir had left Ljarskogar, and went back home.

Chapter L
Grettir Winters With Thorgils At Reykjaholar In Company With The Foster-Brothers

rettir came to Reykjaholar towards the beginning of the winter and asked Thorgils to let him stay the winter with him. Thorgils said he was welcome to his entertainment, like other free men; "but," he said, "we do not pay much attention to the preparation of the food."

Grettir said that would not trouble him.

"There is another little difficulty," Thorgils continued. "Some men are expected here who are a little hot-headed, namely, the foster-brothers Thorgeir and Thormod. I do not know how it will suit you to be together with them. They shall always have entertainment here whenever they wish for it. You may stay here if you will, but I will not have any of you behaving ill to the others."

Grettir said that he would not be the first to raise a quarrel with any man, more especially since the bondi had expressed his wish to him.

Soon after the foster-brothers came up. Thorgeir and Grettir did not take very kindly to one another, but Thormod behaved with propriety. Thorgils said to them what he had said to Grettir, and so great was the deference paid to him that none of them spoke an improper word to the other, although they did not always think alike. In this way the first part of the winter was passed.

Men say that the islands called Olafseyjar, lying in the fjord about a mile and a half from Reykjanes, belonged to Thorgils. He had there a valuable ox, which he had not brought away in the autumn. He was always saying that he wanted him to be brought in before Yule. One day the foster-brothers prepared to go and fetch the ox, but wanted a third man to help them. Grettir offered to go with them and they were very glad to have him. So the three set out in a ten-oared boat. The weather was cold and the wind from the North; the boat was lying at Hvalshausholm. When they left the wind had freshened a little; they reached the island and caught the ox. Grettir asked whether they preferred to ship the ox or to hold the boat, for there was a high surf running on the shore. They told him to hold the boat. He stood by her middle on the side away from the land, the sea reaching right up to beneath his shoulders, but he held the boat firmly so that she could not drift. Thorgeir took the ox by the stern and Thormod by the head, and so they hove him into the boat. Then they started heading for the bay, Thormod taking the bow-oars with Thorgeir amidships and Grettir in the stern. By the time they reached Hafraklett the wind was very high. Thorgeir said: "The stern is slackening."

Grettir said: "The stern will not be left behind if the rowing amidships is all right."

Thorgeir then bent his back to the oars and pulled so violently that both the rowlocks carried away. He said:

"Pull on, Grettir, whilst I mend the rowlocks."

Grettir pulled vigorously whilst Thorgeir mended the rowlocks. But when Thorgeir was about to take over the oars again they were so damaged that on Grettir giving them a shake on the gunwale they broke. Thormod said it would be better to row less and not to break the ship. Then Grettir took two spars which were on board, bored two holes in the gunwale, and rowed so energetically that every timber creaked. As the boat was well found and the men in good condition they reached Hvalshausholm. Grettir asked whether they would go on home with the ox or whether they would beach the boat. They preferred to beach the boat, and they did so with all the water that was in her all frozen. Grettir got off the ox, which was very stiff in its limbs and very fat and tired; when they got to Titlingsstad it could go no more. The foster-brothers went home, for none of them would help the other at his job. Thorgils asked after Grettir; they told him how they had parted, and he sent men out to him. When they came below Hellisholar they saw a man coming towards them with an ox on his back; it was Grettir carrying the ox. They all admired his great feat, but Thorgeir became rather jealous of Grettir's strength.

One day soon after Yule Grettir went out alone to bathe. Thorgeir knew of it and said to Thormod: "Let us go out now and see what Grettir does if I attack him as he comes out of the water."

"I don't care to do that," Thormod said; "and I do not think you will get any good from him."

"I mean to go," Thorgeir said.

He went down to the bank, carrying his axe aloft. Grettir was just coming out of the water, and when they met Thorgeir said: "Is it true, Grettir, that you once said you would not run away from any single person."

"I don't know whether I did," Grettir said; "but I have scarcely run away from you."

Thorgeir raised his axe. In a moment Grettir ran at him and brought him over with a heavy fall. Thorgeir said to Thormod: "Are you going to stand there while this devil knocks me down?"

Thormod then got Grettir by the leg and tried to drag him off Thorgeir but could not. He was wearing a short sword, and was just about to draw it when Thorgils came up and told them to behave themselves and not to fight with Grettir. They did as he bade and made out that it was all play. They had no more strife, so far as has been told, and men thought Thorgils blessed by fortune in having been able to pacify men of such violent tempers.

When the spring set in they all departed. Grettir went on to Thorskafjord. When some one asked him how he liked his entertainment at Reykjaholar he answered: "Our fare was such that I enjoyed my food very much — when I could get it." Then he went West over the heath.

Chapter LI
Grettir's Case Overborne At The All-Thing

Thorgils, the son of Ari, rode to the Thing with a large following. All the magnates were there from all parts of the country, and he soon met with Skapti the Lawman and had some talk with him. Skapti said:

"Is it true, Thorgils, that you have been giving winter entertainment to three of the most unruly men in the country, all three of them outlaws, and that you kept order so well that none of them did any harm to the other?"

Thorgils said it was true.

Skapti said: "Well, I think it shows what authority you possess. But how did their characters appear to you? Who is the most valorous among them?"

"They are all entirely valiant," he answered, "but of two of them I will not say that they never fear; only there is a difference. Thormod fears God, and is a man of great piety; and Grettir fears the dark. He will not, if he may follow his own inclination, venture anywhere after nightfall. But Thorgeir, my kinsman, he I think cannot fear."

"They must be each of them as you say," said Skapti, and there their conversation ended.

At the Thing Thorodd Drapustuf laid his complaint in the matter of the slaying of Thorbjorn Oxmain, for he had failed in the Hunavatn Thing through the influence of Atli's kinsmen. Here he thought that there was less likelihood of his case being overborne. Atli's party sought counsel of Skapti the Lawman; he said that their defence appeared to him a good one, and that full blood-money would have to be paid for Atli. Then the case was brought before the judges, and the opinion of the majority was that the slaying of Atli was set off by that of Thorbjorn. Skapti when he heard of it went to the judges and asked them on what grounds their decision rested; they said that the two slain bondis were of equal rank.

Skapti asked: "Which happened first, the outlawing of Grettir or the death of Atli?"

They reckoned up and found that a week had elapsed between the two events. Grettir was outlawed at the All-Thing and Atli was killed just after it.

"That was what I expected," Skapti said. "You have overlooked the facts; you have treated as a party to the suit a man who was an outlaw, a man who was stopped from appearing either as plaintiff or defendant. I maintain that Grettir has no standing in the case, and that it must be brought by the kinsmen of the deceased who are nearest at law."

Thorodd Drapustuf said: "Who then is to answer for the slaying of my brother Thorbjorn?"

"See to that yourself," said Skapti. "Grettir's kinsmen are not liable to pay for his deeds unless his sentence be removed."

When Thorvald the son of Asgeir learned of Grettir's status in court having been disallowed, inquiry was made for Atli's nearest of kin, and these were found to be Skeggi the son of Gamli at Melar and Ospak the son of Glum of Eyr in Bitra. Both were valiant and strenuous men. Thorodd was then mulcted in blood-money for the slaying of Atli and had to pay two hundreds of silver.

Then Snorri the Godi spoke:

"Men of Hrutafjord! Are you willing now to agree to the remission of the fine in consideration of Grettir's sentence being commuted? I expect that as an outlaw he will bite you sorely."

Grettir's kinsmen welcomed this proposal, and said they did not care about the money if Grettir could have peace and freedom. Thorodd said he saw that his case was beset with difficulties, and that for his part he was willing to accept the proposal. Snorri said that inquiry must first be made whether Thorir of Gard would agree to Grettir being freed. When Thorir heard of it he was furious, and said that never should Grettir either go or come out of his outlawry. So far from consenting to his being amnestied, he would put a higher price upon his head than was put upon any other outlaw.

When they knew that he would take it so ill, nothing more was said about the amnesty. Ospak and Skeggi took the money that was paid and kept it, while Thorodd Drapustuf got no compensation for his brother Thorbjorn. He and Thorir each offered a reward of three marks of silver for Grettir's head; this seemed to men to be an innovation, for never before had more than three marks in all been offered. Snorri said it was very unwise to make such efforts to keep a man outlawed who could do so much mischief, and that many would suffer for it. Then they parted and men rode home from the Thing.

Chapter LII
Grettir Is Captured By Farmers And Released By Thorbjorg

rettir went over the Thorskafjord Heath to Langadal, where he let his hands sweep over the property of the smaller cultivators, taking what he wanted from every one. From some he got weapons, from others clothes. They gave up their property very variously, but when he was gone all said that they had been compelled to do it.

There dwelt on the Vatnsfjord one Vermund the Slender, a brother of Viga-Styr, who had married Thorbjorg the daughter of Olaf Peacock, the son of Hoskuld, called Thorbjorg the Fat. At the time when Grettir was in Langadal Vermund was away at the Thing. He went across the ridge to Laugabol where a man named Helgi was living, one of the principal bondis. Thence Grettir took a good horse belonging to the bondi and rode on to Gervidal, where dwelt a man named Thorkell. He was well provided but in a small way of business. Grettir took from him what he wanted, Thorkell daring neither to withhold anything nor to protest. Thence Grettir went to Eyr and on to the coast of the fjord, obtaining food and clothes from every homestead and making himself generally disagreeable, so that men found it hard to live while he was about.

Grettir went boldly on, taking little care of himself. He went on until he came to Vatnsfjardardal and entered a dairy shelter, where he stayed several nights. There he lay sleeping in the forest, fearing for nothing. When the shepherds learned of it they reported in the homesteads that a fiend had come into the place who they thought would be hard to deal with. All the farmers came together and a band of thirty of them concealed themselves in the forest where Grettir could not know of them. They set one of the shepherds to watch for an opportunity of seizing him, without however knowing very clearly who the man was.

One day when Grettir was lying asleep the farmers came up to him.

They considered how they should take him with least danger to themselves, and arranged that ten should fall upon him while others laid bonds round his feet. They threw themselves on to him, but Grettir struggled so violently that he threw them all off and came down on his hands and knees. Then they threw ropes round his feet. Grettir kicked two of them in the ears and they fell senseless. One came on after the other; long and hard he struggled, but at last they succeeded in getting him down and binding him. Then they began to ask themselves what they were going to do with him. They asked Helgi of Laugabol to take him over and look after him until Vermund returned from the Thing.

He said: "I have something better to do than to keep my men guarding him. I have labour enough with my lands, and he shall not come in my way."

Then they asked Thorkell of Gervidal to take him and said he had sufficient means. He objected strongly and said he had no accommodation for him, "I lie at home with my wife, far from other men. You shall not bring your basket to me."

"Then you, Thoralf of Eyr," they said; "you take Grettir and look after him well while the Thing lasts, or else hand him on to the next farm; only be answerable for his not escaping. Give him over bound, just as you receive him."

He said: "I am not going to take Grettir. I have neither means nor money to keep him, nor was he captured on my property. So far as I can see much more trouble than credit is to be got by taking him or having anything to do with him. He shall not enter my house."

Each of the bondis was asked, but all refused. Some witty person wrote a poem about these confabulations and called it "Grettir's Faring," adding many jests of his own for the dilectification of men. After parleying for a long time they all came to an agreement that they would not throw away their luck, and set to work to raise a gallows there and then in the forest upon which Grettir should hang. Their delight over this proposal was uproarious.

Then they saw three people riding along the valley from below, one of them in a dyed dress. They guessed that it must be Thorbjorg the mistress of

Vatnsfjord on her way to the dairy, and so it was. Thorbjorg was a person of great magnificence, and tremendously wise. She was the leading personage of the district and managed everything when Vermund was away. She came up to where the crowd was gathered and was lifted from her horse; the bondis saluted her respectfully. She said:

"What is your meeting about? Who is this thick-necked man sitting there in bonds?"

Grettir told his name and saluted her.

"What has moved you, Grettir," she said, "to commit violence upon my Thing-men?"

"I cannot overlook everything," he said. "I must be somewhere."

"You are indeed unfortunate," she said, "that a pack of churls like these should have captured you and that none of them should have paid for it. What are you men going to do with him?"

The bondis said that they were going to hoist him on to a gallows for his misdeeds.

She said: "It may be that Grettir has deserved it, but it will bring trouble upon you men of Isafjord if you take the life of a man so renowned and so highly connected as Grettir, ill-starred though he be. Now what will you do for your life, Grettir, if I give it to you?"

"What do you wish me to do?"

"You shall swear never to commit any violence here in Isafjord; nor shall you take revenge upon those who have had a hand in capturing you."

Grettir said it should be as she desired, and he was released. He said it was the greatest effort of self-restraint that he ever made that he did not thrash the men who were there triumphing over him. Thorbjorg told him to come home with her and gave him a horse to ride on. So he went to Vatnsfjord and stayed there well cared for by the mistress until Vermund returned. She gained great renown from this deed through the district. Vermund was very much put out when he got home and asked why Grettir was there. Thorbjorg told him everything which had happened with the Isafjord men.

"To what does he owe it that you gave him his life?" he asked.

"Many reasons there were," she said. "The first is that you might be the more respected as a chief for having a wife who would dare to do such a thing. Next, his kinswoman Hrefna will surely say that I could not let him be slain; and thirdly, because he is in many respects a man of the highest worth."

"You are a wise woman," he said, "in most things. I thank you for what you have done."

Then he said to Grettir: "You have sold yourself very cheap, such a man of prowess as you are, to let yourself be taken by churls. This is what always happens to those who cannot control themselves."

Grettir then spoke a verse:

"Full was my cup in Isafjord
when the old swine held me at ransom."

"What were they going to do with you when they took you?" Vermund
asked.

"To Sigar's lot my neck was destined
when noble Thorbjorg came upon them."

"Would they have hanged you then if they had been left to themselves?"

"My neck would soon have been in the noose,
had she not wisely saved the bard."

"Did she invite you to her home?"

"She bade me home with her to fare.
A steed she gave me, life and peace."

"Great will your life be and troublous," said Vermund; "but now you
have learnt to beware of your foes. I cannot keep you here, for it would
rouse the enmity of many powerful men against me. Your best way is to seek
your kinsmen; there are not many who will be willing to take you in if they
can do anything else; nor are you one who will easily follow the will of
another man."

Grettir remained for a time in Vatnsfjord and went thence to the
Western fjords and tried several of the leading men there, but something
always happened to prevent their taking him in.

Chapter LIII
Grettir Winters In Ljarskogar With Thorsteinn Kuggason

During the autumn Grettir returned to the South and did not stop
till he came to his kinsman Thorsteinn Kuggason in Ljarskogar, who
welcomed him. He accepted Thorsteinn's invitation to stay the winter with
him. Thorsteinn was a man who worked very hard; he was a smith, and

kept a number of men working for him. Grettir was not one for hard work, so that their dispositions did not agree very well. Thorsteinn had had a church built on his lands, with a bridge from his house, made with much ingenuity. Outside the bridge, on the beam which supported it, rings were fastened and bells, which could be heard from Skarfsstadir half a sea-mile distant when any one walked over the bridge. The building of the bridge had cost Thorsteinn, who was a great worker in iron, much labour. Grettir was a first-rate hand at forging the iron, but was not often inclined to work at it. He was very quiet during the winter so that there is not much to relate.

The men of Hrutafjord heard that Grettir was with Thorsteinn, and gathered their forces in the spring. Thorsteinn then told Grettir that he must find some other hiding-place for himself, since he would not work. Men who did nothing did not suit him.

"Where do you mean me to go to?" asked Grettir.

Thorsteinn told him to go South to his kinsmen, but to return to him if he found them of no use.

Grettir did so. He went to Borgarfjord in the South to visit Grim the son of Thorhall, and stayed with him till the Thing was over. Grim sent him on to Skapti the Lawman at Hjalli. He went South over the lower heaths and did not stop before he reached Tunga, where he went to Thorhall, the son of Asgrim the son of Ellidagrim, and paid few visits to the farms around. Thorhall knew of Grettir through the relations which had been between their ancestors; indeed Grettir's name was well known throughout the country because of his exploits. Thorhall was a wise man and treated Grettir well, but did not want to keep him there for very long.

Chapter LIV
Adventure With Lopt

Grettir went from Tunga up the Haukadal valley northwards to Kjol and was there for some time in the summer. For men traveling either to the North or to the South there was no certainty of their not being stripped of what they had on them, for he was hard pressed for the means of living.

One day when Grettir was keeping to the North near Dufunesskeid he saw a man riding South along the Kjol valley. He was a tall man on horseback, riding a good horse with a studded bridle, and was leading another horse loaded with sacks. He had a slouched hat on his head, so that his face was not clearly seen. Grettir was very pleased to see his horse and his property, and went to meet him and asked him his name. He said it was Lopt, and added: "I know what your name is; you are Grettir the Strong, son of Asmund. Whither are you going?"

"I have not made up my mind yet about that," said Grettir. "My present business is to know whether you will lay off some of the property which you are travelling with."

"Why should I give you what belongs to me? What will you give me for the things?"

"Have you not heard that I never pay anything? And yet it seems to most people that I get what I want."

Lopt said: "Make this offer to those who seem good to you; I am not going to give my property away for nothing. Let us each go our own way." Then he whipped on his horse and was about to ride away from Grettir.

"We shall not part so quickly as that," said Grettir, and seized the bridle of Lopt's horse in front of his hands, pulled it from him and held it with both hands.

"Go your own way," said Lopt; "you will get nothing from me as long as I am able to hold it."

"That shall now be tried," said Grettir.

Lopt reached down along the cheek-strap and got hold of the reins between the end ring and Grettir's hands, pulling with such force that Grettir let go, and at last Lopt wrenched the whole bridle away from him. Grettir looked at his palms and thought that this man must have strength in his claws rather than not. Then he looked at him and said: "Where are you going to now?"

He answered:

"To the storm-driven den, over ice-clad heights,
I ride to the rock and the rest of the hand."

Grettir said: "There is no certainty to be had from asking where your dwelling is if you do not speak more clearly." Then Lopt spake and said:

"I seek not to hide thy ways from thy ken.
'Tis the place which the Borgfirdings Balljokull call."

Then they parted. Grettir saw that he had no strength against this man. Then he spoke a verse:

"Illugi brave and Atli were far.
Never again may such hap be mine!
The bridle was torn away from my hand.
Her tears will flow when I am afeared."

After this Grettir left Kjol and went South to Hjalli where he asked Skapti for shelter. Skapti said: "I am told that you are acting with violence and are robbing men of their property; that ill becomes a man so highly connected as you are. It would be easier to negotiate if you gave up robbing. Now as I am called Lawman of this country, it would not be seemly for me to break the law by harbouring outlaws. I would like you to betake yourself somewhere where you do not need to commit robbery."

Grettir said he would be very glad to, but that he could scarcely live alone owing to his fear of the dark. Skapti said he would have to content himself with something short of the best: "And trust no one so fully that what happened to you in the Western fjords may be repeated. Many have been brought to death by over-confidence."

Grettir thanked him for his good advice and turned back to Borgarfjord in the autumn, when he went to his friend Grim, the son of Thorhall, and told him what Skapti had said. Grim advised him to go to the North to Fiskivotn in the Arnarvatn Heath, and he did so.

Chapter LV
Grettir In The Arnarvatn Heath. Death Of Grim The Forest-Man

Grettir went up to the Arnarvatn Heath and built himself a hut there of which the remains are still to be seen. He went there because he wanted to do anything rather than rob, so he got himself a net and a boat and went out fishing to support himself.

It was a weary time for him in the mountains because of his fear of the dark. Other outlaws heard of his having come there and wanted to go and see him, thinking that he would be a great protection to them.

There was an outlaw from the North named Grim. This man was bribed by those of Hrutafjord to kill Grettir. They promised him pardon and money if he succeeded. He went to visit Grettir and asked for his hospitality.

Grettir said: "I do not see how you will be holpen by coming to me, and you men of the forest are untrustworthy. But it is ill to live alone; I have no choice. Only he shall be with me who is willing to work at whatever comes to hand."

Grim said that was just what he wished and pressed Grettir much, until Grettir let himself be persuaded and took him in. He stayed there right into the winter, and watched Grettir closely, but it seemed no easy matter to attack him, for Grettir was suspicious and kept his weapons at hand night and day; when he was awake the man would not venture to approach him.

One morning Grim came home from fishing and went into the hut stamping with his feet and wanting to know whether Grettir was asleep. Grettir lay still and did not move. There was a short sword hanging above his head. Grim thought he would never have a better opportunity. He made a loud noise to see whether Grettir took any notice, but he did not, so Grim felt sure that he was asleep. He crept stealthily to the bed, reached up to the sword, took it down and raised it to strike. Just at the moment when he raised it Grettir sprang up on to the floor, and, seizing the sword with one hand, Grim with the other, hurled him over so that he fell nearly senseless. "This is how you have proved yourself with all your friendly seeming," he said. Then he got the whole truth out of him and killed him. He learned from this what it was to take in a forest-man. So the winter passed. The hardest thing of all to bear was his fear of the dark.

Chapter LVI
Treachery And Death Of Thorir Redbeard

horir of Gard now heard where Grettir had taken up his abode and meant to leave no stone unturned to get him slain. There was a man named Thorir Redbeard, a stout man and a great fighter, on which account he had been declared outlaw throughout the country.

Thorir of Gard sent word to him, and when they met asked Redbeard to undertake the business of slaying Grettir. Redbeard said that was no easy task, as Grettir was very wide awake and very cautious. Thorir told him to try it, saying: "It would be a splendid deed for a valiant man like you; I will get your outlawing removed and give you sufficient money as well."

So Redbeard agreed and Thorir told him how he should go to work to deal with Grettir. Redbeard then went away into the East in order that Grettir might not suspect where he came from. Thence he came to the Arnarvatn Heath, where Grettir had then been for one winter, found Grettir and asked him for entertainment. He said: "I cannot allow people to play with me again as the man did who came here last autumn, pretending to be very friendly; before he had been here very long he began plotting against my life. I cannot risk taking in anymore forest-men."

"I think you have reason," Thorir said, "to mistrust forest-men. It may be you have heard tell of me as a man of blood and a disturber of peace, but never did you hear of such a monstrous deed of me as that I betrayed my host. Ill is the lot of him who has an ill name; for men think of him but as such; nor would I have come here if I had had any better choice. All is not lost for us if we stand together. You might venture so much to begin with as to try how you like me, and then if you find any unfitness in me turn me away."

"Well," said Grettir, "I will risk it with you; but know of a surety that if I suspect you of any treachery it will be your death."

Thorir agreed. Grettir took him in and found that in whatever he did he had the strength of two men. He was ready for anything that Grettir gave him to do. Nothing did Grettir need to do for himself, and he had never lived so comfortably since he had become an outlaw. Nevertheless he was so wary that Thorir got no chance. Two years was Thorir Redbeard with Grettir on the Heath, and at last he began to weary of it. He thought over what he could do to take Grettir off his guard.

One night in the spring a heavy gale sprang up while they were asleep. Grettir awoke and asked where their boat was. Thorir sprang up, ran to the boat, broke her all in pieces, and threw the fragments about so that it looked as if the storm had wrecked her. Then he returned to the hut and said aloud: "You have had bad luck, my friend. Our boat is all broken in pieces and the nets are lying far out in the lake."

"Get them back then," said Grettir. "It seems to me to be your doing that the boat is smashed."

"Of all things which I can do," said Thorir, "swimming is that which suits me least. In almost anything else I think I can hold my own with any ordinary man. You know very well that I have been no burden to you since I came here; nor would I ask you to do this if I were able to do it myself."

Grettir then arose, took his arms and went to the lake. There was a point of land running out into the lake with a large bay on the further side of it. The water was deep up to the shore. Grettir said: "Swim out to the nets and let me see what you are able to do."

"I told you before," Thorir said, "that I cannot swim. I do not know now where all your boldness and daring are gone to."

"I could get the nets," he said; "but betray me not if I trust you."

"Do not think such shameful and monstrous things of me," said Thorir.

"You will prove yourself what you are," Grettir said.

Then he threw off his clothes and his weapons and swam out to the nets. He gathered them together, returned to the shore and cast them up on to the bank. Just as he was about to land Thorir quickly seized his short sword and drew it. He ran towards Grettir as he stepped on to the bank and aimed a blow at him. Grettir threw himself down backwards into the water and sank like a stone. Thorir stood by the shore intending to guard it until he came up. Grettir swam beneath the water, keeping close to the bank so that Thorir could not see him, and so reached the bay behind him, where he landed without letting himself be seen. The first Thorir knew of it was when Grettir lifted him up over his head and dashed him down with such violence that the sword fell out of his hand. Grettir got possession of it and without speaking a word cut off his head. So his life ended. After that Grettir refused to take in any forest-men, and yet he could not live alone.

Chapter LVII
Attack On Grettir By Thorir Of Gard With Eighty Men Repulsed With The Aid Of Hallmund

At the All-Thing Thorir of Gard learned of Thorir Redbeard having been killed. It was evident that the matter was not so easy to deal with. He now determined to ride from the Thing in a westerly direction through the lower heath, and with the aid of about eighty men whom he had with him to take Grettir's life. Grim the son of Thorhall heard of his plans and sent word to Grettir, bidding him beware of himself. Grettir therefore continued closely to watch the movements of men who came and went.

One day he saw a number of men coming in the direction of his place of dwelling. He went into a gorge between two rocks, but did not go right away because he did not see the whole of the troop. Thorir then came up with his whole party and bade them go between his head and his body, saying that the scoundrel had but a poor chance now.

"A filled cup is not yet drunk," answered Grettir. "You have come far to seek me, and some of you shall bear the marks of our game before we part."

Thorir urged his men on to attack him. The gorge was very narrow so that he could easily defend it from one end, and he wondered much that they did not get round to his rear to hurt him. Some of Thorir's men fell and some were wounded, but they effected nothing. Then Thorir said: "I always heard that Grettir was distinguished for his courage and daring, but I never knew that he was so skilled in magic as I now see he is; for there fall half as many again behind his back as before his face, and I see that we have to do with a troll instead of a man."

So he bade his men retire, and they did so. Grettir wondered what the explanation could be, but was terribly exhausted. Thorir and his men withdrew and rode into the northern parts. Their expedition was considered very disgraceful. Thorir had left eighteen men on the ground and had many wounded.

Grettir then went up the gorge and found there a man of huge stature sitting up against the rock and sorely wounded. Grettir asked his name, and he said it was Hallmund, adding: "That you may recognise me I may remind you that you thought I gripped the reins rather tightly when I met you in Kjol last summer. I think I have now made that good."

"Indeed," said Grettir, "I think you have done me a manly service; whenever I can I will repay it."

"Now I wish," said Hallmund, "that you may come to my home, for it must seem wearisome to you here on the Heath."

Grettir said he would come willingly, and they both went together to the foot of the Balljokull, where Hallmund had a large cave. There they found his daughter, a fine and well-grown maiden. They treated Grettir well, and the daughter nursed both the wounded men to health again. Grettir stayed there some time that summer. He composed an ode on Hallmund in which the line occurs: "Hallmund steps from his mountain hall"; further:

"The war-fain sword in Arnarvatn
went forth to hew its bloody path.
Heroes inherit Kelduhverfi.
Hallmund the brave came forth from his den."

It is said that at that encounter Grettir slew six men and Hallmund twelve.

As the summer passed Grettir began to long for the habitations of men, and to see his friends and kinsmen. Hallmund told him to visit him when he returned to the South and Grettir promised to do so. He went westwards to Borgarfjord and thence to Breidafjardardalir and sought counsel of Thorsteinn Kuggason as to where he should go next. Thorsteinn said that his enemies were now becoming so numerous that few would care to take him in; but told him to go to Myrar and see what he found there. So in the autumn he went to Myrar.

Chapter LVIII
Grettir Visits Bjorn The Hitdale Warrior And Takes Refuge In The Fagraskogafjall

here lived in Holm Bjorn the Hitdale Warrior, who was the son of Arngeir, the son of Bersi the Godless, the son of Balki, who was the first settler in Hrutafjord, as has already been told. Bjorn was a great chief and a valiant man, always ready to take in outlaws. He received Grettir well when he came to Holm on account of the friendship which had existed between their former kinsmen. Grettir asked if he would give him shelter, and Bjorn said that he had so many quarrels throughout the land that men would be reluctant to take him in for fear of being outlawed themselves. "But," he said, "I will give you some help if you will leave the men who are under my protection in peace, whatever you do to others in this part."

Grettir promised that he would, and Bjorn continued: "I have thought of something. In the mountain which stretches away from the Hitara river there is a good position for defence, and likewise a good hiding-place if it is skilfully managed. There is a hole through the mountain from which you can see down upon the high road that lies immediately beneath it, and a sandy slope down to the road so steep that few could get up it if it were defended above by one doughty man up in the hollow. It may, I think, be worth your while to consider whether you can stay there; it is easy to go down from there to the Myrar to get your supplies, and to reach the sea."

Grettir said he would trust to his foresight if he would help him a little. Then he went to Fagraskogafjall and made himself a home there. He hung some grey wadmal in front of the hole, and it looked from the road below as if one could see through. Then he began to get in his supplies, but the Myramen thought they had an unhappy visitor in Grettir.

Thord the son of Kolbeinn was an excellent poet who dwelt in Hitarnes. There was a great feud between him and Bjorn at that time, and Bjorn thought it would be more than half useful to him if Grettir were to busy himself with Thord's men or his cattle. Grettir was a great deal with Bjorn and they had many games of strength. It is related in Bjorn's saga that they were considered equal in strength, but the opinion of most people is that Grettir was the strongest man that had been in the land since the days when Orin Storolfsson and Thoralf Skolmsson ceased their trials of strength. Grettir and Bjorn swam in one course the whole length of the Hitara from the lake at its head down to the sea. They brought the stepping-stones into the river which neither floods nor freezing nor icedrifts have since moved from their places. Grettir stayed a year in Fagraskogafjall without any attack being made upon him, and yet many lost their property through his means and got nothing for it, because his position was strong for defence and he was always in good friendship with those who were nearest to him.

Chapter LIX
The Chastisement Of Gisli

There was a man named Gisli; he was the son of that Thorsteinn whom Snorri the Godi had caused to be slain. He was a big strong man, very ostentatious in his dress and in his armour, a man with a high opinion of himself and very boastful. He was a mariner, and landed at the Hvita river in the summer after Grettir had spent a winter in the mountains. Thord the son of Kolbeinn rode to his ship and was welcomed by Gisli, who offered him of his wares whatever he cared to have. Thord accepted his offer and they began to have some talk together. Gisli asked: "Is it true what I hear that you are in difficulty how to rid yourself of a forest-man who is doing you much hurt?"

"We have made no attempt yet," said Thord, "because a great many think he is difficult to reach, and have found it so."

"It seems likely that you will have trouble with Bjorn, unless you drive him away. All the worse it is that I must be too far away next winter to give you any help."

"It is better for you to know of him only by hearsay."

"Don't talk to me about Grettir," said Gisli. "I have been in much greater straits in my campaigns with King Knut the Mighty and in the western seas, where I was always considered to have held my own. Only let me come within reach of him and I will trust myself and my armour."

Thord answered that he should not do it for nothing if he killed Grettir: "There is more money on his head than on that of any other outlaw. First there were six marks of silver, this summer Thorir of Gard added three more, and men think that he who wins it will have had enough trouble."

"Everything will be attempted for money," said Gisli: "especially with us traders. But we must keep quiet about what we have been saying, for Grettir will be more on his guard if he hears that you have taken me into your counsels. I intend next winter to be at Olduhrygg; is there any hiding-place of his on my way there? He will not be prepared for this, and I shall not take many men with me to attack him."

Thord approved of his proposal. He rode home soon after and kept very quiet about it. And now was proved what has often been said, that: Off in the woods is a listener nigh. Men who were friends of Bjorn in Hitardal overheard their conversation and reported it accurately to him. Bjorn told Grettir of it when they met, and said now he should see how to encounter him. "It would be no bad joke," he said, "if you were to injure him in some way without killing him if you can."

Grettir grinned but said little. Towards the time of gathering in the cattle Grettir went down to Flysjuhverfi to get some sheep and got four wethers. The bondis heard of his having come and went after him. They came up just at about the moment when he reached the foot of his mountain and wanted to drive the sheep away from him. But they would not attack him with weapons. There were six of them and they stood across his path to bar his way. He was concerned about his sheep, got angry, seized three of them and threw them down the hill so that they lay senseless. The others when they saw it went at him, but rather halfheartedly. Grettir took the sheep, fastened them together by the horns, threw two over each shoulder and carried them off. Then he went up into his den. The bondis turned back feeling they had had the worst of it, and were more discontented with their lot than ever.

Gisli stayed with his ship that autumn until she was ready to be hauled up. Several things happened to delay him, so that he was late in getting away and rode off very little before the winter nights. Then he rode North and stayed at Hraun on the south bank of the Hitara. Next morning before he rode out he said to his servants: "Now we will ride in red clothes and let the forest-man see that we are not like the other travellers who beat about here every day."

There were three of them and they did as he bade. When they had crossed the river he said: "Here I am told dwells the forest-man, up in that peak; but the way is not an easy one. Would it not please him to come to us and see our array?" They said this was always his habit.

That morning Grettir had got up early. The weather was cold, it was freezing and some snow had fallen, but very little. He saw three men riding from the South across the Hitara, and the light shone from their apparel and from their enamelled shields. It occurred to Grettir who it might be, and he thought he would relieve them of some of their accoutrements. He was very curious to meet a man who went about so ostentatiously. So he took his weapons and hurried down the hillside. Gisli when he heard the clattering of the stones said: "A man, rather tall, is coming down the hill and wants to meet us. Let us act boldly and we shall have good sport." His men said that this fellow had great confidence in himself to run into their hands; but that he who asked should have. Then they got off their horses. Grettir came up to them and laid hold of a bag of clothes which Gisli had behind him on his saddle, saying:

"I must have this; I often stoop to little things."

Gisli said: "You shall not; do not you know with whom you have to do?"

Grettir said: "No; that is not so clear to me. Nor do I make much difference between one man and another since I claim so little."

"May be it seems little to you," said Gisli; "but I would sooner part with thirty hundred ells of wadmal. It seems that extortion is your way. Go for him, boys! Let us see what he can do."

They obeyed. Grettir fell back a little and reached a stone which is still standing by the side of the way and is called Grettishaf, where he stood at bay. Gisli urged on his men, and Grettir saw that he was not quite so valiant as he pretended to be, for he kept well behind them. Grettir got tired of being hemmed in, so he made a lunge with his sword and killed one of Gisli's men, sprang from his stone and assailed them so vigorously that Gisli fell back all along the foot of the hill. Then his other man was killed.

Grettir said: "One would scarcely see that you have achieved much in the world abroad, and you have shamefully forsaken your comrades."

Gisli answered: "The fire is hottest to him who is in it; it is ill dealing with men from Hel."

They had exchanged few more blows when Gisli threw away his arms and bolted right away along the foot of the mountain. Grettir gave him time to throw away whatever he liked, and at every opportunity he threw off something more of his clothes. Grettir never followed him so closely that there was not some distance between them. He ran right away from the mountains, across Kaldardal, round Aslaug's Cliff, above Kolbeinsstad and out to Borgarhraun.

By that time he had nothing left on him but his shirt, and was terribly exhausted. Grettir still followed, keeping now within reach of him. He pulled off a great branch. Gisli did not stop till he reached Haffjardara river, which was all swollen and difficult to ford. Gisli was going right out into the river when Grettir pressed forward and seized him and showed him the difference in their strength.

Grettir got him down, sat on the top of him and asked: "Are you the Gisli who wanted to meet Grettir?"

"I have found him now," he answered; "but I know not how I shall part with him. Keep what you have taken and let me go free."

Grettir said: "You will not understand what I am going to tell you, so I must give you something to remember it by." Then he pulled up Gisli's shirt over his head and let the rod play on both sides of his back. Gisli struggled to get away, but Grettir gave him a sound whipping and then let him go. Gisli thought that he would sooner not learn anything from Grettir than have another such flogging, nor did he do anything more to earn it. Directly he got his feet under him again he ran off to a large pool and swam across the river.

In the evening he reached the settlement called Hrossholt, very exhausted. There he lay for a week, his body covered with blisters, and afterwards went on to his own place.

Grettir turned back, gathered up all the things which Gisli had thrown away and took them home. Gisli never got them back again; many thought be had only got what he deserved for his noisy boasting. Grettir made a verse about their encounter:

> "The horse whose fighting teeth are blunted
> runs from the field before his foe.
> With many an afterthought ran Gisli.
> Gone is his fame, his glory lost!"

In the spring after this Gisli prepared to go on board his ship and forbade in the strongest terms anything which belonged to him being carried South by the way of the mountains; for he said that the Fiend himself was there. Gisli when he went South to join his ship kept all the way along the coast and he never met Grettir again. Nobody considered him worth thinking about, nor do we hear any more of him in this saga. Grettir's relations with Thord the son of Kolbeinn became worse than ever, and Thord tried every means to get Grettir driven away or killed.

Chapter LX
The Battle With The Myramen

When Grettir had been two winters in Fagraskogafjall and the third winter had set in, he went South into Myrar to the farm called Laekjarbug, where he took six wethers without their owner's permission. Then he went down to Akrar and drove off two oxen for slaughter with several sheep, and went up South to the Hitara. When the bondis heard of his exploits they sent word to Thord at Hitarnes and asked him to take the lead in the slaying of Grettir. He was rather reluctant, but as they had asked him he sent his son Arnor, afterwards called Jarlsbard, to go with them, and told them not to let Grettir escape. Messengers were then sent round to all the farms.

There was a man named Bjarni who dwelt in Jorvi in Flysjuhverfi. He collected men on the other side of the Hitara; the intention was that each band should keep on its own side. Grettir had two men with him, one named Eyjolf, a stout man, the son of a bondi in Fagraskogar, and another. The party came on, about twenty in number, under Thorarin from Akrar and Thorfinn of Laekjarbug. Grettir tried to get out across the river, but was met by Arnor and Bjarni coming from the coast. There was a narrow point jutting out into the river on Grettir's side, and when he saw the men approaching he drove his animals on to it, for he never would let go anything of which he had once got possession. The Myramen prepared to attack in good order and Grettir told his companions to guard his rear. They could not all come on at once. There was a hard struggle between them; Grettir used his short sword with both hands and they found it not easy to get at him. Some of the Myramen fell and some were wounded. The men on the other side of the river were rather slow in coming up because there was no ford near. Before they had been fighting very long they fell back. Thorarin of Akrar was a very old man and not able to join in the fighting. When the battle was over there came up his son Thrand, his brother Ingjald's son Thorgils, Finnbogi the son of Thorgeir, the son of Thorhadd of Hitardal, and Steinolf the son of Thorleif of Hraundal. They set on their men and there was a hard struggle.

Grettir saw that there was no choice left but either to flee or else to do his utmost and not spare himself. He pressed on hard and nothing could hold against him, for his foes were so numerous that there was no chance of escaping except by fighting to the last before he fell. He tried always to engage those who seemed most courageous; first he went for Steinolf of Hraundal and cleft his skull down to his shoulders; then he struck at Thorgils the son of Ingjald and almost cut him in two. Then Thrand tried to spring forward and avenge his kinsmen, and Grettir hewed at his right thigh, cutting out all the muscles so that he could fight no more. Next he gave Finnbogi a severe wound. Then Thorarin ordered them off. "The longer you fight," he said, "the worse you will get from him and the more will he choose out the men from your company."

They obeyed and fell back. Ten had fallen; five were wounded to death or crippled, and nearly all who had been in the battle were hurt. Grettir was terribly fatigued but little wounded. The Myramen drew off, having suffered heavy losses, for many a good man had fallen. Those who were beyond the river came over slowly and did not arrive till the fight was over, and when they saw the plight of their men Arnor would not risk himself any further, for which he was much blamed by his father and by others. Men thought he was not much of a warrior. The place where they fought is now called Grettisoddi.

Grettir and his companions were all wounded; they took their horses and rode back along the foot of the mountain. When they reached

Fagraskogar Eyjolf was behind. There was a bondi's daughter there and she asked for their tidings, which Grettir told her fully and spoke a verse:

"Goddess of horn-floods! Steinolf's wounds
are such that scarcely may be healed.
Of Thorgils' life is little hope;
his bones are smashed; eight more are dead."

Then Grettir went to his retreat and spent the winter there.

Chapter LXI
Grettir Winters Under The Geitland Glacier

The next time that Bjorn met Grettir he told him that this was a very serious affair, and that he would not be able to stay there in peace much longer. "You have killed kinsmen and friends of mine, but I will not depart from my promise to you so long as you are here."

Grettir said he was sorry to have given him offence, but that he had to defend his hands and his life. Bjorn said it would have to remain so. Soon there came to him some of the men who had lost their kinsmen through Grettir and petitioned him not to allow such a ruffian as he was to stay there any longer and molest them. Bjorn said he would do as they desired directly the winter was over.

Thrand the son of Thorarin of Akrar had now recovered from his wound. He was a man of much worth, and had married Steinunn the daughter of Hrut of Kambsnes. Steinolf's father Thorleif of Hraundal was a great man; from him are sprung the Hraundal men.

No more meetings are told of between Grettir and the Myramen while he was in the mountains. Bjorn continued in friendship with him, but some of Bjorn's other friends fell away from him because of his allowing Grettir to remain there, for they were annoyed at getting no compensation for the slaying of their kinsmen. When the Thing assembled Grettir left the Myrar district and went to Borgarfjord, where he visited Grim the son of Thorhall and sought counsel of him where he should move to next. Grim said he was not powerful enough to keep him there, so Grettir went off to his friend Hallmund and stayed there till the end of the summer.

In the autumn Grettir went to Geitland, where he stayed till bright weather set in. Then he ascended the Geitlandsjokull and turned his steps South-east along the glacier, taking with him a kettle and fuel. It is supposed that he went there by the counsel of Hallmund, who knew the country far and wide. He went on till he came to a long and rather narrow valley in the glacier, shut in on every side by the ice which overhung the valley. He went about everywhere, and found fair grass-grown banks and brushwood. There were hot springs, and it seemed as if volcanic fires had kept the ice from closing in above the valley.

A little stream flowed down the dale with smooth banks on either side. Little did the light of the sun enter there, and the number of sheep in the valley seemed to him countless. They were much better and fatter than any which he had ever seen.

Grettir stayed there and built himself a hut out of logs which he found about. He caught a sheep to eat, and it was better for slaughter than two in other places. There was a ewe there with her lamb; she had a brown head and excelled all the others in size. He was anxious to have the lamb, so he caught it and slaughtered it and got half a measure of suet out of it, and it was better in every way. When Brownhead missed her lamb she came up every night to Grettir's hut and bleated so that he never could get any sleep. He regretted much having killed the lamb on account of the disturbance which she caused him. Every evening when the twilight set in he heard a voice calling in the valley, and then the sheep used to run together into a place of shelter. Grettir has told us that a blending ruled over the valley, a giant named Thorir, under whose protection he remained. Grettir called the valley after him Thorisdal. He said that Thorir had daughters with whom he had some play, and that they were very pleased, because not many people came there. And when the days of fasting came Grettir remembered to tell them that fat and liver should be eaten in Lent. Nothing particular occurred that winter, and Grettir found it so dull that he could not stay there any longer. He left the valley and went to the South through the glacier, reaching the middle of Skjaldbreid from the North. There he took up a stone, cut a hole in it and said that if a man put his eye to the hole he could see into the gully which flows out of Thorisdal. Then he went across the country South and reached the eastern fjords. He spent the summer and the winter on this journey and visited all the great men, but found them all against him so that nowhere could he get lodging or shelter. So he returned to the North and stayed in various places.

Chapter LXII
Hallmund Is Killed By A Forest-Man Named Grim

oon after Grettir had left the Arnarvatn Heath there came a manthere named Grim, the son of a widow at Kropp. He had killed the son of Eid of Ass, the son of Skeggi, and been outlawed for it. So there he stayed where Grettir had been before him and got plenty of fish out of the lake. Hallmund was not at all pleased at Grim being there instead of Grettir, and said that he should have little advantage from his great catches of fish. One morning Grim had caught a hundred fish, which he brought to the hut and arranged outside. The next morning when he went there every fish was gone. He thought it very strange, but returned to the lake and caught this time two hundred. He carried them home and arranged them; again everything happened as before; in the morning all were gone, evidently through the same agency as before. The third day he caught three hundred, carried them home and kept a watch on his hut. He looked out through a hole in the door to see if any one came, and so he remained for a time. When about one third of the night had passed he heard some one walking near and stepping rather heavily; so he immediately took his axe, which was very sharp, and wanted to know what was the matter. There came a man with a big basket on his back; he put it down and looked round, but saw no one outside. He rummaged about among the fish and seemed to think that they would do for him to lay hands upon. He threw them all into his basket and they quite filled it. The fishes were so large that Grim thought no horse would be able to carry more. This man then took the load and got beneath it. Just as he was about to rise Grim rushed out and taking his axe in both hands struck a blow at his neck which went through the skin. He started in surprise and then ran off towards the south of the hill with his basket. Grim went after him to see whether he had got him. They went south along the foot of the Balljokull where the man entered a cave. There was a bright fire in the cave and a woman standing in it, very tall but shapely. Grim heard her greet her father, calling him Hallmund. He flung down his load and heaved a great sigh. She asked why he was covered with blood. He answered in a verse:

> "No man, I see, may trust his might.
> His luck and heart will fail at death."

Then she pressed him to say what had happened, and he told her everything.

"Hear now," he said, "what I tell you of my adventure. I will tell it to you in verse, and you shall cut it in runes on a staff."

She did so, and he spoke the Hallmundarkvida, in which the following occurs:

"I was strong when Grettir's bridle I seized
I saw him gazing long at his palms.

Then Thorir came on the Heath with his men.
'Gainst eighty we two had play with our spears.
Grettir's hands knew how to strike;
much deeper the marks that were left by mine.
Arms and heads then flew as they tried
to gain my rear; eighteen of them fell.

The giant-kind and the grim rock-dwellers,
demons and blendings fell before me,
elves and devils have felt my hand."

Many exploits of his did Hallmund recount in the lay, for he had been in every land.

The daughter said: "That man was not going to let his catch slip away from him. It was only to be expected, for you treated him very badly. But who is going to avenge you?"

"It is not certain that anybody will, but I think that Grettir would avenge me if he were able. It will not be easy to go against this man's luck; he is destined to great things." Then as the lay continued his strength began to fail. Hallmund died almost at the moment when he finished the song. She grieved much for him and wept sorely. Then Grim came forward and bade her be comforted. "All," he said, "must depart when their fate calls. It was partly his own fault, for I could not look on and see myself robbed."

She said he might speak much about that: "The unjust man prospers ill."

She was somewhat cheered by the talk with him. Grim stayed several nights in the cave and learned the lay; all went well with them. Grim was in the Arnarvatn Heath all the winter after Hallmund's death. Afterwards Thorkell the son of Eyjolf came to the heath and fought with him. The meeting ended by Grim having Thorkell's life in his power, but he would not kill him. Thorkell then took him in, sent him abroad and supplied him with means; each was considered to have acted generously towards the other. Grim became a great traveller and there is a long saga about him.

Chapter LXIII
Grettir's Meeting With Thorir On The Reykja Heath

e now return to Grettir, who came from the eastern fjords, travelling in disguise and hiding his head because he did not wish to meet Thorir. That summer he spent in Modrudal Heath and other places. For a time too he was on Reykja Heath. Thorir heard of his being on Reykja Heath, gathered his men and rode thither, determined not to let him escape. Grettir scarcely knew of their plans before they came upon him. He was in a hill-dairy a little off the road with another man, and when they saw the troop they had to lay their plans quickly. Grettir said they should make their horses lie down inside the house, and they did so. Thorir rode forward across the heath in a northerly direction, missed the place, did not find Grettir and turned back home. When the troop had ridden round to the West, Grettir said: "They will not be pleased with their expedition if they do not meet me. You stay and mind the horses while I go after them. It would be a good jest if they did not recognise me."

His companion tried to dissuade him, but he would go. He changed his dress, put on a wide hat which came down over his face and took a stick in his hand. Then he went along the road towards them. They addressed him and asked whether he had seen any men riding over the heath.

"I have seen the men whom you are seeking," he said, "you very nearly came upon them; they were on your left hand just south of the marshes."

On hearing this they galloped off towards the marshes, which were so swampy that they could not get through and had to spend a great part of the day dragging their horses out. They swore much at the supposed traveller for playing a practical joke upon them.

Grettir returned speedily home to his companion, and when they met spoke a verse:

> "I will not ride to the warriors' arms;
> too great the danger is.
> I dare not meet the storm of Vidri;
> but homeward turn my steps."

They rode off as fast as they could westwards towards the homestead in Gard before Thorir could come there with his company. When they were near the place they met a man on the road who did not know them. There was a young woman standing outside, very much dressed up, and Grettir asked who she was. The man who had come up said she was Thorir's daughter. Then Grettir spoke a verse:

"Maiden, when thy father comes
tell him, little though it please him,
how I rode his dwelling past;
only two who with me rode."

From this the man learnt who it was, and rode to the house to tell them that Grettir had come round. When Thorir returned many men thought that he had been bamboozled by Grettir. He then set spies to watch Grettir's movements. Grettir took the precaution of sending his companion to the western districts with his horse, while he himself went North into the mountains at the beginning of the winter, muffling up his face so that no one should recognise him. Every one thought that Thorir had fared no better but even worse than at their former encounter.

Chapter LXIV
Ghosts In Bardardal

There was dwelling at Eyjardalsa in Bardardal a priest named Steinn, a good farmer and wealthy. His son Kjartan was grown up and was now a fine young man. Thorsteinn the White was a man who dwelt at Sandhaugar to the south of Eyjardalsa; his wife Steinvor was young and of a merry disposition. They had children who at this time were yet young. Their place was generally thought to be much haunted by trolls. Two winters before Grettir came North into those parts, Steinvor the mistress of Sandhaugar went as usual to spend Yule at Eyjardalsa, while her husband stayed at home. Men lay down to sleep in the evening, and in the night they heard a great noise in the room near the bondi's bed. No one dared to get up to see what was the matter because there were so few of them. The mistress of the house returned home the next morning, but her husband had disappeared and no one knew what had become of him. So the next season passed. The following winter the mistress wanted to go to mass, and told her servant to stay at home; he was very unwilling but said she should be obeyed. It happened just as before; this time the servant disappeared. People thought it very strange and found some drops of blood upon the outer door, so they supposed that some evil spirit must have carried off both the men. The story spread all through the district and came to the ears of Grettir, who being well accustomed to deal with ghosts and spectres turned his steps to Bardardal and arrived at Yule-eve at Sandhaugar. He retained his disguise and called himself Gest. The lady of the house saw that he was enormously tall, and the servants were terribly afraid of him. He asked for hospitality; the mistress told him that food was ready for him but that he must see after himself. He said he would, and added: "I will stay in the house while you go to mass if you would like it."

She said: "You must be a brave man to venture to stay in the house."

"I do not care for a monotonous life," he said.

Then she said: "I do not want to remain at home, but I cannot get across the river."

"I will come with you," said Gest. Then she made ready to go to mass with her little daughter. It was thawing outside; the river was flooded and was covered with ice. She said: "It is impossible for either man or horse to cross the river."

"There must be fords," said Gest; "do not be afraid."

"First carry the maiden over," she said; "she is lighter."

"I don't want to make two journeys of it," said he; "I will carry you in my arms."

She crossed herself and said: "That is impossible; what will you do with the girl?"

"I will find a way," he said, taking them both up and setting the girl on her mother's knee as he bore them both on his left arm, keeping his right arm free. So he carried them across. They were too frightened to cry out. The river came up to his breast, and a great piece of ice drove against him, which he pushed off with the hand that was free. Then the stream became so deep that it broke over his shoulder, but he waded on vigorously till he reached the other bank and put them on shore. It was nearly dark by the time he got home to Sandhaugar and called for some food. When he had eaten something he told the servants to go to the other end of the hall. Then he got some boards and loose logs and laid them across the hall to make a great barricade so that none of the servants could get across. No one dared to oppose him or to object to anything. The entrance was in the side wall of the hall under the back gable, and near it was a cross bench upon which Grettir laid himself, keeping on his clothes, with a light burning in the room. So he lay till into the night.

The mistress reached Eyjardalsa for mass and every one wondered how she had crossed the river. She said she did not know whether it was a man or a troll who had carried her over. The priest said it was certainly a man though unlike other men. "Let us keep silence over it; may be that he means to help you in your difficulties."

She stayed there the night.

Chapter LXV
Adventure With A Troll-Woman

We return now to tell of Gest. Towards midnight he heard a loud noise outside, and very soon there walked a huge troll-wife into the room. She carried a trough in one hand and a rather large cutlass in the other. She looked round the room as she entered, and on seeing Gest lying there she rushed at him; he started up and attacked her furiously. They fought long together; she was the stronger but he evaded her skilfully. Everything near them and the panelling of the back wall were broken to pieces. She dragged him through the hall door out to the porch, where he resisted vigorously. She wanted to drag him out of the house, but before that was done they had broken up all the fittings of the outer door and borne them away on their shoulders. Then she strove to get to the river and among the rocks. Gest was terribly fatigued, but there was no choice but either to brace himself or be dragged down to the rocks. All night long they struggled together, and he thought he had never met with such a monster for strength. She gripped him so tightly to herself that he could do nothing with either hand but cling to her waist. When at last they reached a rock by the river he swung the monster round and got his right hand loose. Then he quickly seized the short sword which he was wearing, drew it and struck at the troll's right shoulder, cutting off her right arm and releasing himself. She sprang among the rocks and disappeared in the waterfall. Gest, very stiff and tired, lay long by the rock.

At daylight he went home and lay down on his bed, blue and swollen all over.

When the lady of the house came home she found the place rather in disorder. She went to Gest and asked him what had happened, and why everything was broken to pieces. He told her everything just as it had happened. She thought it a matter of great moment and asked him who he was. He told her the truth, said that he wished to see a priest and asked her to send for one. She did so; Steinn came to Sandhaugar and soon learnt that it was Grettir the son of Asmund who had come there under the name of Gest. The priest asked him what he thought had become of the men who had disappeared; Grettir said he thought that they must have gone among the rocks. The priest said he could not believe his word unless he gave some evidence of it. Grettir said that later it would be known, and the priest went home. Grettir lay many days in his bed and the lady did all she could for him; thus Yule-tide passed. Grettir himself declared that the trollwoman sprang among the rocks when she was wounded, but the men of Bardardal say that the day dawned upon her while they were wrestling; that when he cut off her arm she broke, and that she is still standing there on the mountain in the likeness of a woman. The dwellers in the valley kept Grettir there in hiding.

One day that winter after Yule Grettir went to Eyjardalsa and met the priest, to whom he said: "I see, priest, that you have little belief in what I say. Now I wish you to come with me to the river and to see what probability there is in it."

The priest did so. When they reached the falls they saw a cave up under the rock. The cliff was there so abrupt that no one could climb it, and nearly ten fathoms down to the water. They had a rope with them. The priest said: "It is quite impossible for any one to get down to that."

Grettir answered: "It is certainly possible; and men of high mettle are those who would feel themselves happiest there. I want to see what there is in the fall. Do you mind the rope."

The priest said he could do so if he chose. He drove a stake into the ground and laid stones against it.

Chapter LXVI
Grettir Slays A Giant

rettir now fastened a stone in a loop at the end of the rope, and lowered it from above into the water.

"Which way do you mean to go?" asked the priest.

"I don't mean to be bound when I come into the fall," Grettir said. "So my mind tells me."

Then he prepared to go; he had few clothes on and only a short sword; no other arms. He jumped from a rock and got down to the fall. The priest saw the soles of his feet but after that did not know what had become of him. Grettir dived beneath the fall.

It was very difficult swimming because of the currents, and he had to dive to the bottom to get behind the fall. There was a rock where he came up, and a great cave under the fall in front of which the water poured. He went into the cave, where there was a large fire burning and a horrible great giant most fearful to behold sitting before it. On Grettir entering the giant sprang up, seized a pike and struck at him, for he could both strike and thrust with it. It had a wooden shaft and was of the kind called "heptisax." Grettir struck back with his sword and cut through the shaft. Then the giant tried to reach up backwards to a sword which was hanging in the cave, and at that moment Grettir struck at him and cut open his lower breast and stomach so that all his entrails fell out into the river and floated down the stream. The priest who was sitting by the rope saw some debris being carried down all covered with blood and lost his head, making sure that Grettir was killed. He left the rope and ran off home, where he arrived in the evening and told them for certain that Grettir was dead, and said it was a great misfortune to them to have lost such a man.

Grettir struck few more blows at the giant before he was dead. He then entered the cave, kindled a light and explored. It is not told how much treasure he found there, but there is supposed to have been some. He stayed there till late into the night and found the bones of two men, which he carried away in a skin. Then he came out of the cave, swam to the rope and shook it, thinking the priest was there; finding him gone he had to swarm up the rope and so reached the top. He went home to Eyjardalsa and carried the skin with the bones in it into the vestibule of the church together with a rune-staff, upon which were most beautifully carved the following lines:

"Into the fall of the torrent I went;
dank its maw towards me gaped.
The floods before the ogress' den
Mighty against my shoulder played";

and then:

"Hideous the friend of troll-wife came.
Hard were the blows I dealt upon him.
The shaft of Heptisax was severed.
My sword has pierced the monster's breast."

There too it was told how Grettir had brought the bones from the cave. The priest when he came to the church on the next morning found the staff and all that was with it and read the runes. Grettir had then returned home to Sandhaugar.

Chapter LXVII
Visit To Gudmund The Mighty

When the priest met Grettir again he asked him to say exactly what had happened, and Grettir told him all about where he had been. He said that the priest had held the rope very faithlessly, and the priest admitted that it was true. Men felt no doubt that these monsters were responsible for the disappearance of the men in the valley, nor was there any haunting or ghost-walking there afterwards; Grettir had evidently cleared the land of them. The bones were buried by the priest in the churchyard. Grettir stayed the winter in Bardardal, but unknown to the general public.

Thorir of Gard heard rumours of Grettir being in Bardardal and set some men on to take his life. Men thereupon advised him to depart, and he went into the West to Modruvellir, where he met Gudmund the Mighty and asked him for protection. Gudmund said it would not be convenient for him to take him in.

"You must," he said, "find a place to settle in where you need be in no fear for your life."

Grettir said he did not know where such a place was.

"There is an island," Gudmund said, "in Skagafjord, called Drangey. It is excellent for defence; no one can get up to it without a ladder. If once you can reach it there is no chance of any one attacking you there with arms or with craft, so long as you guard the ladder well."

"That shall be tried," said Grettir. "But I am in such dread of the dark that even for the sake of my life I cannot live alone."

"It may be that it is so," said Gudmund; "but trust no man so well that you trust not yourself better. Many are unfit to be trusted."

Grettir thanked him for his excellent advice and departed from Modruvellir. He went on straight to Bjarg, where his mother and Illugi greeted him joyfully. He stayed there several days and heard of Thorsteinn Kuggason having been slain in the autumn before he went to Bardardal. Fate, he thought, was striking hard against him. Then he rode South to Holtavarda Heath, intending to revenge the death of Hallmund if he could meet with Grim. On reaching Nordrardal he learnt that Grim had left two or three years before, as has already been related. Grettir had not received news of it because he had been in hiding there for two years and a third in Thorisdal and had met no one to tell him of what had happened. Then he turned his steps towards the Breidafjord valleys and waylaid those who passed over Brattabrekka. He continued to let his hands sweep over the property of the small farmers during the height of the summer season.

When the summer was passing away, Steinvor at Sandhaugar gave birth to a son who was named Skeggi. He was at first fathered on Kjartan, the son of Steinn the priest at Eyjardalsa. Skeggi was unlike all his family in his strength and stature. When he was fifteen years old he was the strongest man in the North, and then they put him down to Grettir. There seemed a prospect of his growing into something quite extraordinary, but he died when he was seventeen and there is no saga about him.

Chapter LXVIII
Fight With Thorodd The Son Of Snorri

After the death of Thorsteinn Kuggason, Snorri the Godi was on bad terms with his son Thorodd and with Sam the son of Bork the Fat. It is not clearly stated what they had done to displease him except that they had refused to undertake some important work which he had given them to do; what is known is that Snorri turned off his son Thorodd and told him not to come back until he had slain some forest-man, and so it remained. Thorodd then went to Dalir. There dwelt at Breidabolstad in Sokkolfsdal a certain widow named Geirlaug; she kept as her shepherd a grown-up youth who had been outlawed for wounding some one. Thorodd Snorrason heard of this, rode to Breidabolstad and asked where the shepherd was. The woman said he was with the sheep and asked what Thorodd wanted with him.

"I want to take his life," he said; "he is an outlaw and a forest-man."

She said: "Such a warrior as you has nothing to gain by killing a miserable creature like him. I will show you a much doughtier deed, should you have a mind to try it."

"What is that?" he asked.

"Up there in the mountains," she said, "is Grettir the son of Asmund; deal with him; that will be more fitting for you."

Thorodd liked the proposal and said he would do it. Then he put spurs to his horse and rode up along the valleys. On reaching the hills below the Austra river he saw a light-coloured horse saddled, with a big man in armour, and at once directed his steps towards them. Grettir hailed him and asked who he was. Thorodd told his name and asked: "Why do you not rather ask my business than my name?"

"Because," he said, "it is not likely to be very weighty. Are you a son of Snorri the Godi?"

"So it is indeed; we shall now try which of us is the stronger."

"That is easily done," said Grettir, "but have you not heard that I have not proved a mound of wealth to most of those who have had to do with me?"

"I know that; but I mean to risk something on it now."

Then he drew his sword and went valiantly for Grettir, who defended himself with his shield but would not use his weapons against Thorodd. They fought for a time without his being wounded. Grettir then said:

"Let us stop this play; you will not gain the victory in a battle with me."

Thorodd struck at him most furiously. Grettir was tired of it, so he took hold of him and set him down next to himself, saying: "I could do what I liked with you; but I have no fear of your killing me. I am much more afraid of your grey-headed father, Snorri the Godi, and of his counsels, which have brought many a man to his knees. You should take up tasks which you are able to accomplish; it is no child's play to fight with me."

When Thorodd saw that there was nothing to be done he quieted down, and then they parted. He rode home to Tunga and told his father of his encounter with Grettir. Snorri smiled and said: "Many a man has a high opinion of himself; but the odds against you were too great. While you were aiming blows at him he was doing what he pleased with you. But he was wise not to kill you, for it would not have been my purpose to leave you unavenged. I will now rather use my influence on his side if I ever have to do with his affairs."

Snorri showed his approval of Grettir's action towards Thorodd, for his counsels were always friendly to Grettir.

Chapter LXIX
Grettir's Last Visit To Bjarg And Journey With Illugi To Drangey

Soon after Thorodd left him Grettir rode North to Bjarg and remained there in hiding for a time. His fear of the dark grew so upon him that he dared go nowhere after dusk. His mother offered to keep him there, but said she saw that it would not do for him because of the feuds which he had throughout the land. Grettir said she should not fall into trouble through him, "but," he said, "I can no longer live alone even to save my life."

Illugi his brother was then fifteen years old and was a most goodly young man. He heard what they were saying. Grettir told his mother what Gudmund the Mighty had advised him to do, and declared he would try to get to Drangey if he could. Yet, he said, he could not go there unless he could find some faithful man to stay with him. Then Illugi said: "I will go with you, brother. I know not whether I shall be a support to you, but I will be faithful to you and will not run from you so long as you stand upright. And I shall know the better how it fares with you if I am with you."

Grettir answered: "You are such a one amongst men as I most rejoice in. And if my mother be not against it I would indeed that you should go with me."

Asdis then said: "It has now come to this, that I see two difficulties meeting each other. It is hard for me to lose Illugi, but I know that so much may be said for Grettir's condition that he will find some way out. And though it is much for one to bid farewell to both of you, yet I will consent to it if Grettir's lot is bettered thereby."

Illugi was pleased at her words, for his heart was set upon going with Grettir. She gave them plenty of money to take with them and they made ready for their journey. Asdis took them along the road, and before they parted she said: "Go forth now, my sons twain. Sad will be your death together, nor may any man escape that which is destined for him. I shall see neither of you again; let one fate befall you both. I know not what safety you seek in Drangey, but there shall your bones be laid, and many will begrudge you your living there. Beware of treachery; yet shall you be smitten with weapons, for strange are the dreams which I have had. Guard yourselves against witchcraft, for few things are stronger than the ancient spells."

Thus she spoke and wept much. Grettir said: "Weep not, my mother. It shall be said that you had sons and not daughters if we are attacked with arms. Live well, and farewell."

Then they parted. The two travelled North through the districts and visited their kinsmen while the autumn passed into winter. Then they turned their steps to Skagafjord, then North to Vatnsskard on to Reykjaskard below Saemundarhlid to Langholt, reaching Glaumbaer as the day was waning. Grettir had slung his hat over his shoulder; so he always went when out of doors whether the weather was good or bad. Thence they continued their journey, and when they had gone a short way they met a man with a big head, tall and thin and ill clad. He greeted them and each asked the other's name. They told theirs and he said his name was Thorbjorn. He was a vagrant, had no mind to work and swaggered much. It was the habit of some to make game of him or fool him. He became very familiar and told them much gossip about the district and the people therein. Grettir was much amused. He asked whether they did not want a man to work for them and said he would much like to go with them. So much he got from his talk that they let him join them. It was very cold and there was a driving snow-storm. As the man was so fussy and talkative they gave him a nickname and called him Glaum.

"The people in Glaumbaer," he said, "were much exercised about your going without a hat in this weather, and wanted to know whether you were any the braver for being proof against the cold. There were two sons of bondis there, men of great distinction; the shepherd told them to come out and mind the sheep with him, but they could scarcely get their clothes on for the cold."

Grettir said: "I saw a young man inside the door putting on his mittens, and another going between the cow-house and the dung-heap. Neither of them will frighten me."

Then they went on to Reynines and stayed the night there; then to the sea-shore to a farm called Reykir where a man, a good farmer, named Thorvald, lived. Grettir asked him for shelter and told him of his intention of going to Drangey. The bondi said that men of Skagafjord would not think his a very friendly visit and drew back. Then Grettir took the purse of money which his mother had given him and gave it to the bondi. The man's brows unbent when he saw the money and he told three of his servants to take them out in the night by the moonlight. From Reykir is the shortest distance to the island, about one sea-mile.

When they reached the island Grettir thought it looked quite pleasant; it was all overgrown with grass and had steep cliffs down to the sea so that no one could get on to it except where the ladders were. If the upper ladder was pulled up it was impossible for any one to get on to the island. There was also a large crag full of sea birds in the summer, and there were eighty sheep in the island belonging to the bondis, mostly rams and ewes, which were meant for slaughter.

There Grettir quietly settled down. He had been fifteen or sixteen years an outlaw, so Sturla the son of Thord has recorded.

Chapter LXX
The People Of Skagafjord

When Grettir came to Drangey the following chiefs were in Skagafjord:

Hjalti lived at Hof in Hjaltadal, the son of Thord, the son of Hjalti, the son of Thord Skalp. He was a great chief, very distinguished and very popular. His brother was named Thorbjorn Angle, a big man, strong and hardy and rather quarrelsome. Thord their father had married in his old age, and his then wife was not the mother of these two. She was very much against her stepsons, especially Thorbjorn, because he was intractable and headstrong. One day when he was playing at "tables", his stepmother came up and saw that he was playing at "hnettafl"; they played with big peg pieces. She considered that very lazy of him and spoke some words to which he answered hastily. She took up the piece and struck him on the cheek bone with the peg, and it glanced into his eye which hung down on his cheek. He started up and handled her mercilessly so that she was confined to her bed and soon afterwards died; they say that she was pregnant at the time. After that he became a regular ruffian. He took over his property and went first to live in Vidvik.

Halldor the son of Thorgeir, the son of Thord of Hofdi, lived at Hof in Hofdastrand. He married Thordis the daughter of Thord, the sister of Hjalti and Thorbjorn Angle. Halldor was a worthy bondi and wealthy.

Bjorn was the name of a man who lived at Haganes in Fljot, a friend of Halldor of Hof, and the two held together in every dispute.

Tungu-Steinn dwelt at Steinsstadir. He was the son of Bjorn, the son of Ofeig Thinbeard, the son of Crow-Hreidar, to whom Erik of Guddal gave Tunga below Skalamyr. He was a man of renown.

Erik was the son of Holmgang-Starri, the son of Erik of Guddal, the son of Hroald, the son of Geirmund Straightbeard. He lived at Hof in Guddal.

All these were men of high rank. Two brothers dwelt at a place called Breida in Slettahlid, both named Thord. They were very strong men, but peaceable.

All the men now named had a share in Drangey. It is said that the island was owned by no fewer than twenty men, and none of them would part with his share to the others. The largest share belonged to the sons of Thord since they were the richest.

Chapter LXXI
The Bondis Claim Their Property In Drangey

idwinter was passed, and the bondis prepared to bring in their animals from the island for slaughter. They manned a boat and each had a man of his own on board, some two.

When they reached the island they saw men on it moving about. They thought it very strange, but supposed that some one had been wrecked and had gone on shore there. So they rowed to where the ladders were. The people on the shore pulled the ladders up. This seemed very strange behaviour and they hailed the men and asked who they were. Grettir told his name and those of his companions. The bondis asked who had taken them out to the island.

Grettir answered: "He brought me out who took me here, and had hands, and was more my friend than yours."

The bondis said: "Let us take our animals and come to the land with us. You shall have freely whatever you have taken of our property."

Grettir said: "That is a good offer; but each of us shall have that which he has got. I may tell you at once that hence I go not, unless I am dead or dragged away; nor will I let go that which my hands have taken."

The bondis said no more, but thought that most unhappy visitors had come to Drangey. They offered money and made many fair promises, but Grettir refused them all, and so they had to return home much disgusted, having accomplished nothing. They told all the people of the district of the wolves who had come into the island. This had come upon them unawares and nothing could be done. They talked it over that winter but could think of no way of getting Grettir out of the island.

Chapter LXXII
Grettir Visits The Thing At Hegranes

he time passed on until the spring, when men assembled at the Hegranes Thing. They came in great numbers from all the districts under its jurisdiction, and stayed there a long time, both palavering and merry-making, for there were many who loved merriment in the country round.

When Grettir heard that everybody had gone to the Thing he laid a plan with his friends, for he was always on good terms with those who were nearest to him, and for them he spared nothing which he was able to get. He said he would go to the land to get supplies and that Illugi and Glaum should remain behind. Illugi thought it very imprudent but he let Grettir have his way. He told them to guard the ladder well since everything depended upon that. Then he went to the land and obtained what he wanted. He kept his disguise wherever he went and no one knew that he had come. He heard of the festivities that were going on at the Thing and was curious to see them, so he put on some old clothes that were rather shabby and arrived just as they were going from the Logretta home to their booths. Some of the young men were talking about the weather, said it was good and fair, and that it would be a good thing to have some games and wrestling; they thought it a good proposal. So they sat down in front of their booths. The foremost men in the games were the sons of Thord. Thorbjorn Angle was very uppish and was arranging everything himself for the sports. Every one had to do as he bade, and he took them each by the shoulders and pushed them into the field. The wrestling was begun by the less strong ones in pairs, and there was great sport. When most of them had wrestled except the strongest, there was much talk as to who should tackle the two Thords mentioned above, and there was no one who would do it. They went round inviting men to wrestle, but the more they asked the more their invitation was declined. Thorbjorn Angle looked round and saw a big man sitting there, but could not clearly see his face. He seized hold of him and gave a violent tug, but the man sat still and did not move.

Thorbjorn said: "Nobody has held so firm against me to-day as you. But who is this fellow?"

"My name is Gest."

Thorbjorn said: "You will be wanting to play with us. You are a welcome Guest."

"Things may change quickly," he said. "I cannot join in your games for I have no knowledge of them."

Many of them said that they would take it kindly of him if he, a stranger, would play a little with the men. He asked what they wanted him to do, and they asked him to wrestle with some one. He said he had given up wrestling, though he once used to take pleasure in it. As he did not directly refuse they pressed him all the more.

"Well," he said, "if you want to drag me in you must do one thing for me and grant me peace here at the Thing until I reach my home."

They all shouted and said they would gladly do that. The man who was foremost in urging that peace should be given was one Haf the son of Thorarin, the son of Haf, the son of Thord Knapp, who had settled in the land between Stifla in Fljot and Tungua. He lived at Knappsstad and was a man of many words. He spoke in favour of the peace with great authority and said:

"Hereby do I declare Peace between all men, in particular between this man here seated who is named Gest and all Godord's men, full bondis, all men of war and bearers of arms, all other men of this district of the Hegranes Thing whencesoever they have come, both named and unnamed. I declare Peace and full Immunity in behoof of this newcomer to us unknown, Gest yclept, for the practice of games, wrestling and all kinds of sport, while abiding here, and during his journey home, whether he sail or whether he travel, whether by land or whether by sea. He shall have Peace in all places, named and unnamed, for such time as he needeth to reach his home in safety, by our faith confirmed. And I establish this Peace on the part of ourselves and of our kinsmen, our friends and belongings, alike of women and of men, bondsmen and thralls, youths and adults. Be there any truce-breaker who shall violate this Peace and defile this faith, so be he rejected of God and expelled from the community of righteous men; be he cast out from Heaven and from the fellowship of the holy; let him have no part amongst mankind and become an outcast from society. A vagabond he shall be and a wolf in places where Christians pray and where heathen worship, where fire burneth, where the earth bringeth forth, where the child lispeth the name of mother, where the mother beareth a son, where men kindle fire, where the ship saileth, where shields blink, sun shineth, snow lieth, Finn glideth, fir-tree groweth, falcon flieth the live-long day and the fair wind bloweth straight under both her wings, where Heaven rolleth and earth is tilled, where the breezes waft mists to the sea, where corn is sown. Far shall he dwell from church and Christian men, from the sons of the heathen, from house and cave and from every home, in the torments of Hel. At Peace we shall be, in concord together, each with other in friendly mind, wherever we meet, on mountain or strand, on ship or on snow-shoes, on plains or on glaciers, at sea or on horseback, as friends meet in the water, or brothers by the way, each at Peace with other, as son with father, or father with son, in all our dealings.

"Our hands we lay together, all and every to hold well the Peace and the words we have spoken in this our faith, in the presence of God and of holy men, of all who hear my words and here are present."

Many said that a great word had been spoken. Gest said: "You have declared and spoken well; if you go not back upon it, I will not delay to show that of which I am capable."

Then he cast off his hood and after that all his upper garments. Each looked at the other and woe spread over their lips; for they knew that it was Grettir who had come to them, by his excelling all other men in stature and vigour. All were silent and Haf looked foolish. The men of the district went two and two together, each blaming the other, and most of all blaming him who had declared the peace. Then Grettir said: "Speak plainly to me and declare what is in your minds, for I will not sit here long without my clothes. You have more at stake than I have, whether you hold the peace or not."

They answered little and sat themselves down. The sons of Thord and their brother-in-law Halldor then talked together. Some wished to uphold the peace and some not. Each nodded to the other. Then Grettir spoke a verse:

"Many a man is filled with doubt.
A twofold mask has the prover of shields.
The skilful tongue is put to shame.
They doubt if they shall hold the troth."

Then said Tungu-Steinn: "Think you so, Grettir? Which then will the chieftains do? But true it is that you excel all men in courage. See you not how they are putting their noses together?"

Grettir then said:

"Together they all their noses laid;
They wagged their beards in close converse.
They talked with each other by two and two,
Regretting the peace they afore declared."

Then said Hjalti the son of Thord: "It shall not be so; we will hold the peace with you although our minds have altered. I would not that men should have the example of our having broken the peace which we ourselves gave and declared. Grettir shall depart unhindered whithersoever he will, and shall have peace till such time as he reach his home from this journey. And then this truce shall have expired whatever happen with us." They all thanked him for his speech, and thought he had acted as a chieftain should under such circumstances.

Thorbjorn Angle was silent. Then it was proposed that one or the other of the Thords should close with Grettir, and he said that they might do as they chose.

One of the two brothers Thord then came forward. Grettir stood upright before him and Thord went for him with all his might, but Grettir never moved from his place. Then Grettir stretched over across his back and seizing his breeches tripped up his foot and cast him backwards over his head so that he fell heavily upon his shoulders. Then the people said that both the brothers should tackle him together, and they did so. There arose a mighty tussle, each in turn having the advantage, although Grettir always had one of them down. Now one, now the other was brought to his knees or met with a reverse. So fiercely they gripped that all of them were bruised and bloody. Everybody thought it splendid sport, and when they ceased thanked them for their wrestling. Those that were sitting near judged that the two together were no stronger than Grettir alone, although each had the strength of two strong men. They were so equal that when they strove together neither gained the advantage. Grettir did not stay long at the Thing. The bondis asked him to give up the island, but this he refused to do, and they accomplished nothing.

Grettir returned to Drangey where Illugi rejoiced much at seeing him again. They stayed there in peace and Grettir told them of his journeys; so the summer passed. All thought the men of Skagafjord had acted most honourably in upholding their peace, and from this may be seen what trusty men lived in those days, after all that Grettir had done against them. The less wealthy ones among the bondis began to talk amongst themselves and say that there was little profit in keeping a small share of the island, and now offered to sell their holdings to the sons of Thord, but Hjalti said he did not want to buy them. The bondis stipulated that any one who wanted to buy a share should either kill Grettir or get him away. Thorbjorn Angle said that he was ready to take the lead, and would spare no pains to attack Grettir if they would pay him for it. Hjalti his brother resigned to him his share of the island because Thorbjorn was the more violent and was unpopular. Several other bondis did the same, so that Thorbjorn Angle got a large part of the island at a small price, but he bound himself to get Grettir away.

Chapter LXXIII
Visit Of Thorbjorn Angle To Drangey

At the end of the summer Thorbjorn Angle went with a boat fully manned to Drangey. Grettir and his party came forward on the cliff and they talked together. Thorbjorn begged Grettir to do so much for his asking as to quit the island. Grettir said there was not much hope of that. Thorbjorn said: "It may be that I can give you some assistance which will make it worth your while to do this. Many of the bondis have now given up the shares which they had in the island to me."

Grettir said: "Now for the very reason that you have just told me, because you own the greater part of the island, I am determined never to go hence. We may now divide the cabbage. It is true that I thought it irksome to have the whole of Skagafjord against me, but now neither need spare the other, since neither is suffocated with the love of his fellows. You may as well put off your journeys hither, for the matter is settled so far as I am concerned."

"All abide their time," he said, "and you abide evil."

"I must risk that," he said. And so they parted. Thorbjorn returned home again.

Chapter LXXIV
The Fire Goes Out In Drangey

Grettir had, it is said, been two years in Drangey, and they had slaughtered nearly all the sheep. One ram, it is told, they allowed to live; it was grey below and had large horns. They had much sport with it, for it was very tame and would stand outside and follow them wherever they went. It came to the hut in the evening and rubbed its horns against the door. They lived very comfortably, having plenty to eat from the birds on the island and their eggs, nor had they much trouble in gathering wood for fire. Grettir always employed the man to collect the drift, and there were often logs cast ashore there which he brought home for fuel. The brothers had no need to work beyond going to the cliffs, which they did whenever they chose. The thrall began to get very slack at his work; he grumbled much and was less careful than before. It was his duty to mind the fire every night, and Grettir bade him be very careful of it as they had no boat with them. One night it came to pass that the fire went out. Grettir was very angry and said it would only be right that Glaum should have a hiding. The thrall said he had a very poor life of it to have to lie there in exile and be ill-treated and beaten if anything went wrong. Grettir asked Illugi what was to be done, and he said he could think of nothing else but to wait until a ship brought them some fire.

Grettir said that would be a very doubtful chance to wait for. "I will venture it," he said, "and see whether I can reach the land."

"That is a desperate measure," said Illugi. "We shall be done for if you miscarry."

"I shall not drown in the channel," he said. "I shall trust the thrall less in future since he has failed in a matter of such moment to us."

The shortest passage from the island to the mainland is one sea-mile.

Chapter LXXV
Grettir Swims To The Mainland For Fire

rettir then prepared for his swim. He wore a cloak of coarse material with breeches and had his fingers webbed. The weather was fine; he left the island towards the evening. Illugi thought his journey was hopeless. Grettir had the current with him and it was calm as he swam towards the fjord. He smote the water bravely and reached Reykjanes after sunset. He went into the settlement at Reykir, bathed in the night in a warm spring, and then entered the hall, where it was very hot and a little smoky from the fire which had been burning there all day. He was very tired and slept soundly, lying on right into the day. When it was a little way on in the morning the servants rose, and the first to enter the room were two women, the maid with the bondi's daughter. Grettir was asleep, and his clothes had all fallen off on to the floor. They saw a man lying there and recognised him. The maid said:

"As I wish for salvation, sister, here is Grettir the son of Asmund come. He really is large about the upper part of his body, and is lying bare. But he seems to me unusually small below. It is not at all in keeping with the rest of him."

The bondi's daughter said: "How can you let your tongue run on so? You are more than half a fool! Hold your tongue!"

"I really cannot be silent, my dear sister," said the maid; "I would not have believed it if any one had told me."

Then she went up to him to look more closely, and kept running back to the bondi's daughter and laughing. Grettir heard what she said, sprang up and chased her down the room. When he had caught her he spoke a verse:

(*verse missing in manuscript*)

Soon afterwards Grettir went to the bondi Thorvald, told him his difficulty and asked him to take him out to the island again, which he did, lending him a ship and taking him over. Grettir thanked him for his courtesy. When it became known that Grettir had swum a sea-mile, every one thought his courage extraordinary both on sea and on land. The men of Skagafjord blamed Thorbjorn Angle much for not having ridded Drangey of Grettir, and all wanted their shares back again. That did not suit him and he asked them to have patience.

Chapter LXXVI
Adventure Of Haering In Drangey

That summer a ship came to Gonguskardsos, on board of which was a man named Haering. He was a young man and very active; he could climb any cliff. He went to visit Thorbjorn Angle and stayed there into the autumn. He pressed Thorbjorn much to take him to Drangey, that he might see whether the cliff was so high that he could not get up there. Thorbjorn said it should not be for nothing if he succeeded in getting up on to the island and either killing or wounding Grettir; he made it appear attractive as a task for Haering to undertake.

One day they went to Drangey and he put the Easterner ashore in a certain place, telling him not to let himself be seen if he got to the top. Then they set up the ladder and began a conversation with Grettir's people. Thorbjorn asked him whether he would not leave the island. He said there was nothing on which he was so determined.

"You have played much with us," said Thorbjorn, "and we do not seem likely to have our revenge, but you have not much fear for yourself."

Thus they disputed for long, but came to no agreement.

We have now to tell of Haering. He climbed all about on the cliffs and got to the top in a place which no other man ever reached before or since. On reaching the top he saw the two brothers standing with their backs turned to him. He hoped in a short time to win money and glory from both. They had no inkling of his being there, and thought that nobody could get up except where the ladders were. Grettir was occupied with Thorbjorn's men, and there was no lack of derisive words on both sides. Then Illugi looked round and saw a man coming towards them, already quite close. He said: "Here is a man coming towards us with his axe in the air; he has a rather hostile appearance."

"You deal with him," said Grettir, "while I look after the ladder." Illugi then advanced against the Easterner, who on seeing him turned and ran about all over the island. Illugi chased him to the furthest end of the island; on reaching the edge he leaped down and broke every bone in his body; thus his life ended. The place where he perished was afterwards called Haering's leap. Illugi returned and Grettir asked him how he had parted with his man.

"He would not trust me to manage for him," he said. "He broke his neck over the cliff. The bondis may pray for him as for a dead man."

When Angle heard that he told his men to shove off. "I have now been twice to meet Grettir," he said. "I may come a third time, and if then I return no wiser than I am now, it is likely that they may stay in Drangey, so far as I am concerned. But methinks Grettir will not be there so long in the future as he has been in the past."

They then returned home and this journey seemed even worse than the one before. Grettir stayed in Drangey and saw no more of Thorbjorn that winter. Skapti the Lawman died during the winter, whereby Grettir suffered a great loss, for he had promised to press for a removal of his sentence when he had been twenty years an outlaw, and the events just related were in the nineteenth year. In the spring died Snorri the Godi, and much more happened during this winter season which does not belong to our saga.

Chapter LXXVII
Grettir's Case Before The All-Thing

That summer at the All-Thing Grettir's friends spoke much about his outlawry, and some held that his term was fulfilled when he had completed any portion of the twentieth year. This was disputed by the opposite party, who declared that he had committed many acts deserving of outlawry since, and that, therefore, his sentence ought to be all the longer. A new Lawman had been appointed, Steinn the son of Thorgest, the son of Steinn the Far-traveller, the son of Thorir Autumn-mist. The mother of Steinn the Lawman was Arnora, the daughter of Thord the Yeller. He was a wise man, and was asked for his opinion. He told them to make a search to find out whether this was the twentieth year of his outlawry, and they did so. Then Thorir of Gard went to work to put every possible difficulty in the way, and found out that Grettir had spent one year of the time in Iceland, during which he must be held to have been free of his outlawry. Consequently it had only lasted nineteen years.

The Lawman declared that no man could be outlawed for longer than twenty years in all, even though he committed an outlaw's acts during that time. But before that he would allow no man to be freed.

Thus the endeavour to remove his sentence broke down for the moment, but there seemed a certainty of his being freed in the following summer. The men of Skagafjord were little pleased at the prospect of Grettir being freed, and they told Thorbjorn Angle that he must do one of the two, resign his holding in the island or kill Grettir. He was in great straits, for he saw no way of killing Grettir, and yet he wanted to keep the island. He tried everything he could think of to get the better of Grettir by force or by fraud or in any other way that he could.

Chapter LXXVIII
Thorbjorn's Foster-Mother

Thorbjorn Angle had a foster-mother named Thurid. She was very old and of little use to mankind, but she had been very skilled in witchcraft and magic when she was young and the people were heathen. Now she seemed to have lost it all. Still, although the land was Christian, many sparks of heathendom remained. It was not forbidden by the law of the land to sacrifice or perform other heathen rites in private; only the one who performed them openly was sentenced to the minor exile. Now it happened to many as it is said: The hand turns to its wonted skill, and that which we have learned in youth is always most familiar to us. So Thorbjorn Angle, baffled in all his plans, turned for help to the quarter where it would have been least looked for most people, namely, to his foster-mother, and asked her what she could do for him.

She replied, "Now it seems to me to have come to this, as the saying is: Many go to the goat-house to get wool. What would I less than to think myself above the other men of the country, and then to be as nothing when it comes to the trial? I see not that it fares worse with me than with you, even though I scarce rise from my bed. If you will have my counsel then I must have my way in all that is done."

He consented, and said that she had long given him counsel for his good. The "double month" of the summer was now approaching. One fine day the old woman said to Angle: "The weather is now calm and bright; I will that you go to Drangey and pick a quarrel with Grettir. I will go with you and learn what caution is in his words. I shall have some surety when I see how far they are prospering, and then I will speak over them such words as I please."

Angle said: "Let us not go to Drangey. It is always worse in my mind when I leave that place than when I arrive."

The woman said: "I will not help you if you will not let me do as I like."

"Far be that from me, my foster-mother. I have said that I will go there a third time, that something may come of it for us."

"You may venture it," she said, "much labour will you have before Grettir is laid in the earth; often your lot will be doubtful and hard will it go with you before it is finished. And yet you are so bound that somehow you must get yourself out of it."

Then Thorbjorn Angle had a ten-oared boat manned and went on board with eleven men. The woman was with them and they rowed out to Drangey. When the brothers saw them coming they came forward to the ladder and began once more to talk about their case. Thorbjorn said he had come once more to hear their answer whether Grettir would leave the place. He said he would treat the destruction of his property and Grettir's stay there as a light thing, provided they parted in peace. Grettir said he had no intention of coming to any terms about his going away. "I have often told you," he said, "that there is no use in talking to me about it. You may do whatever you please; I mean to stay here and abide what happens."

Thorbjorn saw that his end would not be gained this time, and said: "I knew very well with what men of Hel I had to do. It is most likely that some days will pass before I come here again."

"It would not hurt me if you never came at all," said Grettir.

The woman was lying in the stern sheets covered up with clothes. Then she began to stir and said:

"These men are brave and unfortunate; there is much difference between you; you offer them good and they refuse everything. There are few more certain tokens of evil than not to know how to accept the good. Now I say this of you, Grettir, that you be deprived of health, of all good luck and fortune, of all protection and counsel, ever the more the longer you live. I wish that your days may be less happy in the future than they have been in the past."

When Grettir heard that he started violently and said: "What fiend is that in the ship with them?"

Illugi said: "I think that must be the old woman, Thorbjorn's foster-mother."

"Curse the hag!" he said. "I could have thought of nothing worse! Nothing that was ever said startled me more than her words, and I know that some evil will befall me from her and her spells. She shall have something to remind her of her visit here."

Then he took up an enormous stone and threw it down into the boat. It fell into the heap of clothes. Thorbjorn had not thought that any man could throw so far. A loud scream was heard, for the stone had struck her thigh and broken it.

Illugi said: "I wish you had not done that."

"Do not blame me for it," said Grettir. "I fear it has been just too little. One old woman would not have been too great a price for us two."

"How will she pay for us? That will be a small sum for the pair of us."

Thorbjorn then returned home; no greeting passed between them when he left. He spoke to the old woman and said: "It has happened as I expected. Little credit has the journey to the island brought you. You have been injured for the rest of your life, and we have no more honour than we had before; we have to endure unatoned one insult after another."

She answered: "This is the beginning of their destruction; I say that from this time onwards they will go downwards. I care not whether I live or not, if I do not have vengeance for the injury they have done me."

"You seem to be in high spirits, foster-mother," he said. Then they arrived home. The woman lay in bed for nearly a month before her leg was set and she was able to walk again. Men laughed much over the journey of Thorbjorn and the old woman. Little luck had come from the meetings with Grettir, first at the peace declaration at the Thing, next when Haering was killed, and now the third time when the woman's thigh was broken, while nothing had been done on their side. Thorbjorn Angle suffered much from their talk.

Chapter LXXIX
The Spell Takes Effect

The autumn passed and but three weeks remained till the winter. The old woman asked to be driven to the sea-shore. Thorbjorn asked what she was going to do.

"A small thing only," she said, "yet maybe the signal of greater things to come."

They did as she asked them. When they reached the shore she hobbled on by the sea as if directed to a spot where lay a great stump of a tree as large as a man could bear on his shoulder. She looked at it and bade them turn it over before her; the other side looked as if it had been burned and smoothed. She had a small flat surface cut on its smooth side; then she took a knife, cut runes upon it, reddened them with her blood and muttered some spells over it. After that she walked backwards against the sun round it, and spoke many potent words. Then she made them push the tree into the sea, and said it should go to Drangey and that Grettir should suffer hurt from it. Then she went back to Vidvik. Thorbjorn said he did not know what would come of it. The woman said he would know more clearly some day. The wind was towards the land up the fjord, but the woman's stump drifted against the wind, and not more slowly than would have been expected.

Grettir was sitting in Drangey with his companions very comfortably, as has been told. On the day following that on which the old woman had cast her spells upon the tree they went down from the hill to look for firewood. When they got to the western side of the island they found a great stump stranded there.

"Here is a fine log for fuel," cried Illugi, "let us carry it home." Grettir gave it a kick with his foot and said: "An ill tree and ill sent. We must find other wood for the fire."

He pushed it out into the sea and told Illugi to beware of carrying it home, for it was sent for their destruction. Then they returned to their hut and said nothing about the tree to the thrall. The next day they found the tree again, nearer to the ladder than on the day before. Grettir put it back into the sea and said he would never carry it home. That night passed and dirty weather set in with rain, so that they did not care to go out and told Glaum to fetch fuel. He grumbled very much and declared it was cruel to make him plague himself to death in every kind of weather. He descended the ladder and found there the woman's log. He thought himself lucky, laboured home with it to the hut and threw it down with a great noise which Grettir heard.

"Glaum has got something; I must go out and see what it is," he said, and went out, taking his wood-cutting axe with him.

"Let your cutting up of it be no worse than my carrying of it home!" said Glaum.

Grettir was irritated with the thrall; he used his axe with both hands and did not notice what tree it was. Directly the axe touched the tree it turned flat and glanced off into Grettir's right leg. It entered above his right knee and pierced to the bone, making a severe wound. Grettir turned to the tree and said: "He who meant me evil has prevailed; it will not end with this. This is the very log which I twice rejected. Two disasters have you now brought about, Glaum; first you let our fire go out, and now you have brought in this tree of ill-fortune. A third mistake will be the death of you and of us all."

Illugi then bound the wound. It bled little; Grettir slept well that night and three days passed without its paining him. When they opened the bandages the flesh had grown together and the wound was almost healed. Illugi said: "I do not think that you will suffer very long with this wound."

"That would be well," said Grettir; "it has happened strangely however it ends; but my mind tells me otherwise."

Chapter LXXX
The Spell Continues To Work

One evening they all went to bed, and about midnight Grettir began to toss about. Illugi asked him why he was so restless. Grettir said his leg was hurting him and he thought there must be some change in its appearance. They fetched a light, unbound the wound and found it swollen and blue as coal. It had opened again and was much worse than at first. He had much pain after that and could not keep quiet, nor would any sleep come to his eyes.

Grettir said: "We must be prepared for it. This illness of mine is not for nothing; there is witchcraft in it. The old woman has meant to punish me for the stone which I threw at her." Illugi said: "I told you that no good would come of that old woman."

"It will be all the same in the end," said Grettir, and spoke a verse:

"Often when men have threatened my life
I have known to defend it against the foe:
but now 'tis a woman has done me to death.
Truly the spells of the wicked are mighty."

"Now we must be on the watch; Thorbjorn Angle will not leave it to end here. You, Glaum, must in future guard the ladder every day and pull it up in the evening. Do this trustily, for much depends thereon. If you betray us your end will be a short one."

Glaum promised most faithfully. The weather now became severe. A north-easterly wind set in and it was very cold. Every evening Grettir asked if the ladder was drawn in.

"Are we now to look for men?" said Glaum. "Is any man so anxious to take your life that he will lose his own for it? This weather is much worse than impossible. Your warlike mood seems to have left you utterly if you think that everything is coming to kill you."

"You will always bear yourself worse than either of us," said Grettir, "whatever happens. But now you must mind the ladder however unwilling you may be."

They drove him out every morning, much to his disgust. The pain of the wound increased, and the whole leg was swollen; the thigh began to fester both above and below the wound, which spread all round, and Grettir thought he was likely to die. Illugi sat with him night and day, paying no heed to anything else. They were now in the second week of his illness.

Chapter LXXXI
Thorbjorn Again Visits Drangey

Thorbjorn Angle was now at home in Vidvik, much put out at not having been able to overcome Grettir. When about a week had passed from the day when the old woman had bewitched the log, she came to speak with Thorbjorn and asked whether he did not mean to visit Grettir. He said there was nothing about which he was more determined.

"But do you wish to meet him, foster-mother?" he asked.

"I have no intention of meeting him," she said; "I have sent him my greeting, which I expect he has received. But I advise you to set off at once and go quickly to see him, otherwise it will not be your fate to overcome him."

He replied: "I have made so many inglorious journeys there that I am not going again. This weather is reason enough; it would not be possible, however pressing it were."

"You are indeed without counsel if you see not through these wiles. Now, I will advise you. First go and collect men; ride to your brother-in-law Halldor in Hof and get help from him. Is it too wild a thing to suppose that I may have to do with this breeze that is now playing?"

Thorbjorn thought it might be that the woman saw further than he supposed, so he sent through the country for men. Answer came very quickly that none of those who had given up their shares would do anything to help him. They said that both the island and the Grettir affair were Thorbjorn's. Tungu-Steinn gave him two men, Hjalti his brother three, Erik in Guddal sent him one. Of his own he had six. These twelve rode out from Vidvik to Hof, where Halldor invited them to stay and asked their news. Thorbjorn told him everything fully. Halldor asked who had done it all; he said his foster-mother had urged him much.

"That will lead to no good. She is a sorceress, and sorcery is now forbidden."

"I cannot overlook everything," said Thorbjorn; "I am determined that it shall now be brought to an end somehow. But how shall I go to work to get on to the island?"

"It seems to me," said Halldor, "that you are relying upon something, but I know not whether it is anything good. If you want to accomplish anything go out to my friend Bjorn in Haganes in Fljot. He has a good boat; ask him from me to lend it to you, and then you will be able to sail on to Drangey. It seems to me that if you find Grettir well and hearty your journey will have been in vain. One thing know for certain: do not slay him in open fight, for there are enough men to avenge him. Do not slay Illugi if you can help it. I fear that my counsel may not appear altogether Christian."

Halldor then gave him six men; one was named Kar, another Thorleif, the third Brand. The names of the others are not mentioned.

These eighteen men then went to Fljot, reached Haganes, and gave Halldor's message to Bjorn. He said it was his duty to do it for Halldor's sake, but that he was under no obligation to Thorbjorn.

He said it was an insane journey to make, and tried hard to dissuade them. They answered that they could not turn back, so they went down to the sea and launched the boat, which was ready with all her gear in the boat-house. Then they made ready to sail. All those who were standing on the shore thought it impossible to cross. They hoisted the sail and the boat was soon under way, far out in the fjord. When they got right out to sea the weather quieted and was no longer too heavy. In the evening as it was getting dark they reached Drangey.

Chapter LXXXII
The Last Battle — Death Of Grettir And Illugi

It has now to be told how Grettir became so ill that he could not stand on his feet. Illugi sat with him and Glaum had to hold watch. He still continued to object, and said they might think their lives were going to fall out of them, but there was no reason for it. He went out, but most unwillingly. When he came to the ladder he said to himself that there was no need to draw it up. He felt very sleepy, lay down and slept all day, and did not wake until Thorbjorn reached the island. They saw then that the ladder was not drawn up. Thorbjorn said: "The situation has changed from what it used to be; there are no men moving about, and the ladder is in its place. It may be that more will come of our journey than we expected at first. Now let us go to the hut and not let our courage slacken. If they are well we may know for certain that there will be need for each to do his very best."

They went up the ladder, looked round and saw close to the ascent a man lying and snoring aloud. Thorbjorn recognised Glaum, went up to the rascal and told him to wake up, striking his ear with the hilt of his sword and saying: "Truly he is in a bad case whose life is entrusted to your keeping."

Glaum looked up and said: "They are going on as usual. Do you think my freedom such a great thing while I am lying here in the cold?"

Angle said: "Have you lost your wits? Don't you see that your enemies are upon you and about to kill you all?"

Glaum said nothing, but on recognising the men cried out as loud as he could.

"Do one thing or the other," said Angle; "either be silent this moment and tell me all about your household, or be killed."

Glaum was as silent as if he had been dipped in water.

Thorbjorn said: "Are the brothers in the hut? Why are they not about?"

"That would not be so easy," said Glaum, "for Grettir is sick and nigh to death and Illugi is sitting with him."

Thorbjorn asked about his condition, and what had happened. Then Glaum told him all about Grettir's wound.

Angle laughed and said: "True is the ancient saying that old friends are the last to break away, and also this, that It is ill to have a thrall for your friend — such a one as you, Glaum! You have shamefully betrayed your liege lord, though there was little good in him."

Then the others cast reproaches at him for his villainy; they beat him almost helpless and left him lying there. Then they went on to the hut and knocked violently at the door.

Illugi said: "Greybelly is knocking at the door, brother."

"He is knocking rather loud," said Grettir; "most unmercifully." Then the door broke in pieces. Illugi rushed to his arms and defended the door so that they could not get in. They assailed it long, but could get nothing in but the points of their spears, all of which Illugi severed from their shafts. Seeing that they could do nothing, they sprang on to the roof and began to break it in. Then Grettir got on to his feet, seized a spear and thrust it between the rafters. It struck Kar, Halldor's man from Hof, and went right through him. Angle told them to go to work warily and be careful of themselves. "We shall only overcome them," he said, "if we act with caution."

Then they laid open the end of one of the timbers and bore upon it until it broke. Grettir was unable to rise from his knees, but he seized the sword Karsnaut at the moment when they all sprang in from the roof, and a mighty fray began. Grettir struck with his sword at Vikar, a man of Hjalti the son of Thord, reaching his left shoulder as he sprang from the roof. It passed across his shoulder, out under his right arm, and cut him right in two. His body fell in two parts on the top of Grettir and prevented him from recovering his sword as quickly as he wished, so that Thorbjorn Angle was able to wound him severely between the shoulders. Grettir said: "Bare is his back who has no brother!"

Illugi threw his shield before Grettir and defended him so valiantly that all men praised his prowess.

Grettir said to Angle: "Who showed you the way to the island?"

"Christ showed us the way," he said.

"I guess," said Grettir, "that it was the wicked old woman, your foster-mother, who showed you; hers were the counsels that you relied upon."

"It shall now be all the same to you," said Angle, "upon whom I relied."

They returned to the attack; Illugi defended himself and Grettir courageously, but Grettir was unfit for fighting, partly from his wounds, partly from his illness. Angle then ordered them to bear Illugi down with their shields, saying he had never met with his like amongst older men than he. They did so, and pressed upon him with a wall of armour against which resistance was impossible. They took him prisoner and kept him. He had wounded most of those who were attacking him and killed three. Then they went for Grettir, who had fallen forward on his face. There was no resistance in him for he was already dead from his wounded leg; his thigh was all mortified up to the rectum. Many more wounds they gave him, but little or no blood flowed.

When they thought he was quite dead Angle took hold of his sword, saying he had borne it long enough, but Grettir's fingers were so tightly locked around the hilt that he could not loosen them. Many tried before they gave it up, eight of them in turn, but all failed. Angle then said: "Why should we spare a forest-man? Lay his hand upon the log."

They did so, and he hewed off the hand at the wrist. Then the fingers straightened and were loosed from the hilt. Angle took his sword in both hands and hewed at Grettir's head. So mighty was the blow that the sword could not hold against it, and a piece was broken out of the edge. When asked why he spoilt a good weapon, he replied: "It will be more easily known if there be any question."

They said this was unnecessary, as the man was dead before. "I will do more," he said, and struck two or three blows at Grettir's neck before he took off his head. Then he said:

"Now I know for certain that Grettir is dead; a great man of war have we laid even with the earth. We will take his head with us, for I have no wish to lose the money which was put upon it. There shall not be any doubt that it was I who slew Grettir."

They said he might do as he pleased, but they felt much disgusted, and thought his conduct contemptible.

Then Angle said to Illugi: "It is a great pity that a man so valiant as you should have committed such a folly as to cast in your lot with this outlaw and follow his evil ways, at last to die unatoned."

Illugi answered: "When the All-Thing is over next summer you shall know who are outlawed. Neither you nor the woman, your foster-mother, shall judge this case, for it is your spells and sorcery that have killed Grettir, though you bore your iron weapons against him when he was at the door of death. Many a base deed did you do over and above your witchcraft."

Angle said: "You speak bravely, but it shall not be so. I will show how I value you by sparing your life if you will swear by your honour to take no vengeance upon any person who has been with us on this occasion."

"I might have thought of it," he said, "if Grettir had been able to defend himself or if you had killed him in honourable battle. But now you need not hope that I will try to save my life by becoming a poltroon like you. I tell you at once that if I live no man shall be more burdensome to you than I. Long will it be before I forget how you have dealt with Grettir; far sooner will I choose to die."

Then Thorbjorn consulted with his companions whether they should allow Illugi to live. They said he should decide their doings himself, as he was the leader of the expedition. Angle said he was not going to have a man threatening his head who would not promise to hold faith. When Illugi knew that they intended to slay him he laughed and said: "Now you have resolved upon that which was nearest to my heart."

When the day broke they led him to the eastern side of the island and there slew him. All praised his courage, and said there was no man of his years who was like him. They buried both the brothers in the island, but took Grettir's head with all weapons and clothes which had any value away with them. His good sword Angle would not allow to come amongst the spoils for division, but bore it long himself. They took Glaum with them, still complaining and resisting. The weather had calmed down in the night, and in the morning they rowed to the mainland. Angle sailed for the most convenient place, and sent the ship on to Bjorn. When they came near to Osland, Glaum became so obstreperous that they refused to carry him any further and slew him there where he was, crying as loud as he could until he was killed. Angle went home to Vidvik and considered that on this journey he had been successful. They laid Grettir's head in salt and put it for the winter in the out-house called Grettisbur in Vidvik. Angle was much blamed for this affair when men came to know that Grettir had been overcome by sorcery. He remained quietly at home till after Yule. Then he went to seek Thorir in Gard and told him of the slayings, adding that he considered that he had a right to the money which had been put on Grettir's head.

Thorir said that he would not deny that he had brought about Grettir's sentence. "I have often suffered wrong from him; but I would not to take his life have become an evil-doer as you have done. I will not pay the money to you, for you seem to me as one who will be doomed to death for magic and witchcraft."

Angle said: "I think it is much more avarice and meanness on your part than any scruples about the way in which Grettir was killed."

Thorir said there was an easy way of settling it between them; they need only wait for the All-Thing and accept what seemed right to the Lawman. They then parted with nothing but ill-feeling between Thorir and Thorbjorn Angle.

Chapter LXXXIII
Thorbjorn Visits Grettir's Mother At Bjarg

The kinsmen of Grettir and Illugi were deeply grieved when they heard of their death. They held that Angle had done a dastardly deed in slaying a man at the point of death, and they also accused him of practising sorcery. They applied to the most learned men, and Angle's case was ill-spoken of.

Four weeks after the beginning of summer he rode Westwards to Midfjord. When Asdis heard of his being in the neighbourhood she gathered her men around her. She had many friends, Gamli and Glum, Skeggi, called Short-hand, and Ospak, who was mentioned before. So much beloved was she that the whole of Midfjord rose to help her, even those who had once been Grettir's enemies. Chief among these was Thorodd Drapustuf, who was joined by most of the Hrutafjord men.

Angle reached Bjarg with a following of twenty men, bringing Grettir's head with him. All those who had promised their support had not yet come in. Angle's party entered the room with the head and set it on the floor. The mistress of the house was there and several others; no greeting passed between them. Angle spoke a verse:

> "Grettir's head I bring thee here.
> Weep for the red-haired hero, lady.
> On the floor it lies; 'twere rotten by this,
> but I laid it in salt. Great glory is mine."

She sat silent while he spoke his verse; then she said:

> "The swine would have fled like sheep from the fox if
> Grettir had stood there hearty and strong.
> Shame on the deeds that were done in the North!
> Little the glory you gain from my lay."

Many said it was small wonder that she had brave sons, so brave was she herself before the insults which she had received. Ospak was outside and was talking with those of Angle's men who had not gone in. He asked about the fray, and they all praised Illugi for the defence that he had made. They also told of Grettir's firm grip on his sword after he was dead, and the men thought it marvellous. Then a number of men were seen riding from the West; they were the friends of Asdis with Gamli and Skeggi, who had come from Melar.

Angle had intended to have an execution against Illugi and to claim all his property, but when all these men came up he saw that it would not do. Ospak and Gamli were very forward in wanting to fight with Angle, but the wiser heads told them to get the advice of their kinsmen Thorvald and other chiefs, and said that the more men of knowledge occupied themselves with the affair the worse it would be for Angle. Through their intervention Angle got away and took with him Grettir's head, which he intended to produce at the All-Thing. He rode home thinking that matters were going badly for him, for nearly all the chiefs in the land were either relations or connections of Grettir and Illugi.

That summer Skeggi Short-hand married the daughter of Thorodd Drapustuf, who then took part in the case on the side of Grettir's kinsmen.

Chapter LXXXIV
Thorbjorn Is Exiled At The Thing

Men now rode to the Thing. Angle's party was smaller than he had expected, because the matter had come to be badly spoken of. Halldor asked whether they were to take Grettir's head with them to the All-Thing. Angle said he meant to take it.

"That is an ill-advised thing to do," said Halldor; "there are quite enough men against you as it is, without your doing such a thing as that to re-awaken their grief."

They were then on the road, and meant to ride South by Sand, so Angle let him take the head and bury it in a sand-hill, which is now called Grettisthuf.

The Thing was very full. Angle brought forward his case, making the most of his own deeds. He told them how he had killed the forest-man on whose head the highest price had been laid, and he claimed the money. Thorir replied as before. Then the Lawman was asked for his opinion. He said that he wished to hear whether any counter-charge was made, by which Angle should forfeit the outlaw money; if not, the money offered for Grettir's head must be paid. Then Thorvald the son of Asgeir asked Short-hand to bring the case before the court, and he declared a first summons against Thorbjorn Angle for witchcraft and sorcery through which Grettir had met with his death, and a second for having killed a man who was half dead, crimes which he said were punishable with outlawry.

There was a great division of parties, but those who supported Thorbjorn were few. It went very unexpectedly for him, for Thorvald and his son-in-law Isleif held that to do a man to death by sorcery was a crime worthy of death. Finally, by the counsel of wise men sentence was passed that Thorbjorn was to leave Iceland that summer and not to return during the lifetime of any of the men concerned in the case on the side of Illugi and Grettir. It was enacted as a law that all sorcerers should be outlawed.

When Thorbjorn saw what his fate was going to be he got away from the Thing, for Grettir's friends were making preparations to attack him. None of the money that was set upon Grettir's head did he get; Steinn the Lawman would not allow it because of his dishonourable conduct; nor was any blood-money paid for the men who had fallen on his side in Drangey; they were set off against Illugi, an arrangement, however, with which Illugi's kinsmen were not at all pleased.

Men rode home from the Thing, and all the feuds which had arisen on Grettir's account were now at an end. Skeggi the son of Gamli, son-in-law of Thorodd Drapustuf and sister's son of Grettir, went North to Skagafjord with the assistance of Thorvald Asgeirsson and of his son-in-law Isleif, who afterwards became bishop of Skalaholt. After obtaining the consent of the whole community he took ship and went to Drangey, where he found the bodies of Grettir and Illugi and brought them to Reykir in Reykjastrand and buried them in the church. Testimony of Grettir lying there is in the fact that in the days of the Sturlungs, when the church at Reykir was moved to another place, Grettir's bones were dug up, and were found to be enormously big and strong. Illugi was buried later on the north side of the church, and Grettir's head was buried in the church at his home in Bjarg.

Asdis remained in Bjarg and was so beloved that no one molested her any more than they did while Grettir was an outlaw. The property at Bjarg passed after her death to Skeggi Short-hand, who became a great man. His son was Gamli, the father of Skeggi of Skarfsstad and of Alfdis the mother of Odd the Monk, from whom many are descended.

Chapter LXXXV
Thorbjorn Goes To Norway And Constantinople

Thorbjorn Angle embarked at Gasar with as much of his own property as he was able to get. His lands went to his brother Hjalti, including Drangey, which Angle gave him. Hjalti became a great chief later on, but is not mentioned again in our story.

Angle went to Norway and still made himself very important. He was supposed to have done a great deed of valour in slaying Grettir, and many who did not know how it really happened honoured him accordingly; but there were some to whom Grettir's fame was known. He only told so much of the story as tended to his own glory, but whatever was less creditable to him he omitted. In the autumn his account reached Tunsberg and came to the ears of Thorsteinn Dromund, who kept very quiet, for he had been told that Angle was a very doughty man and valiant. He remembered the talk which he had had with Grettir in days long past about his arms, and obtained news of Angle's movements. They were both in Norway that winter, but Thorbjorn was in the North and Thorsteinn in Tunsberg, so that they did not see each other. Angle knew, however, that Grettir had a brother in Norway, and did not feel very secure in a strange country; so he asked advice as to what he had better do. In those days many of the Norsemen used to go to Mikligard to take service. Thorbjorn thought it would suit him very well to go there and earn wealth and glory instead of staying in the northern parts where there were relations of Grettir. So he made ready to leave Norway, embarked, and did not stop until he reached Constantinople, and obtained service there.

Chapter LXXXVI
Grettir's Death Avenged By His Brother Thorsteinn Dromund

Thorsteinn Dromund was a wealthy man and highly thought of. On hearing of Angle's departure to Constantinople he handed over his property to his kinsmen and followed him, dogging his movements as he went, without Angle knowing. He reached Constantinople very soon after Angle, intending at all costs to kill him. Neither knew of the other.

Both wanted to be received into the Varangian Guards, and their offer was well received directly it was known that they were Norsemen. At that time Michael Catalactus was king over Constantinople. Thorsteinn Dromund watched for an opportunity of meeting Angle where he might recognise him, but failed amidst the crowd, so he kept on the watch, caring little for his own well-being and ever thinking how much he had lost.

The next thing that happened was that the Varangians were ordered on field service for the defence of the country. The custom and the law were that before they marched a review was held for the inspection of their weapons; this was done on the present occasion. On the day appointed for the review all the Varangians and all who were marching with them had to appear and show their arms. Thorsteinn and Angle both presented themselves. Thorbjorn was the first to show his weapons and he presented the sword Grettisnaut. As he showed it all marvelled and declared that it was indeed a noble weapon, but said it was a bad fault that a piece was out of the middle of the edge, and they asked how that had come about. Angle said that was a tale worth telling.

"The first thing I must tell you," he said, "is that out in Iceland I slew a hero named Grettir the Strong. He was a tremendous warrior and so valorous that no one could succeed in killing him until I came. But as I was destined to be his slayer, I overcame him, although he was many times stronger than I am. I cut off his head with this sword and broke a piece out of the edge."

Those who stood by said he must have had a hard skull, and they showed the sword round. From this Thorsteinn came to know which was Angle, and asked to be shown the sword with the others. Angle willingly showed it to him, for they were all praising his strength and courage, and he, having no notion of its being Thorsteinn or any relation of Grettir, thought he would do likewise. Dromund took the sword, at once raised it aloft and struck a blow at Angle. It came into his head with such force that it penetrated to his jaw and Thorbjorn fell dead to the ground. Thereupon all the men became silent. The officer of the place put Thorsteinn under arrest and asked him why he had committed such a breach of discipline in the sanctity of the Assembly. Thorsteinn said he was a brother of Grettir the Strong and that he had never been able to obtain his vengeance till that moment. Then many of them stood up for him and said there was much excuse for a man who had come such a long way to avenge his brother. The elders of the town thought that this might be true, but as there was no one present to bear out his word they fell back upon their own law, which declared that any man who slew another should lose nothing else than his life.

Judgment was quickly passed upon Thorsteinn, and it was rather hard. He was to sit in a dark chamber in a dungeon and there await his death unless some one came to pay a ransom for him. When he reached the dungeon he found a man who had been there a long time and was all but dead from misery. It was both foul and cold. Thorsteinn asked him: "How do you find your life?"

"Most evil," he replied; "no one will help me, for I have no kinsmen to pay a ransom."

"There are many ways out of a difficulty," said Thorsteinn, "let us be happy and do something to cheer ourselves."

The man said he had no joy in anything.

"We will try it," said Thorsteinn.

Then he began to sing songs. He was such a singer that it would be hard to find his like, and he spared nothing. The dungeon was close to the public road and Thorsteinn sang so loud that it resounded from the walls; the man who before was half dead had much joy therefrom. In this way he sang every evening.

Chapter LXXXVII
The Lady Spes

There was a very distinguished lady in that town, the owner of a large establishment, very rich and highly born. Her name was Spes. Her husband's name was Sigurd; he too was wealthy, but of lower birth than she was. She had been married to him for his money. There was not much love between them, and the marriage was thought an unhappy one. She was very proud, and had much dignity.

One evening when Thorsteinn was diverting himself she happened to pass along the street near the dungeon and heard singing so sweet that she declared she had never heard the like. She was walking with several retainers, and told them to go in and find out who it was that had such a magnificent voice. They called out and asked who was there in such close confinement. Thorsteinn told his name. Spes said:

"Are you as good at other things as you are at singing?"

He said there was not much in that.

"What have you done," she asked, "that they should torture you here to death?"

He said he had killed a man and avenged his brother; "but I have no witness to prove it," he said; "so I have been put here unless some one comes to release me, of which there seems little hope, since I have no relations here."

"A great loss would it be if you were killed," she said. "Was your brother then a man of such renown, he who you avenged?"

Thorsteinn said he was half as good a man again as himself.

She asked what token there was of that. Then Thorsteinn spoke this verse:

"Goddess of rings! No eight could meet him,
or gain the sword from his vanquished hand.
Brave was Grettir; his foemen doughty
severed the hand of the ruler of ships."

Those who understood the song declared that it told of great nobility. When she heard that she asked:

"Will you receive your life at my hands if the choice is offered you?"

"Indeed I will," he said, "if this companion of mine sitting here is released along with me. If not, we must both remain sitting here together."

She answered: "I think you are more worth paying for than he is."

"However that may be," he said, "either we both of us come out from here together or neither of us comes out." So she went to the Varangians' quarters and asked for the release of Thorsteinn, offering money. They agreed. With her interest and her wealth she brought it about that both of them were released. Directly Thorsteinn came out of the dungeon he went to pay his respects to the lady Spes. She welcomed him and kept him there secretly. From time to time he went campaigning with the Varangians, and was distinguished for his courage in all their engagements.

Chapter LXXXVIII
Adventures Of Thorsteinn And Spes

At that time Harald the son of Sigurd was in Constantinople, and Thorsteinn became friendly with him. Thorsteinn was now a very great personage, for Spes kept him well supplied with money, and they became very much attached to one another. She was a great admirer of his skill. Her expenses were very great because she tried to keep up many friends. Her husband noticed a great change in her character and her behaviour, and especially that she had become very extravagant. Treasures of gold and other property which were in her keeping disappeared. One day her husband Sigurd spoke with her and said that he was much surprised at her conduct. "You pay no attention to our affairs," he said, "and squander money in many ways. You seem as if you were in a dream, and never wish to be where I am. I am certain that something is going on."

She replied: "I told you as I told my kinsmen when we married that I meant to be my own mistress in all matters which concern myself; that is why I do not spare your money. Or is there anything more than this that you wish to speak about with me? Do you accuse me of anything shameful?"

He said: "I am not without my suspicions that you are keeping some man whom you prefer to me."

"I do not know," she said, "that there would be very much in that; and yet of a surety there is no truth in what you say. I will not speak with you alone if you bring such improper accusations against me."

He dropped the subject for the time. She and Thorsteinn continued to carry on as before, and were not very heedful of the talk of evil-minded people; they relied upon her wits and her popularity. They were often sitting together and diverting themselves.

One evening when they were sitting in an upper room in which her treasures were kept she asked Thorsteinn to sing something, and thinking that her husband was as usual sitting at drink she fastened the door. When he had sung for a time there was a banging at the door, and some one called to them to open it. It was her husband with a number of his followers. The lady had opened a large chest to show Thorsteinn the treasures. When she knew who was outside she refused to open the door, and said to Thorsteinn: "Quickly! Jump into the chest and keep very quiet."

He did so. She locked the chest and sat upon it. Her husband then entered, having forced his way in. She said:

"What are you coming here for with all this uproar? Are there robbers after you?"

He said: "Now it is well that you yourself give proof of what you are. Where is the man who was letting his voice run on so grandly? No doubt you think his voice is better than mine."

"No man is a fool if he keeps silence," she said; "that applies to you. You think yourself very cunning, and would like to fasten your lies on to me, as in this case. Well, if you have spoken the truth, find the man. He will not escape through the walls or the roof."

He searched all through the room and found nothing.

"Why don't you take him," she said, "if you are so certain?"

He was silent and knew not how he could have been deceived. He asked his men whether they had not heard what he heard, but when they saw that the lady was displeased there was nothing to be got out of them; they said that one was often mistaken about sounds. He then went away, not doubting that he knew the truth, though he could not find the man. After that he ceased for some time to pry into his wife's concerns.

On another occasion, much later, Thorsteinn and Spes were sitting in a tiring-room where dresses were kept which belonged to them, both made up and in the piece. She showed many of the cloths to Thorsteinn and spread them out. When they were least expecting it her husband came up with a troop of men and broke into the room. While they were forcing their way in she covered Thorsteinn up with a bundle of clothes and leaned against the heap when they entered.

"Do you again deny," he said, "that there was a man here with you? There are those present here now who saw you both."

She told him not to be so violent. "You will not fail to catch him now," she said. "Only leave me in peace and do not push me about."

They searched the room, but finding nothing had to give it up.

"It is always good to have better proofs than people suppose. It was only to be expected that you would not find what was not there. Now, my husband, will you admit your folly and free me from this slanderous accusation?"

"By no means will I free you," he said, "for I know that what I have accused you of is true, and it will cost you an effort to free yourself of the charge."

She said she was quite ready to do that, and therewith they parted.

After this Thorsteinn remained entirely with the Varangians. Men say that he acted by the advice of Harald the son of Sigurd, and it is thought that they would not have got out of it as they did if they had not made use of him and his wits.

After a time Sigurd gave out that he was about to go abroad on some business. His wife did not try to dissuade him. When he was gone Thorsteinn came to Spes and they were always together. Her house was built on the very edge of the sea and there were some of the rooms under which the sea flowed.

Here it was that Spes and Thorsteinn always sat. There was a small trap-door in the floor, known to no one but these two, and it was kept open in case of its being wanted in a hurry.

Sigurd, it must be told, did not go away, but concealed himself so as to be able to watch his wife's doings. One evening when they were sitting unconcernedly in the room over the sea and enjoying themselves, in came her husband with a party of men, taking them by surprise. He had taken some of the men to the window of the room that they might see whether it was not as he had said. They all said that he had spoken truly, and that it must have been so too on the former occasions. Then they rushed into the room.

On hearing the noise Spes said to Thorsteinn: "You must go down here whatever it costs. Give me some sign that you have got away from the house."

He promised that he would, and descended through the floor. The lady closed the trap-door with her foot, and it fell back into its place so that no one could see any mark of the floor having been touched. Sigurd entered the room with his men, searched, and of course found nothing. The room was uninhabited and there was no furniture in it, but only the bare floor and a bed, on which the lady was sitting and twirling her fingers. She paid little attention to them and seemed as if their business did not concern her. Sigurd thought it altogether ridiculous and asked his followers if they had not seen the man. They declared that they had seen him most assuredly.

The lady said: "Now we may say as the proverb has it: All good things are in threes. This is your case, Sigurd. Three times you have disturbed me, if I remember rightly; and now are you any the wiser than you were in the beginning?"

"This time I am not alone to tell the story," he said. "For all that you will have to clear yourself, for on no terms will I allow your shameful deeds to go unpunished."

"It seems," she said, "that you require the very thing which I would myself propose. It will please me well to show the falsehood of this accusation, which has been so thoroughly aired that I shall be disgraced if I cannot refute it."

"At the same time," he said, "you will have to deny that you have expended my money and my property."

She replied: "At the time when I clear myself I will refute all the matters which you brought against me, and you may consider how it will all end. I mean to go at once, to-morrow morning, before the bishop that he may grant me full compurgation from this charge."

Her husband was satisfied with this and went away with his men.

In the meantime Thorsteinn had swum away from the house and landed at a convenient place, where he got a firebrand and held it aloft so that it could be seen from the lady's house. She stayed long outside in the evening and the night, for she was anxious to know whether Thorsteinn had reached the land. When she saw the light she knew that he had landed, for that was the signal which they had agreed upon.

The next morning Spes proposed to her husband that they should speak with the bishop on their matter. This he was quite ready to do, so they went before the bishop and Sigurd repeated his accusation. The bishop asked whether she had ever been accused of misbehaviour before, but nobody had heard of such a thing. Then he asked upon what evidence this charge was brought against her, and Sigurd produced the men who had seen her sitting in a room with the door locked and a man with her. Her husband said that this was ground enough for supposing that the man meant to seduce her.

The bishop said that she might very well purge herself from this accusation if she so desired. She replied that she desired it very much. "I hope," she said, "that I shall have many women to swear for me on this charge."

The form of the oath which she was to swear was then communicated to her and the day for the compurgation fixed. She returned home and was quite happy. She and Thorsteinn met and laid their plans.

Chapter LXXXIX
The Ordeal

The day now arrived when Spes was to make oath. She invited all her friends and relations, and appeared in the finest clothes that she possessed, with many a fine lady in her train. It was raining heavily and the roads were flooded; on the way to the church there was a swamp to be passed. When Spes came with her company to the swamp there was a great crowd on the high road, and a multitude of poor people asking for alms, for all who knew her thought it a duty to give her a greeting and wish her well because of the kindnesses which they had often received from her.

Amongst these poor people there was a beggar very large of stature and with a long beard. The women halted at the swamp; being people of high rank they did not like to cross the dirty slough. The big beggar, seeing that Spes was better dressed than the other ladies, said to her: "Good lady, have the condescension to allow me to carry you over the swamp. It is the duty of us gaberlunzies to serve you in whatever way we can."

"How can you carry me," she said, "when you can scarcely carry yourself?"

"Nevertheless, it would be a great condescension. I cannot offer you more than I have, and you will prosper the better in other things for having had no pride with a poor man."

"Know then for a surety," she said, "that if you carry me not properly the skin shall be flayed from your back."

"Gladly will I venture upon that," he said, and waded out into the stream. She pretended to dislike very much being carried by him; nevertheless, she got upon his back. He staggered along very slowly, using two crutches, and when they reached the middle he was reeling in every direction. She told him to pull himself together. "If you drop me here," she said, "it shall be the worst journey that you ever made."

The poor wretch gathered up all his strength and still went on. By dint of a valiant effort he had all but reached the shore when he struck his foot against something and fell forwards, projecting her on to the bank while he himself fell into the mire up to his armpits. There as he lay he put out his hands, not on her clothes, but on her legs. She sprang up cursing and said she always suffered ill from low vagabonds. "It would only be right that you should have a good beating," she said, "were I not ashamed to beat such a miserable creature as you are."

He said: "Unequal is the lot of man. I thought to earn some benefit and to receive alms from you, and you only give me abuse and insult without any reward." And he pretended to be very much disgusted. Many felt pity for him, but she said he was a very cunning rascal. When they all began to beg for him she took out her purse, wherein was many a golden penny. She shook out the money, saying: "Take that, fellow! It would not be right that you should go unpaid for all my scoldings. You are now paid for what you have done."

He gathered up the money and thanked her for her liberality. Spes then went to the church, which was full of people. Sigurd proceeded with energy and told her to clear herself of the charge which he had brought against her.

"I pay no heed to your accusation," she said; "but I want to know what man it was whom you pretend to have seen in the room with me, because there is always some proper man near me; there is nothing to be ashamed of in that. But this I will swear, that to no man have I given money and that by no man has my body been defiled excepting by my husband and by that beggar, who put his muddy hands upon my leg to-day when I was carried over the ditch."

Many then were satisfied and declared that her oath was perfectly good and that she was in no way disgraced by a man having touched her unwittingly. She said she had to tell the story just as it happened, and then she swore the oath in the words appointed for her. Many said that she would be observing the saying that: Nothing should be omitted from an oath. But she replied that wise men would hold that there was no cause for suspicion. Then her relations began to talk with her and said that it was a great insult to a woman of high birth that such lies should be told about her and go unpunished, for they said it was an offence punishable with death if a woman were proved to have been unfaithful to her husband. So Spes asked he bishop to divorce her from Sigurd, saying that she would not endure the lies which he had told. Her kinsmen supported her, and with their help her request was granted. Sigurd got little of the property and had to leave the country. So it happened as usual that the weaker had to bow, nor could he accomplish anything although the right was on his side. Spes took all the money and was held in high esteem, but when men came to consider her oath they thought it was not altogether above suspicion, and they concluded that very skilful men had composed the Latin formula for her. They ferreted out that the beggar who carried her was Thorsteinn Dromund. But Sigurd got no redress.

Chapter XC
Thorsteinn And Spes Return To Norway

While the affair was being talked about Thorsteinn Dromund remained with the Varangians, where he was held in such high estimation that his prowess was considered to be beyond that of nearly every man who had come to them. Especially Harald the son of Sigurd did him honour, and claimed kinship with him; it was supposed to have been by his advice that Thorsteinn had acted.

Soon after Sigurd was driven from the country Thorsteinn proposed marriage to Spes; she was quite agreeable, but referred it to her kinsmen. There were family meetings and all agreed that she herself ought to decide. Matters were settled between them; their union was most prosperous and they had plenty of money. Thorsteinn was considered lucky to have got out of his difficulties in such a way. After they had lived together for two years in Constantinople, Thorsteinn told her that he would like to visit his property once more in Norway. She said he should do as he pleased, and he then sold his property so as to have some ready money. They left the country with a good company of followers and sailed all the way to Norway. Thorsteinn's kinsmen welcomed them both, and soon saw that Spes was both generous and noble; accordingly she quickly became very popular. They had three children, and remained on their property very well contented with their condition.

The king of Norway was at that time Magnus the Good. Thorsteinn soon went to meet him, and was well received because of the fame which he had earned through having avenged Grettir the Strong. Scarcely an example was known of a man from Iceland having been avenged in Constantinople, excepting Grettir the son of Asmund. It is said that Thorsteinn entered his bodyguard. Thorsteinn remained nine years in Norway, both he and his wife being in high honour. After that King Harald the son of Sigurd returned from Constantinople, and King Magnus gave him the half of Norway. Both kings were together in Norway for a time. After Magnus's death some who had been his friends were less contented, for he was beloved of all, but Harald was not easy to get on with, since he was hard and severe. Thorsteinn Dromund then began to grow old, but was still very vigorous. Sixteen winters had now passed since the death of Grettir.

Chapter XCI
Absolution In Rome

There were many who urged Thorsteinn to visit King Harald and become his man, but he would not. Spes said to him: "I would not, Thorsteinn, that you go to Harald, for a larger debt remains unpaid to another King, whereto we must now turn our thoughts. Our youth is now passed; we are both becoming old, and we have lived more after our desires than after Christian doctrine or regard for righteousness. Now I know that neither kinsmen nor wealth may pay this debt if we pay it not ourselves. I would therefore that we now change our way of life and leave the country to betake ourselves to Pafagard. I have hope that so I shall be absolved from my sin." Thorsteinn answered: "The matter of which you speak is as well known to me as it is to you. It is right that you should rule now, and most seemly, since you allowed me to rule when our matter was much less hopeful. And so shall it be now in all that you say."

This resolve of theirs took men by surprise. Thorsteinn was then two years past of sixty-five, but still vigorous in all that he undertook. He summoned all his kinsmen and connections to him and told them his plans. The wiser men approved of his resolve, while holding his departure a great misfortune for themselves. Thorsteinn said there was no certainty of his return. He said:

"I wish now to thank you all for the care of my goods which you took while I was absent. Now I ask you to take over my children along with my property, and to bring them up in your own ways; for I am now come to such an age that even if I live there is much doubt about whether I shall return. Manage all that I leave behind as if I should never return to Norway."

The men answered that matters would be more easily managed if his wife remained to look after them.

She answered: "I left my own country and came from Mikligard with Thorsteinn, I bade farewell to my kinsmen and my possessions, because I wished that one fate should befall us both. And now it has seemed pleasant to me here, but no desire have I to remain in Norway or in these Northern lands after he has departed. There has always been goodwill between us and no dissension. Now we must both depart together; for we ourselves know best about many things which have happened since we first met."

When they had thus dealt with their own condition, Thorsteinn appointed certain impartial men to divide his property in two parts. Thorsteinn's kinsmen took over the half which was to go to the children, and brought them up with their father's relations. They became in time men of the utmost valour, and a large posterity in the Vik is sprung from them. Thorsteinn and Spes divided their share, giving some to the church for the good of their souls and keeping some for themselves. So they set off for Rome, bearing the good wishes of many with them.

Chapter XCII
The End Of Thorsteinn And Spes

They travelled then the whole way to Rome, and appeared before him who was appointed to hear confessions. They related truly all that had happened, all the cunning tricks wherewith they had achieved their union. They submitted with humility to the penances laid upon them, and by reason of their having voluntarily turned their hearts to desire absolution from their sins, without any pressure from the elders of the church, their penance was lightened so far as it was possible, and they were gently admonished to arrange their lives with wisdom for the well-being of their souls, and, after receiving absolution in full, to live henceforward in purity. They were declared to have acted wisely and well.

Then the lady Spes said: "Now, I think it has gone well; and now we have not suffered only misfortune together. It may be that foolish men will follow the example of our former lives. Let us now end in such way that we may be an example to the good. We will come to an agreement with some men skilled in building to erect for each of us a stone retreat, thus may we atone for all the offences which we have committed against God."

So Thorsteinn advanced money to stone-masons and such other persons as might be needed, that they might not be without the means of subsistence. When these works were completed and all matters were settled, a fitting time was chosen for them to part company with each other, each to live alone, in order more surely to partake of the eternal life in another world. They remained each in their own retreat, living as long as it pleased God to spare them, and thus ending their lives.

Most men consider Thorsteinn Dromund and Spes to have been most fortunate in escaping from the difficulties which they had fallen into. None of their children or posterity are mentioned as having come to Iceland.

Chapter XCIII
The Testimony Of Sturla The Lawman

Sturla the Lawman has declared that no outlaw was ever so distinguished as Grettir the Strong. For this he assigns three reasons. First, that he was the cleverest, inasmuch as he was the longest time an outlaw of any man without ever being captured, so long as he was sound in health. Secondly, that he was the strongest man in the land of his age, and better able than any other to deal with spectres and goblins. Thirdly, that his death was avenged in Constantinople, a thing which had never happened to any other Icelander.

Further, he says that Thorsteinn Dromund was a man who had great luck in the latter part of his life.

Here endeth the story of Grettir the son of Asmund.

The Life and Death of Kormac the Skald

Kormac's Fore-Elders

Harald Fairhair was king of Norway when this tale begins. There was a chief in the kingdom in those days and his name was Kormac; one of the Vik-folk by kindred, a great man of high birth. He was the mightiest of champions, and had been with King Harald in many battles.

He had a son called Ogmund, a very hopeful lad; big and sturdy even as a child; who when he was grown of age and come to his full strength, took to sea-roving in summer and served in the king's household in winter. So he earned for himself a good name and great riches.

One summer he went roving about the British Isles and there he fell in with a man named Asmund Ashenside, who also was a great champion and had worsted many vikings and men of war. These two heard tell of one another and challenges passed between them. They came together and fought. Asmund had the greater following, but he withheld some of his men from the battle: and so for the length of four days they fought, until many of Asmund's people were fallen, and at last he himself fled. Ogmund won the victory and came home again with wealth and worship.

His father said that he could get no greater glory in war, -- "And now," said he, "I will find thee a wife. What sayest thou to Helga, daughter of Earl Frodi?"

"So be it," said Ogmund.

Upon this they set off to Earl Frodi's house, and were welcomed with all honour. They made known their errand, and he took it kindly, although he feared that the fight with Asmund was likely to bring trouble. Nevertheless this match was made, and then they went their ways home. A feast was got ready for the wedding and to that feast a very great company came together.

Helga the daughter of Earl Frodi had a nurse that was a wise woman, and she went with her. Now Asmund the viking heard of this marriage, and set out to meet Ogmund. He bade him fight, and Ogmund agreed.

Helga's nurse used to touch men when they went to fight: so she did with Ogmund before he set out from home, and told him that he would not be hurt much.

Then they both went to the fighting holm and fought. The viking laid bare his side, but the sword would not bite upon it. Then Ogmund whirled about his sword swiftly and shifted it from hand to hand, and hewed Asmund's leg from under him: and three marks of gold he took to let him go with his life.

How Kormac Was Born and Bred

About this time King Harald Fairhair died, and Eric Bloodaxe reigned in his stead. Ogmund would have no friendship with Eric, nor with Gunnhild, and made ready his ship for Iceland.

Nor Ogmund and Helga had a son called Frodi: but when the ship was nearly ready, Helga took a sickness and died; and so did their son Frodi.

After that, they sailed to sea. When they were near the land, Ogmund cast overboard his high-seat-pillars; and where the high-seat-pillars had already been washed ashore, there they cast anchor, and landed in Midfiord.

At this time Skeggi of Midfiord ruled the countryside. He came riding toward them and bade them welcome into the firth, and gave them the pick of the land: which Ogmund took, and began to mark out ground for a house. Now it was a belief of theirs that as the measuring went, so would the luck go: if the measuring-wand seemed to grow less when they tried it again and again, so would that house's luck grow less: and if it grew greater, so would the luck be. This time the measure always grew less, though they tried it three times over.

So Ogmund built him a house on the sandhills, and lived there ever after. He married Dalla, the daughter of Onund the Seer, and their sons were Thorgils and

Kormac. Kormac was dark-haired, with a curly lock upon his forehead: he was bright of blee and somewhat like his mother, big and strong, and his mood was rash and hasty. Thorgils was quiet and easy to deal with.

When the brothers were grown up, Ogmund died; and Dalla kept house with her sons. Thorgils worked the farm, under the eye of Midfiord-Skeggi.

How Kormac Fell In Love

There was a man named Thorkel lived at Tunga (Tongue). He was a wedded man, and had a daughter called Steingerd who was fostered in Gnupsdal (Knipedale).

Now it was one autumn that a whale came ashore at Vatnsnes (Watsness), and it belonged to the brothers, Dalla's sons. Thorgils asked Kormac would he rather go shepherding on the fell, or work at the whale. He chose to fare on the fell with the house-carles.

Tosti, the foreman, it was should be master of the sheep-gathering: so he and Kormac went together until they came to Gnupsdal. It was night: there was a great hall, and fires for men to sit at.

That evening Steingerd came out of her bower, and a maid with her. Said the maid, "Steingerd mine, let us look at the guests."

"Nay," she said, "no need": and yet went to the door, and stepped on the threshold, and spied across the gate. Now there was a space between the wicker and the threshold, and her feet showed through. Kormac saw that, and made this song:

> "At the door of my soul she is standing,
> So sweet in the gleam of her garment:
> Her footfall awakens a fury,
> A fierceness of love that I knew not,
> Those feet of a wench in her wimple,
> Their weird is my sorrow and troubling,
> --Or naught may my knowledge avail me—
> Both now and for aye to endure."

Then Steingerd knew she was seen. She turned aside into a corner where the likeness of Hagbard was carved on the wall, and peeped under Hagbard's beard. Then the firelight shone upon her face.

"Kormac," said Tosti, "seest eyes out yonder by that head of Hagbard?"

Kormac answered in song: --

"There breaks on me, burning upon me,
A blaze from the cheeks of a maiden,
—I laugh not to look on the vision—
In the light of the hall by the doorway.
So sweet and so slender I deem her,
Though I spy bug a glimpse of an ankle
By the threshold -- and through me there flashes
A thrill that shall age never more."

And then he made another song:

"The moon of her brow, it is beaming
'Neath the bright-litten heaven of her forehead:
So she gleams in her white robe, and gazes
With a glance that is keen as the falcon's.
But the star that is shining upon me
What spell shall it work by its witchcraft?
Ah, that moon of her brow shall be mighty
With mischief to her—and to me?"

Said Tosti, "She is fairly staring at thee!" — And he answered:

"She's a ring-bedight oak of the ale-cup,
And her eyes never left me unhaunted.
The strife in my heart I could hide not,
For I hold myself bound in her bondage.
O gay in her necklet, and gainer
In the game that wins hearts on her chessboard,
When she looked at me long from the doorway
Where the likeness of Hagbard is carved."

Then the girls went into the hall, and sat down. He heard what they said about his looks -- the maid, that he was black and ugly, and Steingerd, that he was handsome and everyway as best could be -- "There is only one blemish," said she, "his hair is tufted on his forehead:" — and he said:

"One flaw in my features she noted
—With the flame of the wave she was gleaming
All white in the wane of the twilight—
And that one was no hideous blemish.
So highborn, so haughty a lady
—I should have such a dame to befriend me:

But she trows me uncouth for a trifle,
For a tuft in the hair on my brow!"

Said the maid, "Black are his eyes, sister, and that becomes him not." Kormac heard her, and said in verse:

"Yes, black are the eyes that I bring ye,
O brave in your jewels, and dainty.
But a draggle-tail, dirty-foot slattern
Would dub me ill-favoured and sallow.
Nay, many a maiden has loved me,
Thou may of the glittering armlet:
For I've tricks of the tongue to beguile them
And turn them from handsomer lads."

At this house they spent the night. In the morning when Kormac rose up, he went to a trough and washed himself; then he went into the ladies' bower and saw nobody there, but heard folk talking in the inner room, and he turned and entered. There was Steingerd, and women with her.

Said the maid to Steingerd, "There comes thy bonny man, Steingerd."

"Well, and a fine-looking lad he is," said she.

Now she was combing her hair, and Kormac asked her, "Wilt thou give me leave?"

She reached out her comb for him to handle it. She had the finest hair of any woman. Said the maid, "Ye would give a deal for a wife with hair like Steingerd's, or such eyes!"

He answered:

"One eye of the far of the ale-horn
Looking out of a form so bewitching,
Would a bridegroom count money to buy it
He must bring for it ransom three hundred.
The curls that she combs of a morning,
White-clothed in fair linen and spotless,
They enhance the bright hoard of her value,
Five hundred might barely redeem them!"

Said the maid, "It's give and take with the two of ye! But thou'lt put a big price upon the whole of her!" He answered:

"The tree of my treasure and longing,
It would take this whole Iceland to win her:
She is dearer than far-away Denmark,
And the doughty domain of the Hun-folk.

With the gold she is combing, I count her
More costly than England could ransom:
So witty, so wealthy, my lady
Is worth them-- and Ireland beside!"

Then Tosti came in, and called Kormac out to some work or other; but he said:

"Take swift-footed steel for thy tiding,
Ay, and stint not the lash to him, Tosti:
On the desolate downs ye may wander
And drive him along till he weary.
I care not o'er mountain and moorland
The murrey-brown weathers to follow,
Far liefer, I'd linger the morning
In long, cosy chatter with Steingerd."

Tosti said he would find it a merrier game, and went off; so Kormac sat down to chess, and right gay he was. Steingerd said he talked better than folk told of; and he sat there all the day; and then he made this song:

" 'Tis the dart that adorneth her tresses,
The deep, dewy grass of her forehead.
So kind to my keeping she gave it,
That good comb I shall ever remember!
A stranger was I when I sought her
-- Sweet stem with the dragon's hoard shining — "
With gold like the sea-dazzle gleaming —
The girl I shall never forget."

Tosti came off the fell and they fared home. After that Kormac used to go to Gnupsdal often to see Steingerd: and he asked his mother to make him good clothes, so that Steingerd might like him the most that could be. Dalla said there was a mighty great difference betwixt them, and it was far from certain to end happily if Thorkel at Tunga got to know.

How Kormac Liked Black-Puddings

W ell Thorkel soon heard what was going forward, and thought it would turn out to his own shame and his daughter's if Kormac would not pledge himself to take her or leave her. So he sent for Steingerd, and she went home.

Thorkel had a man called Narfi, a noisy, foolish fellow, boastful, and yet of little account. Said he to Thorkel, "If Kormac's coming likes thee not, I can soon settle it."

"Very well," says Thorkel.

Now, in the autumn, Narfi's work it was to slaughter the sheep. Once, when Kormac came to Tunga, he saw Steingerd in the kitchen. Narfi stood by the kettle, and when they had finished the boiling, he took up a black-pudding and thrust it under Kormac's nose, crying:

> "Kormac, how would ye relish one?
> Kettle-worms I call them."

To which he answered:

> "Black-puddings boiled, quoth Ogmund's son,
> Are a dainty-- fair befall them!"

And in the evening when Kormac made ready to go home he saw Narfi, and bethought him of those churlish words. "I think, Narfi," said he, "I am more like to knock thee down, than thou to rule my coming and going." And with that struck him an axe- hammer-blow, saying:

> "Why foul with thy clowning and folly,
> The food that is dressed for thy betters?
> Thou blundering archer, what ails thee
> To be aiming thy insults at me?"

And he made another song about:

> "He asked me, the clavering cowherd
> If I cared for — what was it he called them?--
> The worms of the kettle. I warrant
> He'll be wiping his eyes by the hearth-stone.
> I deem that yon knave of the dunghill

Who dabbles the muck on the meadow
—Yon rook in his mud-spattered raiment—
Got a rap for his noise—like a dog."

They Waylay Kormac: And The Witch Curses Him

There was a woman named Thorveig, and she knew a deal too much. She lived at Steins-stadir (Stonestead) in Midfiord, and had two sons; the elder was Odd, and the younger Gudmund. They were great braggarts both of them.

This Odd often came to see Thorkel at Tunga, and used to sit and talk with Steingerd. Thorkel made a great show of friendship with the brothers, and egged them on to waylay Kormac. Odd said it was no more than he could do.

So one day when Kormac came to Tunga, Steingerd was in the parlour and sat on the dais. Thorveig's sons sat in the room, ready to fall upon him when he came in; and Thorkel had put a drawn sword on one side of the door, and on the other side Narfi had put a scythe in its shaft. When Kormac came to the hall-door the scythe fell down and met the sword, and broke a great notch in it. Out came Thorkel and began to upbraid Kormac for a rascal, and got fairly wild with his talk: then flung into the parlour and bade Steingerd out of it. Forth they went by another door, and he locked her into an outhouse, saying that Kormac and she would never meet again.

Kormac went in: and he came quicker than folk thought for, and they were taken aback. He looked about, and no Steingerd: but he saw the brothers whetting their weapons: so he turned on his heel and went, saying:

"The weapon that mows in the meadow
It met with the gay painted buckler,
When I came to encounter a goddess
Who carries the beaker of wine.
Beware! for I warn you of evil
When warriors threaten me mischief.
It shall not be for nought that I pour ye
The newly mixed mead of the gods."

And when he could find Steingerd nowhere, he made this song:

"She has gone, with the glitter of ocean
Agleam on her wrist and her bosom,
And my heart follows hard on her footsteps,
For the hall is in darkness without her.
I have gazed, but my glances can pierce not
The gloom of the desolate dwelling;
And fierce is my longing to find her,
The fair one who only can heal me."

After a while he came to the outhouse where Steingerd was, and burst it open and had talk with her.

"This is madness," cried she, "to come talking with me; for Thorveig's sons are meant to have thy head."

But he answered:

"There wait they within that would snare me;
There whet they their swords for my slaying.
My bane they shall be not, the cowards,
The brood of the churl and the carline.
Let the twain of them find me and fight me
In the field, without shelter to shield them,
And ewes of the sheep should be surer
To shorten the days of the wolf."

So he sat there all day. By that time Thorkel saw that the plan he had made was come to nothing; and he bade the sons of Thorveig waylay Kormac in a dale near his garth. "Narfi shall go with ye two," said he; "but I will stay at home, and bring you help if need be."

In the evening Kormac set out, and when he came to the dale, he saw three men, and said in verse:

"There sit they in hiding to stay me
From the sight of my queen of the jewels:
But rude will their task be to reave me
From the roof of my bounteous lady.
The fainer the hatred they harbour
For him that is free of her doorway,
The fainer my love and my longing
For the lass that is sweeter than samphire."

Then leaped up Thorveig's sons, and fought Kormac for a time: Narfi the while skulked and dodged behind them. Thorkel saw from his house that they were getting but slowly forward, and he took his weapons. In that nick of time Steingerd came out and saw what her father meant. She laid hold on his hands, and he got no nearer to help the brothers. In the end Odd fell, and Gudmund was so wounded that he died afterwards. Thorkel saw to them, and Kormac went home.

A little after this Kormac went to Thorveig and said he would have her no longer live there at the firth. "Thou shalt flit and go thy way at such a time," said he, "and I will give no blood-money for thy sons."

Thorveig answered, "It is like enough ye can hunt me out of the countryside, and leave my sons unatoned. But this way I'll reward thee. Never shalt thou have Steingerd."

Said Kormac, "That's not for thee to make or to mar, thou wicked old hag!"

Kormac Wins His Bride and Loses Her

After this, Kormac went to see Steingerd the same as ever: and once when they talked over these doings she said no ill of them: whereupon he made this song:

"There sat they in hiding to slay me
From the sight of my bride and my darling:
But weak were the feet of my foemen
When we fought on the island of weapons.
And the rush of the mightiest rivers
Shall race from the shore to the mountains
Or ever I leave thee, my lady,
And the love that I feast on to-day!"

"Say no such big words about it," answered she; "Many a thing may stand in the road."

Upon which he said:

"O sweet in the sheen of thy raiment,
The sight of thy beauty is gladdening!
What man that goes marching to battle,
What mate wouldst thou choose to be thine?"

And she answered:

"O giver of gold, O ring-breaker,
If the gods and the high fates befriend me,
I'd pledge me to Frodi's blithe brother
And bind him that he should be mine."

Then she told him to make friends with her father and get her in marriage. So for her sake Kormac gave Thorkel good gifts. Afterwards many people had their say in the matter; but in the end it came to this -- that he asked for her, and she was pledged to him, and the wedding was fixed: and so all was quiet for a while.

Then they had words. There was some falling-out about settlements. It came to such a pass that after everything was ready, Kormac began to cool off. But the real reason was, that Thorveig had bewitched him so that they should never have one another.

Thorkel at Tunga had a grown-up son, called Thorkel and by-named Tooth-gnasher. He had been abroad some time, but this summer he came home and stayed with his father.

Kormac never came to the wedding at the time it was fixed, and the hour passed by. This the kinsfolk of Steingerd thought a slight, deeming that he had broken off the match; and they had much talk about it.

How Steingerd Was Married To Somebody Else

Bersi lived in the land of Saurbae, a rich man and a good fellow: he was well to the fore, a fighter, and a champion at the holmgang. He had been married to Finna the Fair: but she was dead: Asmund was their son, young in years and early ripe. Helga was the sister of Bersi: she was unmarried, but a fine woman and a pushing one, and she kept house for Bersi after Finna died.

At the farm called Muli (the Mull) lived Thord Arndisarson: he was wedded to Thordis, sister of Bork the Stout. They had two sons who were both younger than Asmund the son of Bersi.

There was also a man with Vali. His farm was named Vali's stead, and it stood on the way to Hrutafiord.

Now Thorveig the spaewife went to see Holmgang Bersi and told him her trouble. She said that Kormac forbade her staying in Midfiord: so Bersi bought land for her west of the firth, and she lived there for a long time afterwards.

Once when Thorkel at Tunga and his son were talking about Kormac's breach of faith and deemed that it should be avenged, Narfi said, "I see a plan that will do. Let us go to the west- country with plenty of goods and gear, and come to Bersi in

Saurbae. He is wifeless. Let us entangle him in the matter. He would be a great help to us."

That counsel they took. They journeyed to Saurbae, and Bersi welcomed them. In the evening they talked of nothing but weddings. Narfi up and said there was no match so good as Steingerd, "And a deal of folk say, Bersi, that she would suit thee."

"I have heard tell," he answered, "that there will be a rift in the road, though the match is a good one."

"If it's Kormac men fear," cried Narfi, "there is no need; for he is clean out of the way."

When Bersi heard that, he opened the matter to Thorkel Toothgnasher, and asked for Steingerd. Thorkel made a good answer, and pledged his sister to him.

So they rode north, eighteen in all, for the wedding. There was a man named Vigi lived at Holm, a big man and strong of his hands, a warlock, and Bersi's kinsman. He went with them, and they thought he would be a good helper. Thord Arndisarson too went north with Bersi, and many others, all picked men.

When they came to Thorkel's, they set about the wedding at once, so that no news of it might get out through the countryside: but all this was sore against Steingerd's will.

Now Vigi the warlock knew every man's affairs who came to the steading or left it. He sat outmost in the chamber, and slept by the hall door.

Steingerd sent for Narfi, and when they met she said, "I wish thee, kinsman, to tell Kormac the business they are about: I wish thee to take this message to him."

So he set out secretly; but when he was a gone a little way Vigi came after, and bade him creep home and hatch no plots. They went back together, and so the night passed.

Next morning Narfi started forth again; but before he had gone so far as on the evening, Vigi beset him, and drove him back without mercy.

When the wedding was ended they made ready for their journey. Steingerd took her gold and jewels, and they rode towards Hrutafiord, going rather slowly. When they were off, Narfi set out and came to Mel. Kormac was building a wall, and hammering it with a mallet. Narfi rode up, with his shield and sword, and carried on strangely, rolling his eyes about like a hunted beast. Some men were up on the wall with Kormac when he came, and his horse shied at them. Said Kormac, "What news, Narfi? What folk were with you last night?"

"Small tidings, but we had guests enough," answered he.

"Who were the guests?"

"There was Holmgang Bersi, with seventeen more to sit at his wedding."

"Who was the bride?"

"Bersi wed Steingerd Thorkel's daughter," said Narfi. "When they were gone she sent me here to tell thee the news."

"Thou hast never a word but ill," said Kormac, and leapt upon him and struck at the shield: and as it slipped aside he was smitten on the breast and fell from his horse; and the horse ran away with the shield hanging to it.

Kormac's brother Thorgils said this was too much. "It serves him right," cried Kormac. And when Narfi woke out of his swoon they got speech of him.

Thorgils asked, "What manner of men were at the wedding?"

Narfi told him.

"Did Steingerd know this before?"

"Not till the very evening they came," answered he; and then told of his dealings with Vigi, saying that Kormac would find it easier to whistle on Steingerd's tracks and go on a fool's errand than to fight Bersi. Then said Kormac:

"Now see to thy safety henceforward,
And stick to thy horse and thy buckler;
Or this mallet of mine, I can tell thee,
Will meet with thine ear of a surety.
Now say no more stories of feasting,
Though seven in a day thou couldst tell of,
Or bumps thou shalt comb on thy brainpan,
Thou that breakest the howes of the dead.

Thorgils asked about the settlements between Bersi and Steingerd. Her kinsmen, said Narfi, were now quit of all farther trouble about that business, however it might turn out; but her father and brother would be answerable for the wedding.

How Kormac Chased Bersi And His Bride

Kormac took his horse and weapons and saddle-gear.

"What now, brother?" asked Thorgils.

He answered:

"My bride, my betrothed has been stolen,
And Bersi the raider has robbed me.
I who offer the song-cup of Odin—
Who else? -- should be riding beside her.
She loved me—no lord of them better:
I have lost her—for me she is weeping:
The dear, dainty darling that kissed me,
For day upon day of delight."

Said Thorgils, "A risky errand is this, for Bersi will get home before you catch him. And yet I will go with thee."

Kormac said he would away and bide for no man. He leapt on his horse forthwith, and galloped as hard as he could. Thorgils made haste to gather men -- they were eighteen in all -- and came up with Kormac on the hause that leads to Hrutafiord, for he had foundered his horse. So they turned to Thorveig the spaewife's farmsteading, and found that Bersi was gone aboard her boat.

She had said to Bersi, "I wish thee to take a little gift from me, and good luck follow it."

This was a target bound with iron; and she said she reckoned Bersi would hardly be hurt if he carried it to shield him, "but it is little worth beside this steading thou hast given me." He thanked her for the gift, and so they parted. Then she got men to scuttle all the boats on the shore, because she knew beforehand that Kormac and his folk were coming.

When they came and asked her for a boat, she said she would do them no kindness without payment; "Here is a rotten boat in the boathouse which I would lend for half a mark."

Thorgils said it would be in reason if she asked two ounces of silver. Such matters, said Kormac, should not stand in the way; but Thorgils said he would sooner ride all round the water-head. Nevertheless Kormac had his will, and they started in the boat; but they had scarcely put off from shore when it filled, and they had hard work to get back to the same spot.

"Thou shouldst pay dearly for this, thou wicked old hag," said Kormac, "and never be paid at all."

That was no mighty trick to play them, she said; and so Thorgils paid her the silver; about which Kormac made this song:

"I'm a tree that is tricked out in war-gear,
She, the trim rosy elf of the shuttle:
And I break into singing about her
Like the bat at the well, never ceasing.
With the dew-drops of Draupnir the golden
Full dearly folk buy them their blessings;
Then lay down three ounces and leave them
For the leaky old boat that we borrowed."

Bersi got hastily to horse, and rode homewards; and when Kormac saw that he must be left behind, he made this song:

"I tell you, the goddess who glitters
With gold on the perch of the falcon,
The bride that I trusted, by beauty,
From the bield of my hand has been taken.

On the boat she makes glad in its gliding
She is gone from me, reft from me, ravished!
O shame, that we linger to save her,
Too sweet for the prey of the raven!

They took their horses and rode round the head of the firth. They met Vali and asked about Bersi; he said that Bersi had come to Muli and gathered men to him, "A many men."

"Then we are too late," said Kormac, "if they have got men together."

Thorgils begged Kormac to let them turn back, saying there was little honour to be got; but Kormac said he must see Steingerd.

So Vali went with them and they came to Muli where Bersi was and many men with him. They spoke together. Kormac said that Bersi had betrayed him in carrying off Steingerd, "But now we would take the lady with us, and make him amends for his honour."

To this said Thord Arndisarson, "We will offer terms to Kormac, but the lady is in Bersi's hands."

"There is no hope that Steingerd will go with you," said Bersi; "but I offer my sister to Kormac in marriage, and I reckon he will be well wedded if take Helga."

"This is a good offer," said Thorgils; "let us think of it, brother."

But Kormac started back like a restive horse.

Of Another Witch, And Two Magic Swords

T here was a woman called Thordis—and a shrew she was—who lived at Spakonufell (Spaequean's-fell), in Skagastrand. She, having foresight of Kormac's goings, came that very day to Muli, and answered this matter on his behalf, saying, "Never give him yon false woman. She is a fool, and not fit for any pretty man. Woe will his mother be at such a fate for her lad!"

"Aroint thee, foul witch!" cried Thord. They should see, said he, that Helga would turn out fine. But Kormac answered, "Said it may be, for sooth it may be: I will never think of her."

"Woe to us, then," said Thorgils, "for listening to the words of yon fiend, and slighting this offer!"

Then spoke Kormac, "I bid thee, Bersi, to the holmgang within half a month, at Leidholm, in Middal."

Bersi said he would come, but Kormac should be the worse for his choice.

After this Kormac went about the steading to look for Steingerd. When he found her he said she had betrayed him in marrying another man.

"It was thou that made the first breach, Kormac," said she, "for this was none of my doing."

Then said he in verse:

"Thou sayest my faith has been forfeit,
O fair in thy glittering raiment;
But I wearied my steed and outwore it,
And for what but the love that bare thee?
O fainer by far was I, lady,
To founder my horse in the hunting —
Nay, I spared not the jade when I spurred it —
Than to see thee the bride of my foe."

After this Kormac and his men went home. When he told his mother how things had gone, "Little good," she said, "will thy luck do us. Ye have slighted a fine offer, and you have no chance against Bersi, for he is a great fighter and he has good weapons."

Now, Bersi owned the sword they call Whitting; a sharp sword it was, with a life-stone to it; and that sword he had carried in many a fray.

"Whether wilt thou have weapons to meet Whitting?" she asked. Kormac said he would have an axe both great and keen.

Dalla said he should see Skeggi of Midfiord and ask for the loan of his sword, Skofnung. So Kormac went to Reykir and told Skeggi how matters stood, asking him to lend Skofnung. Skeggi said he had no mind to lend it. Skofnung and Kormac, said he, would never agree: "It is cold and slow, and thou art hot and hasty."

Kormac rode away and liked it ill. He came home to Mel and told his mother that Skeggi would not lend the sword. Now Skeggi had the oversight of Dalla's affairs, and they were great friends; so she said, "He will lend the sword, though not all at once."

That was not what he wanted, answered Kormac -- "If he withhold it not from thee, while he does withhold it from me." Upon which she answered that he was a thwart lad.

A few days afterwards Dalla told him to go to Reykir. "He will lend thee the sword now," said she. So he sought Skeggi and asked for Skofnung.

"Hard wilt thou find it to handle," said Skeggi. "There is a pouch to it, and that thou shalt let be. Sun must not shine on the pommel of the hilt. Thou shalt not wear it until fighting is forward, and when ye come to the field, sit all alone and then draw it. Hold the edge toward thee, and blow on it. Then will a little worm creep from under the hilt. Then slope thou the sword over, and make it easy for that worm to creep back beneath the hilt."

"Here's a tale of tricks, thou warlock!" cried Kormac

"Nevertheless," answered Skeggi, "it will stand thee in good stead to know them."

So Kormac rode home and told his mother, saying that her will was of great avail with Skeggi. He showed the sword, and tried to draw it, but it would not leave the sheath.

"Thou are over wilful, my son," said she.

Then he set his feet against the hilts, and pulled until he tore the pouch off, at which Skofnung creaked and groaned, but never came out of the scabbard.

Well, the time wore on, and the day came. He rode away with fifteen men; Bersi also rode to the holm with as many. Kormac came there first, and told Thorgils that he would sit apart by himself. So he sat down and ungirt the sword.

Now, he never heeded whether the sun shone upon the hilt, for he had girt the sword on him outside his clothes. And when he tried to draw it he could not, until he set his feet upon the hilts. Then the little worm came, and was not rightly done by; and so the sword came groaning and creaking out of the scabbard, and the good luck of it was gone.

The Fight On Leidarholm

After that Kormac went to his men. Bersi and his party had come by that time, and many more to see the fight.

Kormac took up Bersi's target and cut at it, and sparks flew out.

Then a hide was taken and spread for them to stand on. Bersi spoke and said, "Thou, Kormac, hast challenged me to the holmgang; instead of that, I offer thee to fight in simple sword-play. Thou art a young man and little tried; the holmgang needs craft and cunning, but sword-play, man to man, is an easy game."

Kormac answered, "I should fight no better even so. I will run the risk, and stand on equal footing with thee, every way."

"As thou wilt," said Bersi.

It was the law of the holmgang that the hide should be five ells long, with loops at its corners. Into these should be driven certain pins with heads to them, called tjosnur. He who made it ready should go to the pins in such a manner that he could see sky between his legs, holding the lobes of his ears and speaking the forewords used in the rite called "The Sacrifice of the tjosnur." Three squares should be marked round the hide, each one foot broad. At the outermost corners of the squares should be four poles, called hazels; when this is done, it is a hazelled field. Each man should have three shields, and when they were cut up he must get upon the hide if he had given way from it before, and guard himself with his weapons alone thereafter. He who had been challenged should strike the first stroke. If one was wounded so that blood fell upon the hide, he should fight no longer. If either set one foot outside the hazel poles "he went on his heel," they said; but he "ran" if both feet were outside. His own man was to hold the shield before each of the fighters. The one who was wounded should pay three marks of silver to be set free.

So the hide was taken and spread under their feet. Thorgils held his brother's shield, and Thord Arndisarson that of Bersi. Bersi struck the first blow, and cleft Kormac's shield; Kormac struck at Bersi to the like peril. Each of them cut up and spoilt three shields of the other's. Then it was Kormac's turn. He struck at Bersi, who parried with Whitting. Skofnung cut the point off Whitting in front of the ridge. The sword-point flew upon Kormac's hand, and he was wounded in the thumb. The joint was cleft, and blood dropped upon the hide. Thereupon folk went between them and stayed the fight.

Then said Kormac, "This is a mean victory that Bersi has gained; it is only from my bad luck; and yet we must part."

He flung down his sword, and it met Bersi's target. A shard was broken out of Skofnung, and fire flew out of Thorveig's gift.

Bersi asked the money for release, Kormac said it would be paid; and so they parted.

The Songs That Were Made About The Fight

Steinar was the name of a man who was the son of Onund the Seer, and brother of Dalla, Kormac's mother. He was an unpeaceful man, and lived at Ellidi.

Thither rode Kormac from the holme, to see his kinsman, and told him of the fight, at which he was but ill pleased. Kormac said he meant to leave the country, - "And I want thee to take the money to Bersi."

"Thou art no bold man," said Steinar, "but the money shall be paid if need be." Kormac was there some nights; his hand swelled much, for it was not dressed.

After that meeting, Holmgang Bersi went to see his brother. Folk asked how the holmgang had gone, and when he told them they said that two bold men had struck small blows, and he had gained the victory only through Kormac's mishap. When Bersi met Steingerd, and she asked how it went, he made this verse:

"They call him, and truly they tell it,
A tree of the helmet right noble:
But the master of manhood must bring me

Three marks for his ransom and rescue.
Though stout in the storm of the bucklers
In the stress of the Valkyrie's tempest
He will bid me no more to the battle,
For the best of the struggle was ours."

Steinar and Kormac rode from Ellidi and passed through Saurbae. They saw men riding towards them, and yonder came Bersi. He greeted Kormac and asked how the wound was getting on. Kormac said it needed little to be healed.

"Wilt thou let me heal thee?" said Bersi; "though from me thou didst get it: and then it will be soon over."

Kormac said nay, for he meant to be his lifelong foe. Then answered Bersi:

"Thou wilt mind thee for many a season
How we met in the high voice of Hilda.
Right fain I go forth to the spear-mote
Being fitted for every encounter.
There Kormac's gay shield from his clutches
I clave with the bane of the bucklers,
For he scorned in the battle to seek me
If we set not the lists of the holmgang."

Thus they parted; and then Kormac went home to Mel and saw his mother. She healed his hand; it had become ugly and healed badly. The notch in Skofnung they whetted, but the more they whetted the bigger it was. So he went to Reykir, and flung Skofnung at Skeggi's feet, with this verse:

"I bring thee, thus broken and edgeless,
The blade that thou gavest me, Skeggi!
I warrant thy weapon could bite not:
I won not the fight by its witchcraft.
No gain of its virtue nor glory
I got in the strife of the weapons,
When we met for to mingle the sword-storm
For the maiden my singing adorns."

Said Skeggi, "It went as I warned thee." Kormac flung forth and went home to Mel: and when he met with Dalla he made this song

"To the field went I forth, O my mother
The flame of the armlet who guardest,
To dare the cave-dweller, my foeman
And I deemed I should smite him in battle.
But the brand that is bruited in story

It brake in my hand as I held it;
And this that should thrust men to slaughter
Is thwarted and let of its might.

For I borrowed to bear in the fighting
No blunt-edged weapon of Skeggi:
There is strength in the serpent that quivers
By the side of the land of the girdle.
But vain was the virtue of Skofnung
When he vanquished the sharpness of Whitting;
And a shard have I shorn, to my sorrow,
From the shearer of ringleted mail.

Yon tusker, my foe, wrought me trouble
When targe upon targe I had carven:
For the thin wand of slaughter was shattered
And it sundered the ground of my handgrip.
Loud bellowed the bear of the sea-king
When he brake from his lair in the scabbard,
At the hest of the singer, who seeketh
The sweet hidden draught of the gods.

Afar must I fare, O my mother,
And a fate points the pathway before me,
For that white-wreathen tree may woo not
— Two wearisome morrows her outcast.
And it slays me, at home to be sitting,
So set is my heart on its goddess,
As a lawn with fair linen made lovely
-- I can linger no third morrow's morn."

After that, Kormac went one day to Reykir and talked with Skeggi, who said
the holmgang had been brought to scorn. Then answered Kormac:

"Forget it, O Frey of the helmet,
— Lo, I frame thee a song in atonement—
That the bringer of blood, even Skofnung,
I bare thee so strangely belated.
For by stirrers of storm was I wounded;
They smote me where perches the falcon:
But the blade that I borrowed, O Skeggi,
Was borne in the clashing of edges.

I had deemed, O thou Grey of fighting,
Of the fierce song of Odin, my neighbour,
I had deemed that a brand meet for bloodshed
I bare to the crossways of slaughter.
Nay, thy glaive, it would gape not nor ravin
Against him, the rover who robbed me:
And on her, as the surge on the shingle,
My soul beats and breaks evermore."

Bersi's Bad Luck At The Thor's-Ness Thing

In the winter, sports were held at Saurbae. Bersi's lad, Asmund, was there, and likewise the sons of Thord; but they were younger than he, and nothing like so sturdy. When they wrestled Asmund took no heed to stint his strength, and the sons of Thord often came home blue and bleeding. Their mother Thordis was ill pleased, and asked her husband would he give Bersi a hint to make it up on behalf of his son. Nay, Thord answered, he was loath to do that.

"Then I'll find my brother Bork," said she, "and it will be just as bad in the end."

Thord bade her do no such thing. "I would rather talk it over with him," said he; and so, at her wish, he met Bersi, and hinted that some amends were owing.

Said Bersi, "Thou art far too greedy of getting, nowadays. This kind of thing will end in losing thee thy good name. Thou wilt never want while anything is to be got here."

Thord went home, and there was a coolness between them while that winter lasted.

Spring slipped by, until it was time for the meeting at Thor's-ness. By then, Bersi thought he saw through this claim of Thord's, and found Thordis at the bottom of it. For all that, he made ready to go to the Thing. By old use and wont these two neighbours should have gone riding together; so Bersi set out and came to Muli, but when he got there Thord was gone.

"Well," said he, "Thord has broken old use and wont in awaiting me no longer."

"If breach there be," answered Thordis, "it is thy doing. This is nothing to what we owe thee, and I doubt there will be more to follow."

They had words. Bersi said that harm would come of her evil counsel; and so they parted.

When he left the house he said to his men, "Let us turn aside to the shore and take a boat; it is a long way to ride round the waterhead." So they took a boat—it was one of Thord's—and went their way.

They came to the meeting when most other folks were already there, and went to the tent of Olaf Peacock of Hjardarholt (Herdholt), for he was Bersi's chief. It was crowded inside, and Bersi found no seat. He used to sit next to Thord, but that place was filled. In it there sat a big and strong-looking man, with a bear-skin coat, and a hood that shaded his face. Bersi stood a while before him, but the seat was not given up. He asked the man for his name, and was told he might call him Bruin, or he might call him Hoodie—which-ever he liked; whereupon he said in verse:

> "Who sits in the seat of the warriors,
> With the skin of the bear wrapped around him,
> So wild in his look? Ye have welcomed
> A wolf to your table, good kinsfolk!
> Ah, now may I know him, I reckon!
> Doth he name himself Bruin, or Hoodie?
> We shall meet once again in the morning,
> And maybe he'll prove to be—Steinar."

"And it's no use for thee to hide thy name, thou in the bearskin," said he.

"No more it is," he answered. "Steinar I am, and I have brought money to pay thee for Kormac, if so be it is needed. But first I bid thee to fight. It will have to be seen whether thou get the two marks of silver, or whether thou lose them both."

Upon which quoth Bersi:

> "They that waken the storm of the spear-points—
> For slaughter and strife they are famous—
> To the island they bid me for battle,
> Nor bitter I think it nor woeful;
> For long in that craft am I learned
> To loosen the Valkyrie's tempest
> In the lists, and I fear not to fight them—
> Unflinching in battle am I.

"Well I wot, though," said he, "that ye and your gang mean to make away with me. But I would let you know that I too have something to say about it—something that will set down your swagger, maybe."

"It is not thy death we are seeking," answered Steinar; "all we want is to teach thee thy true place."

Bersi agreed to fight him, and then went out to a tent apart and took up his abode there.

Now one day the word went round for bathing in the sea. Said Steinar to Bersi, "Wilt try a race with me, Bersi?"

"I have given over swimming," said he, "and yet I'll try."

Bersi's manner of swimming was to breast the waves and strike out with all his might. In so doing he showed a charm he wore round his neck. Steinar swam at him and tore off the lucky-stone with the bag it was in, and threw them both into the water, saying in verse:

"Long I've lived,
And I've let the gods guide me;
Brown hose I never wore
To bring the luck beside me.
I've never knit
All to keep me thriving
Round my neck a bag of worts,
—And lo! I'm living!"

Upon that they struck out to land.

But this turn that Steinar played was Thord's trick to make Bersi lose his luck in the fight. And Thord went along the shore at low water and found the luck-stone, and hid it away.

Now Steinar had a sword that was called after Skrymir the giant: it was never fouled, and no mishap followed it. On the day fixed, Thord and Steinar went out of the tent, and Kormac also came to the meeting to hold the shield of Steinar. Olaf Peacock got men to help Bersi at the fight, for Thord had been used to hold his shield, but this time failed him. So Bersi went to the trysting-place with a shield-bearer who is not named in the story, and with the round target that once had belonged to Thorveig.

Each man was allowed three shields. Bersi cut up two, and then Kormac took the third. Bersi hacked away, but Whitting his sword stuck fast in the iron border of Steinar's shield. Kormac whirled it up just when Steinar was striking out. He struck the shield-edge, and the sword glanced off, slit Bersi's buttock, sliced his thigh down to the knee-joint, and stuck in the bone. And so Bersi fell.

"There!" cried Steinar, "Kormac's fine is paid."

But Bersi leapt up, slashed at him, and clove his shield. The sword-point was at Steinar's breast when Thord rushed forth and dragged him away, out of reach.

"There!" cried Thord to Bersi, "I have paid thee for the mauling of my sons."

So Bersi was carried to the tent, and his wound was dressed. After a while, Thord came in; and when Bersi saw him he said:

"When the wolf of the war-god was howling
Erstwhile in the north, thou didst aid me:
When it gaped in my hand, and it girded
At the Valkyries' gate for to enter.

But now wilt thou never, O warrior,
At need in the storm-cloud of Odin
Give me help in the tempest of targes
-- Untrusty, unfaithful art thou.

"For when I was a stripling I showed me
To the stems of the lightning of battle
Right meet for the mist of the war-maids;
— Ah me! that was said long ago.
But now, and I may not deny it
My neighbours in earth must entomb me,
At the spot I have sought for grave-mound
Where Saurbae lies level and green."

Said Thord, "I have no wish for thy death; but I own it is no sorrow to see thee down for once."

To which Bersi answered in song:

"The friend that I trusted has failed me
In the fight, and my hope is departed:
I speak what I know of; and note it,
Ye nobles, I tell ye no leasing.
Lo, the raven is ready for carnage,
But rare are the friends who should succour.
Yet still let them scorn me and threaten,
I shrink not, I am not dismayed."

After this, Bersi was taken home to Saurbae, and lay long in his wounds.

But when he was carried into the tent, at that very moment Steinar spoke thus to Kormac:

"Of the reapers in harvest of Hilda
— Thou hast heard of it—four men and eight men
With the edges of Skrymir to aid me
I have urged to their flight from the battle.
Now the singer, the steward of Odin,
Hath smitten at last even Bersi
With the flame of the weapon that feedeth
The flocks of the carrion crows."

"I would have thee keep Skrymir now for thy own, Kormac," said he, "because I mean this fight to be my last."

After that, they parted in friendly wise: Steinar went home, and Kormac fared to Mel.

Steingerd Leaves Bersi

Next it is told of Bersi. His wound healed but slowly. Once on a time a many folk were met to talk about that meeting and what came of it, and Bersi made this song:

> "Thou didst leave me forlorn to the sword-stroke,
> Strong lord of the field of the serpent!
> And needy and fallen ye find me,
> Since my foeman ye shielded from danger.
> Thus cunning and counsel are victors,
> When the craft of the spear-shaft avails not;
> But this, as I think, is the ending,
> O Thord, of our friendship for ever!"

A while later Thord came to his bedside and brought back the luck-stone; and with it he healed Bersi, and they took to their friendship again and held it unbroken ever after.

Because of these happenings, Steingerd fell into loathing of Bersi and made up her mind to part with him; and when she had got everything ready for going away she went to him and said: "First ye were called Eygla's-Bersi, and then Holmgang-Bersi, but now your right name will be Breech-Bersi!" and spoke her divorce from him.

She went north to her kinsfolk, and meeting with her brother Thorkel she bade him seek her goods again from Bersi—her pin-money and her dowry, saying that she would not own him now that he was maimed. Thorkel Toothgnasher never blamed her for that, and agreed to undertake her errand; but the winter slipped by and his going was put off.

The Bane Of Thorkel Toothgnasher

Afterwards, in the spring, Thorkel Toothgnasher set out to find Bersi and to seek Steingerd's goods again. Bersi said that his burden was heavy enough to bear, even though both together underwent the weight of it. "And I shall not pay the money!" said he.

Said Thorkel, "I bid thee to the holmgang at Orrestholm beside Tjaldanes (Tentness)."

"That ye will think hardly worth while," said Bersi, "such a champion as you are; and yet I undertake for to come."

So they came to the holme and fell to the holmgang. Thord carried the shield before Bersi, and Vali was Thorkel's shield-bearer. When two shields had been hacked to splinters, Bersi bade Thorkel take the third; but he would not. Bersi still had a shield, and a sword that was long and sharp.

Said Thorkel, "The sword ye have, Bersi, is longer than lawful."

"That shall not be," cried Bersi; and took up his other sword, Whitting, two-handed, and smote Thorkel his deathblow. Then sang he:

> "I have smitten Toothgnasher and slain him,
> And I smile at the pride of his boasting.
> One more to my thirty I muster,
> And, men! say ye this of the battle:
> In the world not a lustier liveth
> Among lords of the steed of the oar-bench;
> Though by eld of my strength am I stinted
> To stain the black wound-bird with blood."

After these things Vali bade Bersi to the holmgang, but he answered in this song:

> "They that waken the war of the mail-coats,
> For warfare and manslaying famous,
> To the lists they have bid me to battle,
> Nor bitter I think it not woeful.
> It is sport for yon swordsmen who goad me
> To strive in the Valkyries' tempest
> On the holme; but I fear not to fight them —
> Unflinching in battle am I!"

The were even about to begin fighting, when Thord came and spoke to them saying: "Woeful waste of life I call it, if brave men shall be smitten down for the sake of any such matters. I am ready to make it up between ye two."

To this they agreed, and he said: "Vali, this methinks is the most likely way of bringing you together. Let Bersi take thy sister Thordis to wife. It is a match that may well be to thy who worship."

Bersi agreed to this, and it was settled that the land of Brekka should go along with her as a dowry; and so this troth was plighted between them. Bersi afterwards had a strong stone wall built around his homestead, and sat there for many winters in peace.

The Rescue Of Steinvor Slim-ankles

There was a man named Thorarin Alfsson, who lived in the north at Thambardal; that is a dale which goes up from the fiord called Bitra. He was a big man and mighty, and he was by-named Thorarin the Strong. He had spent much of his time in seafaring (as a chapman) and so lucky was he that he always made the harbour he aimed at.

He had three sons; one was named Alf, the next Loft, and the third Skofti. Thorarin was a most overbearing man, and his sons took after him. They were rough, noisy fellows.

Not far away, at Tunga (Tongue) in Bitra, lived a man called Odd. His daughter was named Steinvor, a pretty girl and well set up; her by-name was Slim-ankles. Living with Odd were many fisherman; among them, staying there for the fishing-season, was one Glum, an ill-tempered carle and bad to deal with.

Now once upon a time these two, Odd and Glum, were in talk together which were the greatest men in the countryside. Glum reckoned Thorarin to be foremost, but Odd said Holmgang Bersi was better than he in every way.

"How can ye make that out?" asked Glum.

"Is there any likeness whatever," said Odd, "between the bravery of Bersi and the knavery of Thorarin?"

So they talked about this until they fell out, and laid a wager upon it.

Then Glum wend and told Thorarin. He grew very angry and made many a threat against Odd. And in a while he went and carried off Steinvor from Tunga, all to spite her father; and he gave out that if Odd said anything against it, the worse for him: and so took her home to Thambardal.

Things went on so for a while, and then Odd went to see Holmgang Bersi, and told him what had happened. He asked him for help to get Steinvor back and to wreak vengeance for that shame. Bersi answered that such words had been better unsaid, and bade him go home and take no share in the business. "But yet," added he, "I promise that I will see to it."

No sooner was Odd gone than Bersi made ready to go from home. He rode fully armed, with Whitting at his belt, and three spears; he came to Thambardal when the day was far spent and the women were coming out of the bower. Steinvor saw him and turning to meet him told of her unhappiness.

"Make ready to go with me," said he; and that she did.

He would not go to Thambardal for nothing, he said; and so he turned to the door where men were sitting by long fires. He knocked at the door, and out there came a man—his name was Thorleif. But Thorarin knew Bersi's voice, and rushed forth with a great carving-knife and laid on to him. Bersi was aware of it, and drew Whitting, and struck him his death-blow.

Then he leapt on horseback and set Steinvor on his knee and took his spears which she had kept for him. He rode some way into the wood, where in a hidden spot he left his horse and Steinvor, bidding her await him. Then he went to a narrow gap through which the high-road ran, and there made ready to stand against his foes.

In Thambardal there was anything but peace. Thorleif ran to tell the sons of Thorarin that he lay dead in the doorway. They asked who had done the deed. He told them. Then they went after Bersi and steered the shortest way to the gap, meaning to get there first; but by that time he was already first at the gap.

When they came near him, Bersi hurled a spear at Alf, and it went right through him. Then Loft cast at Bersi, but he caught the spear on his target and it dropped off. Then Bersi threw at Loft and killed him, and so he did by Skofti.

When all was over, the house-carles of the brothers came up. Thorleif turned back to meet them, and they all went home together.

After that Bersi went to find Steinvor, and mounted his horse. He came home before men were out of bed. They asked him about his journey and he told them. When Odd met him he asked about the fight and how it had passed, and Bersi answered in this verse:

> "There was one fed the wolves has encountered
> His weird in the dale of the Bowstring —
> Thorarin the Strong, 'neath the slayer
> Lay slain by the might of my weapon.
> And loss of their lives men abided
> When Loft fell, and Alf fell, and Skofti.
> They were four, yonder kinsmen, and fated —
> They were fey — and I met them, alone!"

After that Odd went home, but Steinvor was with Bersi, though it misliked Thordis, his wife. By this time his stone wall was some-what broken down, but he had it built up again; and it is said that no blood-money was ever paid for Thorarin and his sons. So the time went on.

How Vali Fell Before An Old Man And A Boy

Once on a day when Thordis and Bersi were talking together, said he, "I have been thinking I might ask Olaf Peacock for a child of his to foster."

"Nay," said she, "I think little of that. It seems to me a great trouble, and I doubt if folk will reckon more of us for it."

"It means that I should have a sure friend," answered he. "I have many foes, and I am growing heavy with age."

So he went to see Olaf, and asked for a child to foster. Olaf took it with thanks, and Bersi carried Halldor home with him and got Steinvor to be nurse. This too misliked Thordis, and she laid hands on every penny she could get (for fear it should go to Steinvor and the foster-child).

At last Bersi took to ageing much. There was one time when men riding to the Thing stayed at his house. He sat all by himself, and his food was brought him before the rest were served. He had porridge while other folk had cheese and curds. Then he made this verse:

"To batten the black-feathered wound-bird
With the blade of my axe have I stricken
Full thirty and five of my foemen;
I am famed for the slaughter of warriors.
May the fiends have my soul if I stain not
My sharp-edged falchion once over!
And then let the breaker of broadswords
Be borne—and with speed—to the grave!"

"What?" said Halldor; "hast thou a mind to kill another man, then?"

Answered Bersi, "I see the man it would rightly serve!"

Now Thordis let her brother Vali feed his herds on the land of Brekka. Bersi bade his house-carles work at home, and have no dealings with Vali; but still Halldor thought it a hardship that Bersi had not his own will with his own wealth. One day Bersi made this verse:

"Here we lie,
    Both on one settle—
Halldor and I,
    Men of no mettle.
Youth ails thee,
    But thou'lt win through it;
Age ails me,
    And I must rue it!"

"I do hate Vali," said Halldor; and Bersi answered thus in verse:

"Yon Vali, so wight as he would be,
Well wot I our pasture he grazes;
Right fain yonder fierce helmet-wearer

Under foot my dead body would trample!
But often my wrongs have I wreaked
In wrath on the mail-coated warrior —
On the stems of the sun of the ocean
I have stained the wound-serpent for less!"

And again he said:

"With eld I am listless and lamed —
I, the lord of the gold of the armlet:
I sit, and am still under many
A slight from the warders of spear-meads.
Though shield-bearers shape for the singer
To shiver alone in the grave-mound,
Yet once in the war would I redden
The wand that hews helms ere I fail."

"Thy heart is not growing old, foster-father mine!" cried Halldor.

Upon that Bersi fell into talk with Steinvor, and said to her "I am laying a plot, and I need thee to help me."

She said she would if she could.

"Pick a quarrel," said he, "with Thordis about the milk-kettle, and do thou hold on to it until you whelm it over between you. Then I will come in and take her part and give thee nought but bad words. Then go to Vali and tell him how ill we treat thee."

Everything turned out as he had planned. She went to Vali and told him that things were no way smooth for her; would he take her over the gap (to Bitra to her father's) and so he did.

But when he was on the way back again, out came Bersi and Halldor to meet him. Bersi had a halberd in one hand and a staff in the other, and Halldor had Whitting. As soon as Vali saw them he turned and hewed at Bersi. Halldor came at his back and fleshed Whitting in his rough-sinews. Thereupon he turned sharply and fell upon Halldor. Then Bersi set the halberd-point betwixt his shoulders. That was his death-wound.

Then they set his shield at his feet and his sword at his head, and spread his cloak over him; and after that got on horseback and rode to five homesteads to make known the deed they had done and then rode home. Men went and buried Vali, and the place where he fell has ever since been called Vali's fall.

Halldor was twelve winters old when these doings came to pass.

How Steingerd Was Married Again

Now there was a man named Thorvald, the son of Eystein, bynamed the Tinker: he was a wealthy man, a smith, and a skald; but he was mean-spirited for all that. His brother Thorvard lived in the north country at Fliot (Fleet); and they had many kinsmen, -- the Skidings they were called-- but little luck or liking.

Now Thorvald the Tinker asked Steingerd to wife. Her folk were for it, and she said nothing against it; and so she was wed to him in the very same summer in which she left Bersi.

When Kormac heard the news he made as though he knew nothing whatever about the matter; for a little earlier he had taken his goods aboard ship, meaning to go away with his brother. But one morning early he rode from the ship and went to see Steingerd; and when he got talk with her, he asked would she make him a shirt. To which she answered that he had no business to pay her visits; neither Thorvald nor his kinsmen would abide it, she said, but have their revenge.

Thereupon he made his voice:

> "Nay, think it or thole it I cannot,
> That thou, a young fir of the forest
> Enwreathed in the gold that thou guardest,
> Shouldst be given to a tinkering tinsmith.
> Nay, scarce can I smile, O thou glittering
> In silk like the goddess of Baldur,
> Since thy father handfasted and pledged thee,
> So famed as thou art, to a coward."

"In such words," answered Steingerd, "an ill will is plain to hear. I shall tell Thorvald of this ribaldry: no man would sit still under such insults."

Then sang Kormac:

> "What gain is to get if he threatens,
> White goddess in raiment of beauty,
> The scorn that the Skidings may bear me?
> I'll set them a weft for their weaving!
> I'll rhyme you the roystering caitiffs
> Till rocks go afloat on the water;
> And lucky for them if they loosen
> The line of their fate that I ravel!"

Thereupon they parted with no blitheness, and Kormac went to his ship.

Kormac's Voyage To Norway

The two brothers had but left the roadstead, when close beside their ship, uprose a walrus. Kormac hurled at it a pole-staff, which struck the beast, so that it sank again: but the men aboard thought that they knew its eyes for the eyes of Thorveig the witch. That walrus came up no more, but of Thorveig it was heard that she lay sick to death; and indeed folk say that this was the end of her.

Then they sailed out to sea, and at last came to Norway, where at that time Hakon, the foster-son of Athelstan, was king. He made them welcome, and so they stayed there the winter long with all honour.

Next summer they set out to the wars, and did many great deeds. Along with them went a man called Siegfried, a German of good birth; and they made raids both far and wide. One day as they were gone up the country eleven men together came against the two brothers, and set upon them; but this business ended in their overcoming the whole eleven, and so after a while back to their ship. The vikings had given them up for lost, and fain were their folk when they came back with victory and wealth.

In this voyage the brothers got great renown: and late in the summer, when winter was coming on, they made up their minds to steer for Norway. They met with cold winds; the sail was behung with icicles, but the brothers were always to the fore. It was on his voyage that Kormac made the song:

> "O shake me yon rime from the awning;
> Your singer's a-cold in his berth;
> For the hills are all hooded, dear Skardi,
> In the hoary white veil of the firth.
> There's one they call Wielder of Thunder
> I would were as chill and as cold;
> But he leaves not the side of his lady
> As the lindworm forsakes not its gold."

"Always talking of her now!" said Thorgils; "and yet thou wouldst not have her when thou couldst."

"That was more the fault of witchcraft," answered Kormac, "that any want of faith in me."

Not long after they were sailing hard among crags, and shortened sail in great danger.

"It is a pity Thorvald Tinker is not with us here!" said Kormac.

Said Thorgils with a smile, "Most likely he is better off than we, to-day!"

But before long they came to land in Norway.

How Kormac Fought In Ireland, And Went Home To Iceland; And How He Met Steingerd Again

While they were abroad there had been a change of kings; Hakon was dead, and Harald Greyfell reigned in his stead. They offered friendship to the king, and he took their suit kindly; so they went with him to Ireland, and fought battles there.

Once upon a time when they had gone ashore with the king, a great host came against him, and as the armies met, Kormac made this song:

> "I dread not a death from the foemen,
> Though we dash at them, buckler to buckler,
> While our prince in the power of his warriors
> Is proud of me foremost in battle.
> But the glimpse of a glory comes o'er me
> Like the gleam of the moon on the skerry,
> And I faint and I fail for my longing,
> For the fair one at home in the North."

"Ye never get into danger," said Thorgils, "but ye think of Steingerd!"

"Nay," answered Kormac, "but it's not often I forget her."

Well: this was a great battle, and king Harald won a glorious victory. While his men drove the rout before him, the brothers were shoulder to shoulder; and they fell upon nine men at once and fought them. And while they were at it, Kormac sang:

> "Fight on, arrow-driver, undaunted,
> And down with the foemen of Harald!
> What are nine? they are nought! Thou and I, lad,
> Are enough—they are ours!-- we have won them!
> But—at home-- in the arms of an outlaw
> That all the gods loathe for a monster,
> So white and so winsome she nestles
> —Yet once she was loving to me!"

"It always comes down to that!" said Thorgils. When the fight was over, the brothers had got the victory, and the nine men had fallen before them; for which they won great praise from the king, and many honours beside.

But while they were ever with the king in his warfarings, Thorgils was aware that Kormac was used to sleep but little; and he asked why this might be. This was the song Kormac made in answer:

> "Surf on a rock-bound shore of the sea-king's blue domain —
> Look how it lashes the crags, hark how it thunders again!
> But all the din of the isles that the Delver heaves in foam
> In the draught of the undertow glides out to the sea-gods' home.
> Now, which of us two should test? Is it thou, with thy heart at ease,
> Or I that am surf on the shore in the tumult of angry seas?
> Drawn, if I sleep, to her that shines with the ocean-gleam,
> Dashed, when I wake, to woe, for the want of my glittering dream."

"And now let me tell you this, brother," he went on. "Hereby I give out that I am going back to Iceland."

Said Thorgils, "There is many a snare set for thy feet, brother, to drag thee down, I know not whither."

But when the king heard of his longing to begone, he sent for Kormac, and said that he did unwisely, and would hinder him from his journey. But all this availed nothing, and aboard ship he went.

At the outset they met with foul winds, so that they shipped great seas, and the yard broke. Then Kormac sang:

> "I take it not ill, like the Tinker
> If a trickster had foundered his muck-sled;
> For he loves not rough travelling, the losel,
> And loath would he be of this uproar.
> I flinch not — nay, hear it, ye fearless
> Who flee not when arrows are raining,
> Though the steeds of the ocean be storm-bound
> And stayed in the harbour of Solund."

So they pushed out to sea, and hard weather they tholed. Once on a time when the waves broke over the deck and drenched them all, Kormac made this song:

> "O the Tinker's a lout and a lubber,
> And the life of a sailor he dares not,
> When the snow-crested surges caress us
> And sweep us away with their kisses,
> He bides in a berth that is warmer,
> Embraced in the arms of his lady;
> And lightly she lulls him to slumber,
> But long she has reft me of rest!"

They had a very rough voyage, but landed at last in Midfiord, and anchored off shore. Looking landward they beheld where a lady was riding by; and Kormac knew at once that it was Steingerd. He bade his men launch a boat, and rowed ashore. He went quickly from the boat, and got a horse, and rode to meet her. When they met, he leapt from horseback and helped her to alight, making a seat for her beside him on the ground.

Their horses wandered away: the day passed on, and it began to grow dark. At last Steingerd said, "It is time to look for our horses."

Little search would be needed, said Kormac; but when he looked about, they were nowhere in sight. As it happened, they were hidden in a gill not far from where the two were sitting.

So, as night was hard at hand, they set out to walk, and came to a little farm, where they were taken in and treated well, even as they needed. That night they slept each on either side of the carven wainscot that parted bed from bed: and Kormac made this song:

> "We rest, O my beauty, my brightest,
> But a barrier lies ever between us.
> So fierce are the fates and so mighty
> —I feel it—that rule to their rede.
> Ah, nearer I would be, and nigher,
> Till nought should be left to dispart us,
> —The wielder of Skofnung the wonder,
> And the wearer of sheen from the deep."

"It was better thus," said Steingerd: but he sang:

> "We have slept 'neath one roof-tree—slept softly,
> O sweet one, O queen of the mead-horn,
> O glory of sea-dazzle gleaming,
> These grim hours, these five nights, I count them.
> And here in the kettle-prow cabined
> While the crow's day drags on in the darkness,
> How loathly me seems to be lying,
> How lonely, so near and so far!"

"That," said she, "is all over and done with; name it no more." But he sang:

> "The hot stone shall float, ay, the hearth-stone
> Like a husk of the corn on the water,
> Ah, woe for the wight that she loves not!
> And the world, ah, she loathes me! shall perish,
> And the fells that are famed for their hugeness

Shall fail and be drowned in the ocean,
Or ever so gracious a goddess
Shall grow into beauty like Steingerd."

Then Steingerd cried out that she would not have him make songs upon her: but he went on:

"I have known it and noted it clearly,
O neckleted fair one, in visions,
Is it doom for my hopes, is it daring
To dream? O so oft have I seen it!
Even this, that the boughs of thy beauty,
O braceleted fair one, shall twine them
Round the hill where the hawk loves to settle,
The hand of thy lover, at last."

"That," said she, "never shall be, if I can help it. Thou didst let me go, once for all; and there is no more hope for thee."

So then they slept the night long; and in the morning, when Kormac was making ready to be gone, he found Steingerd, and took the ring off his finger to give her.

"Fiend take thee and thy gold together!" she cried. And this is what he answered:

"To a dame in her broideries dainty
This drift of the furnace I tendered;
O day of ill luck, for a lover
So lured, and so heartlessly cheated!
Too blithe in the pride of her beauty —
The bliss that I crave she denies me;
So rich that no boon can I render,
And my ring she would hurl to the fiends!"

So Kormac rode forth, being somewhat angry with Steingerd, but still more so with the Tinker. He rode home to Mel, and stayed there all the winter, taking lodgings for his chapmen near the ship.

Of A Spiteful Song That Kormac Never Made; And How Angry Steingerd Was

Now Thorvald the Tinker lived in the north-country at Svinadal (Swindale), but his brother Thorvard at Fliot. In the winter Kormac took his way northward to see Steingerd; and coming to Svinadal he dismounted and went into the chamber. She was sitting on the dais, and he took his seat beside her; Thorvald sat on the bench, and Narfi by him.

Then said Narfi to Thorvald, "How canst thou sit down, with Kormac here? It is no time, this, for sitting still!"

But Thorvald answered, "I am content; there is no harm done it seems to me, though they do talk together."

"That is ill," said Narfi.

Not long afterwards Thorvald met his brother Thorvard and told him about Kormac's coming to his house.

"Is it right, think you," said Thorvard, "to sit still while such things happen?"

He answered that there was no harm done as yet, but that Kormac's coming pleased him not.

"I'll mend that," cried Thorvard, "if you dare not. The shame of it touches us all."

So this was the next thing, that Thorvard came to Svinadal, and the Skiding brothers and Narfi paid a gangrel beggar-man to sing a song in the hearing of Steingerd, and to say that Kormac had made it, which was a lie. They said that Kormac had taught this song to one called Eylaug, a kinswoman of his; and these were the words:

"I wish an old witch that I know of,
So wealthy and proud of her havings,
Were turned to a steed in the stable
—Called Steingerd—and I were the rider!
I'd bit her, and bridle, and saddle,
I'd back her and drive her and tame her;
So many she owns for her masters,
But mine she will never become!"

Then Steingerd grew exceedingly angry, so that she would not so much as hear Kormac named. When he heard that, he went to see her. Long time he tried in vain to get speech with her; but at last she gave this answer, that she misliked his holding her up to shame, "And now it is all over the country-side!"

Kormac said it was not true; but she answered, "Thou mighest flatly deny it, if I had not heard it."

"Who sang it in thy hearing?" asked he.

She told him who sang it, "And thou needest not hope for speech with me if this prove true."

He rode away to look for the rascal, and when he found him the truth was forced out at last. Kormac was very angry, and set on Narfi and slew him. That same onset was meant for Thorvald, but he hid himself in the shadow and skulked, until men came between then and parted them. Said Kormac:

> "There, hide in the house like a coward,
> And hope not hereafter to scare me
> With the scorn of thy brethren the Skidings,
> I'll set them a weft for their weaving!
> I'll rhyme on the swaggering rascals
> Till rocks go afloat on the water;
> And lucky for you if ye loosen
> The line of your fate that I ravel!"

This went all over the country-side and the feud grew fiercer between them. The brothers Thorvald and Thorvard used big words, and Kormac was wroth when he heard them.

How Thorvard Would Not Fight, But Tried To Get The Law Of Kormac

After this Thorvard sent word from Fliot that he was fain to fight Kormac, and he fixed time and place, saying that he would now take revenge for that song of shame and all other slights.

To this Kormac agreed; and when the day came he went to the spot that was named, but Thorvard was not there, nor any of his men. Kormac met a woman from the farm hard by, who greeted him, and they asked each other for news.

"What is your errand?" said she; "and why are you waiting here?"

Then he answered with this song:

> "Too slow for the struggle I find him,
> That spender of fire from the ocean,
> Who flung me a challenge to fight him
> From Fleet in the land of the North.

That half-witted hero should get him
A heart made of clay for his carcase,
Though the mate of the may with the necklace
Is more of a fool than his fere!"

"Now," said Kormac, "I bid Thorvard anew to the holmgang, if he can be
called in his right mind. Let him be every man's nithing if he come not!" and then
he made this song:

"The nithing shall silence me never,
Though now for their shame they attack me,
But the wit of the Skald is my weapon,
And the wine of the gods will uphold me.
And this they shall feel in its fulness;
Here my fame has its birth and beginning;
And the stout spears of battle shall see it,
If I 'scape from their hands with my life."

Then the brothers set on foot a law-suit against him for libel. Kormac's
kinsmen backed him up to answer it, and he would let no terms be made, saying
that they deserved the shame put upon them, and no honour; he was not unready
to meet them, unless they played him false. Thorvard had not come to the
holmgang when he had been challenged, and therefore the shame had fallen of
itself upon him and his, and they must put up with it.

So time passed until the Huna-water Thing. Thorvard and Kormac both went
to the meeting, and once they came together.

"Much enmity we owe thee," said Thorvard, "and in many ways. Now
therefore I challenge thee to the holmgang, here at the Thing."

Said Kormac, "Wilt thou be fitter than before? Thou hast drawn back time after
time."

"Nevertheless," said Thorvard, "I will risk it. We can abide thy spite no
longer."

"Well," said Kormac, "I'll not stand in the way;" and went home to Mel.

What The Witch Did For Them In Their Fights.

At Spakonufell (Spae-wife's-fell) lived Thordis the spae-wife, of whom
we have told before. with her husband Thorolf. They were both at the Thing. and

many a man thought her good-will was of much avail. So Thorvard sought her out, to ask her help against Kormac, and gave her a fee; and she made him ready for the holmgang according to her craft.

Now Kormac told his mother what was forward, and she asked if he thought good would come of it.

"Why not?" said he.

"That will not be enough for thee," said Dalla. "Thorvard will never make bold to fight without witchcraft to help him. I think it wise for thee to see Thordis the spae-wife, for there is going to be foul play in this affair."

"It is little to my mind," said he; and yet went to see Thordis, and asked her help.

"Too late ye have come," said she. "No weapon will bite on him now. And yet I would not refuse thee. Bide here to-night, and seek thy good luck. Anyway, I can manage so that iron bite thee no more than him."

So Kormac stayed there for the night; and, awaking, found that some one was groping round the coverlet at his head. "Who is there?" he asked, but whoever it was made off, and out at the house-door, and Kormac after. And then he saw it was Thordis, and she was going to the place where the fight was to be, carrying a goose under her arm.

He asked what it all meant, and she set down the goose, saying, "Why couldn't ye keep quiet?"

So he lay down again, but held himself awake, for he wanted to know what she would be doing. Three times she came, and every time he tried to find out what she was after. The third time, just as he came out, she had killed two geese and let the blood run into a bowl, and she had taken up the third goose to kill it.

"What means this business, foster-mother?" said he.

"True it will prove, Kormac, that you are a hard one to help," said she. "I was going to break the spell Thorveig laid on thee and Steingerd. Ye could have loved one another and been happy if I had killed the third goose and no one seen it."

"I believe nought of such things," cried he; and this song he made about it:

"I gave her an ore at the ayre,
That the arts of my foe should not prosper;
And twice she has taken the knife,
And twice she has offered the offering;
But the blood is the blood of a goose —
What boots it if two should be slaughtered?
Never sacrifice geese for a Skald
Who sings for the glory of Odin!"

So they went to the holmgang: but Thorvald gave the spae-wife a still greater fee, and offered the sacrifice of geese; and Kormac said:

"Trust never another man's mistress!
For I know, on this woman who weareth
The fire of the field of the sea-king
The fiends have been riding to revel.
The witch with her hoarse cry is working
For woe when we go to the holmgang,
And if bale be the end of the battle
The blame, be assured, will be hers."

"Well," she said, "I can manage so that none shall know thee." Then Kormac began to upbraid her, saying she did nought but ill, and wanting to drag her out to the door to look at her eyes in the sunshine. His brother Thorgils made him leave that: "What good will it do thee?" said he.

Now Steingerd gave out that she had a mind to see the fight; and so she did. When Kormac saw her he made this song:

"I have fared to the field of the battle,
O fair one that wearest the wimple!
And twice for thy sake have I striven;
What stays me as now from thy favour?
This twice have I gotten thee glory,
O goddess of ocean! and surely
To my dainty delight, to my darling
I am dearer by far than her mate."

So then they set to. Kormac's sword bit not at all, and for a long while they smote strokes one upon the other, but neither sword bit. At last Kormac smote upon Thorvard's side so great a blow that his ribs gave way and were broken; he could fight no more, and thereupon they parted. Kormac looked and saw where a bull was standing, which he slew for a sacrifice; and being heated, he doffed his helmet from his head, saying this song:

"I have fared to the field of the battle,
O fair one that wearest the bracelet!
Even three times for thee have I striven,
And this thou canst never deny me.
But the reed of the fight would not redden,
Though it rang on the shield-bearer's harness;
For the spells of a spae-wife had blunted
My sword that was eager for blood."

He wiped the sweat from him on the corner of Steingerd's mantle; and said:

"So oft, being wounded and weary,
I must wipe my sad brow on thy mantle.
What pangs for thy sake are my portion,
O pine-tree with red gold enwreathed!
Yet beside thee he snugs on the settle
As thou seamest thy broidery, that rhymester!
And the shame of it whelms me in sorrow,
O Steingerd! -- that rascal unslain!"

And then Kormac prayed Steingerd that she would go with him: but Nay, she said; she would have her own way about men. So they parted, and both were ill pleased.

Thorvard was taken home, and she bound his wounds. Kormac was now always meeting with Steingerd. Thorvard healed but slowly; and when he could get on his feet he went to see Thordis, and asked her what was best to help his healing.

"A hill there is," answered she, "not far away from here, where elves have their haunt. Now get you the bull that Kormac killed, and redden the outer side of the hill with its blood, and make a feast for the elves with its flesh. Then thou wilt be healed."

So they sent word to Kormac that they would buy the bull. He answered that he would sell it, but then he must have the ring that was Steingerd's. So they brought the ring, took the bull, and did with it as Thordis bade them do. On which Kormac made a song:

"When the workers of wounds are returning,
And with them the sacrifice reddened,
Then a lady in raiment of linen,
Who loved me, time was-- she will ask--
My ring, have ye robbed me? -- where is it?
I have wrought them no little displeasure:
For the swain that is swarthy has won it,
The son of old Ogmund, the skald."

It fell out as he guessed. Steingerd was very angry because they had sold her ring.

How Kormac Beat Thorvard Again

After that, Thorvard was soon healed, and when he thought he was strong again, he rode to Mel and challenged Kormac to the holmgang.

"It takes thee long to tire of it," said Kormac: "but I'll not say thee nay."

So they went to the fight, and Thordis met Thorvard now as before, but Kormac sought no help from her. She blunted Kormac's sword, so that it would not bite, but yet he struck so great a stroke on Thorvard's shoulder that the collarbone was broken and his hand was good for nothing. Being so maimed he could fight no longer, and had to pay another ring for his ransom.

Then Thorolf of Spakonufell set upon Kormac and struck at him. He warded off the blow and sang this song:

> "This reddener of shields, feebly wrathful,
> His rusty old sword waved against me,
> Who am singer and sacred to Odin!
> Go, snuffle, most wretched of men, thou!
> A thrust of thy sword is as thewless
> As thou, silly stirrer of battle.
> What danger to me from thy daring,
> Thou doited old witch-woman's carle?"

Then he killed a bull in sacrifice according to use and wont, saying, "Ill we brook your overbearing and the witchcraft of Thordis:" and he made this song:

> "The witch in the wave of the offering
> Has wasted the flame of the buckler,
> Lest its bite on his back should be deadly
> At the bringing together of weapons.
> My sword was not sharp for the onset
> When I sought the helm-wearer in battle;
> But the cur got enough to cry craven,
> With a clout that will mind him of me!"

After that each party went home, and neither was well pleased with these doings.

How They All Went Out To Norway

Now all the winter long Kormac and Thorgils laid up their ship in Hrutafiord; but in spring the chapmen were off to sea, and so the brothers made up their minds for the voyage. When they were ready to start, Kormac went to see Steingerd: and before they two parted he kissed her twice, and his kisses were not at all hasty. The Tinker would not have it; and so friends on both sides came in, and it was settled that Kormac should pay for this that he had done.

"How much?" asked he.

"The two rings that I parted with," said Thorvard. Then Kormac made a song:

> "Here is gold of the other's well gleaming
> In guerdon for this one and that one,
> Here is treasure of Fafnir the fire-drake
> In fee for the kiss of my lady.
> Never wearer of ring, never wielder
> Of weapon has made such atonement;
> Never dearer were deeply-drawn kisses,
> For the dream of my bliss is betrayed."

And then, when he started to go aboard his ship he made another song:

> "One song from my heart would I send her
> Ere we shall, ere I leave her and lose her,
> That dainty one, decked in her jewels
> Who dwells in the valley of Swindale.
> And each word that I utter shall enter
> The ears of that lady of bounty,
> Saying—Bright one, my beauty, I love thee,
> Ah, better by far than my life!"

So Kormac went abroad and his brother Thorgils went with him; and when they came to the king's court they were made welcome.

Now it is told that Steingerd spoke to Thorvald the Tinker that they also should abroad together. He answered that it was mere folly, but nevertheless he could not deny her. So they set off on their voyage: and as they made their way across the sea, they were attacked by vikings who fell on them to rob them and to carry away Steingerd. But it so happened that Kormac heard of it: and he made after them and gave good help, so that they saved everything that belonged to them, and came safely at last to the court of the king of Norway.

One day Kormac was walking in the street, and spied Steingerd sitting within doors. So he went into the house and sat down beside her, and they had a talk together which ended in his kissing her four kisses. But Thorvald was on the watch. He drew his sword, but the women-folk rushed in to part them, and word was sent to King Harald. He said they were very troublesome people to keep in order. "But let me settle this matter between you," said he; and they agreed.

Then spake the king: "One kiss shall be atoned for by this, that Kormac helped you to get safely to land. The next kiss is Kormac's, because he saved Steingerd. For the other two he shall pay two ounces of gold."

Upon which Kormac sang the same song that he had made before:

"Here is gold of the otter's well gleaming
In guerdon for this one and that one,
Here is treasure of Fafnir the fire-drake
In fee for the kiss of my lady.
Never wearer of ring, never wielder
Of weapon has made such atonement;
Never dearer were deeply-drawn kisses —
And the dream of my bliss is betrayed."

Another day he was walking in the street and met Steingerd again. He turned to her and prayed her to walk with him. She would not; whereupon he laid hand on her, to lead her along. She cried out for help; and as it happened, the king was standing not far off, and went up to them. He thought this behaviour most unseemly, and took her away, speaking sharply to Kormac. King Harald made himself very angry over this affair; but Kormac was one of his courtiers, and it was not long before he got into favour again, and then things went fair and softly for the rest of the winter.

How They Cruised With The King's Fleet, And Quarrelled, And Made It Up

In the following spring King Harald set forth to the land of Permia with a great host. Kormac was one of the captains in that warfaring, and in another ship was Thorvald: the other captains of ships are not named in our story.

Now as they were all sailing in close order through a narrow sound, Kormac swung his steering-oar and hit Thorvald a clout on the ear, so that he fell from his place at the helm in a swoon; and Kormac's ship hove to, when she lost her rudder. Steingerd had been sitting beside Thorvald; she laid hold of the tiller, and ran Kormac down. When he saw what she was doing, he sang:

"There is one that is nearer and nigher
To the noblest of dames than her lover:
With the haft of the helm is he smitten
On the hat-block—and fairly amidships!
The false heir of Eystein—he falters—
He falls in the poop of his galley!
Nay! steer not upon me, O Steingerd,
Though stoutly ye carry the day!"

So Kormac's ship capsized under him; but his crew were saved without loss of time, for there were plenty of people round about. Thorvald soon came round again, and they all went on their way. The king offered to settle the matter between them; and when they both agreed, he gave judgment that Thorvald's hurt was atoned for by Kormac's upset.

In the evening they went ashore; and the king and his men sat down to supper. Kormac was sitting outside the door of a tent, drinking out of the same cup with Steingerd. While they were busy at it, a young fellow for mere sport and mockery stole the brooch out of Kormac's fur cloak, which he had doffed and laid aside; and when he came to take his cloak again, the brooch was gone. He sprang up and rushed after the young fellow, with the spear that he called Vigr (the spear) and shot at him, but missed. This was the song he made about it:

"The youngster has pilfered my pin,
As I pledged the gay dame in the beaker;
And now must we brawl for a brooch
Like boys when they wrangle and tussle.
Right well have I shafted my spear,
Though I shot nothing more than the gravel:
But sure, if I missed at my man,
The moss has been prettily slaughtered!"

After this they went on their way to the land of Permia, and after that they went home again to Norway.

How Kormac Saved Steingerd Once More From Pirates; And How They Parted For Good And All

Thorvald the Tinker fitted out his ship for a cruise to Denmark, and Steingerd sailed with him. A little afterwards the brothers set out on the same voyage, and late one evening they made the Brenneyjar.

There they saw Thorvald's ship riding, and found him aboard with part of his crew; but they had been robbed of all their goods, and Steingerd had been carried off by Vikings. Now the leader of those Vikings was Thorstein, the son of that Asmund Ashenside, the old enemy of Ogmund, the father of Kormac and Thorgils.

So Thorvald and Kormac met, and Kormac asked how came it that his voyage had been so unlucky.

"Things have not turned out for the best, indeed," said he.

"What is the matter?" asked Kormac. "Is Steingerd missing?"

"She is gone," said Thorvald, "and all our goods."

"Why don't you go after her?" asked Kormac.

"We are not strong enough," said Thorvald.

"Do you mean to say you can't?" said Kormac.

"We have not the means to fight Thorstein," said Thorvald. "But if thou hast, go in and fight for thy own hand."

"I will," said Kormac.

So at nightfall the brothers went in a boat and rowed to the Viking fleet, and boarded Thorstein's ship. Steingerd was in the cabin on the poop; she had been allotted to one of the Vikings; but most of the crew were ashore round the cooking-fires. Kormac got the story out of the men who were cooking, and they told all the brothers wanted to know. They clambered on board by the ladder; Thorgils dragged the bridegroom out to the gunwale, and Kormac cut him down then and there. Then he dived into the sea with Steingerd and swam ashore; but when he was nearing the land a swarm of eels twisted round his hands and feet, so that he was dragged under. On which he made this song:

"They came at me yonder in crowds,
O kemp of the shield-serpents' wrangle!
When I fared on my way through the flood,
That flock of the wights of the water.
And ne'er to the gate of the gods
Had I got me, if there had I perished;
Yet once and again have I won,
Little woman, thy safety in peril!"

So he swam ashore and brought Steingerd back to her husband.

Thorvald bade Steingerd to go, at last, along with Kormac, for he had fairly won her, and manfully. That was what he, too, desired, said Kormac; but "Nay," said Steingerd, "she would not change knives."

"Well," said Kormac, "it was plain that this was not to be. Evil beings," he said, "ill luck, had parted them long ago." And he made this song:

> "Nay, count not the comfort had brought me,
> Fair queen of the ring, thy embrace!
> Go, mate with the man of thy choosing,
> Scant mirth will he get of thy grace!
> Be dearer henceforth to thy dastard,
> False dame of the coif, than to me;
> I have spoken the word; I have sung it;
> I have said my last farewell to thee."

And so he bade her begone with her husband.

The Swan-Songs of Kormac

After these things the brothers turned back to Norway, and Thorvald the Tinker made his way to Iceland. But the brothers went warfaring round about Ireland, Wales, England and Scotland, and they were reckoned to be the most famous of men. It was they who first built the castle of Scarborough; they made raids into Scotland, and achieved many great feats, and led a mighty host; and in all that host none was like Kormac in strength and courage.

Once upon a time, after a battle, Kormac was driving the flying foe before him while the rest of his host had gone back aboard ship. Out of the woods there rushed against him one as monstrous big as an idol—a Scot; and a fierce struggle began. Kormac felt for his sword, but it had slipped out of the sheath; he was overmatched, for the giant was possessed; but yet he reached out, caught his sword, and struck the giant his death-blow. Then the giant cast his hands about Kormac, and gripped his sides so hard that the ribs cracked, and he fell over, and the dead giant on top of him, so that he could not stir. Far and wide his folk were looking for him, but at last they found him and carried him aboard ship. Then he made this song:

"When my manhood was matched in embraces
With the might of yon horror, the strangler,
Far other I found it than folding
That fair one ye know in my arms!
On the high-seat of heroes with Odin
From the horn of the gods I were drinking
O'er soon—let me speak it to warriors—
If Skrymir had failed of his aid."

Then his wounds were looked to; they found that his ribs were broken on both sides. He said it was no use trying to heal him, and lay there in his wounds for a time, while his men grieved that he should have been so unwary of his life.

He answered them in song:

"Of yore never once did I ween it,
When I wielded the cleaver of targets,
That sickness was fated to foil me—
A fighter so hardy as I.
But I shrink not, for others must share it,
Stout shafts of the spear though they deem them,
—O hard at my heart is the death-pang --
Thus hopeless the bravest may die."

And this song also:

"He came not with me in the morning,
Thy mate, O thou fairest of women,
When we reddened for booty the broadsword,
So brave to the hand-grip, in Ireland:
When the sword from its scabbard was loosened
And sang round my cheeks in the battle
For the feast of the Fury, and blood-drops
Fell hot on the neb of the raven."

And then he began to fail.
This was his last song:

"There was dew from the wound smitten deeply
That drained from the stroke of the sword-edge;
There was red on the weapon I wielded
In the war with the glorious and gallant:
Yet not where the broadsword -- the blood wand --

Was borne by the lords of the falchion,
But low in the straw like a laggard,
O my lady, dishonoured I die!"

He said that his will was to give Thorgils his brother all he had, the goods he owned and the host he led; for he would like best, he said, that his brother should have the use of them.

So then Kormac died. Thorgils became captain over the host, and was long time in viking.

And so ends the story.